NATIONAL IDENTITY IN
RUSSIAN CULTURE

What is Russia? Who are Russians? What is "Russianness"? The question of national identity has long been a vexed one in Russia, and is particularly pertinent in the post-Soviet period. For a thousand years, these questions have been central to the work of Russian writers, artists, musicians, film-makers, critics, politicians, and philosophers. Questions of national self-identity permeate Russian cultural self-expression. This wide-ranging study, designed for students of Russian literature, culture, and history, explores aspects of national identity in Russian culture from medieval times to the present day. Written by an international team of scholars, the volume offers an accessible overview and a broad, multi-faceted introductory account of this central feature of Russian cultural history. The book is comprehensive and concise; it combines general surveys with a wide range of specific examples to convey the rich texture of Russian cultural expression over the past thousand years.

SIMON FRANKLIN is Professor of Russian Studies at the University of Cambridge. He has published widely on Russian history and culture, especially the Medieval period, and his recent books include *Writing, Society and Culture in early Rus: c.950–1300* (Cambridge, 2002), winner of the Alexander Nove Prize for 2002.

EMMA WIDDIS is Lecturer in the Department of Slavonic Studies at the University of Cambridge. She is author of *Visions of a New Land: Soviet Film from the Revolution to the Second World War* (New Haven, 2003) and *Alexander Medvedkin* (London, 2004).

NATIONAL IDENTITY IN RUSSIAN CULTURE

An Introduction

EDITED BY

SIMON FRANKLIN AND EMMA WIDDIS

CAMBRIDGE UNIVERSITY PRESS

PUBLISHED BY THE PRESS SYNDICATE OF THE UNIVERSITY OF CAMBRIDGE
The Pitt Building, Trumpington Street, Cambridge, United Kingdom

CAMBRIDGE UNIVERSITY PRESS
The Edinburgh Building, Cambridge, CB2 2RU, UK
40 West 20th Street, New York, NY 10011–4211, USA
477 Williamstown Road, Port Melbourne, VIC 3207, Australia
Ruiz de Alarcón 13, 28014 Madrid, Spain
Dock House, The Waterfront, Cape Town 8001, South Africa

http://www.cambridge.org

First published 2004

Printed in the United Kingdom at the University Press, Cambridge

Typeface Adobe Garamond 11/12.5 pt.   *System* LaTeX 2ε [TB]

A catalogue record for this book is available from the British Library

Library of Congress Cataloguing in Publication data
National Identity in Russian Culture: An Introduction / edited by Simon Franklin and Emma Widdis.
p.   cm.
Includes bibliographical references and index.
ISBN 0 521 83926 2
1. National characteristics, Russian.   2. Russians – Ethnic identity.   3. Russia – Civilization.
I. Franklin, Simon.   II. Widdis, Emma, 1970–
DK510.34.N38   2004
305.891′71 – dc22   2003068743

ISBN 0 521 83926 2 hardback

Contents

v

Illustrations

Notes on contributors

ANTHONY CROSS has been Professor of Slavonic Studies at the University of Cambridge since 1985. He has written and edited over twenty books and written over 200 articles on all aspects of eighteenth-century Russia and Anglo-Russian relations. He is currently writing a book entitled *Petersburg and the British: The City through British Eyes over Three Centuries*.

SIMON FRANKLIN is Professor of Russian Studies at the University of Cambridge. His main research interests are the history and culture of early Rus, and nineteenth-century Russian literature. Publications include *The Emergence of Rus 750–1200* (with Jonathan Shepard: London, 1996) and *Writing, Society and Culture in Early Rus c.950–1300* (Cambridge, 2002).

MARINA FROLOVA-WALKER is Lecturer in Music at the University of Cambridge and a Fellow of Clare College, Cambridge. Her principal fields of research are German Romanticism, Russian and Soviet music, and nationalism in music. She is currently writing *Russia: Music and Nation*, commissioned by Yale University Press.

BORIS GASPAROV is Professor of Slavic Linguistics and Russian Literature at Columbia University, New York. He is the author and editor of numerous books and articles on the philosophy of language, Slavic historical linguistics, and Russian culture of the nineteenth and twentieth centuries. Recent publications include: *Language and Memory* (Moscow, 1996, in Russian), *Old Church Slavonic* (Munich, 2001), and *Five Operas and a Symphony: Russian Music and Its Cultural Environment* (forthcoming at Yale University Press).

LINDSEY HUGHES is Professor of Russian History and Director of the Centre for Russian Studies at the School of Slavonic and East European Studies, University College London. Her recent publications include

Russia in the Age of Peter the Great (Yale University Press, 1998) and *Peter the Great, A Biography* (Yale, 2002). She is currently working on a study of responses to key monuments of Russian culture.

HUBERTUS JAHN is Senior Lecturer in Russian History at the University of Cambridge and a Fellow of Clare College, Cambridge. His recent publications include *Patriotic Culture in Russia during World War I* (Cornell University Press). He has just finished a history of begging and poverty in Russian history.

CATRIONA KELLY is Professor of Russian at the University of Oxford. She has published widely on Russian literature and cultural history, including *Russian Literature: A Very Short Introduction* (Oxford University Press, 2001), *Utopias: Russian Modernist Texts 1905–1940* (Penguin, 1999), and a history of politeness in Russia. She also co-edited *Constructing Russian Culture in the Age of Revolution* and *An Introduction to Russian Cultural Studies* (both Oxford University Press, 1998). She is currently working on a history of childhood in twentieth-century Russia (for Yale) and a book about Pavlik Morozov, who betrayed his father to the authorities (for Granta).

STEPHANIE SANDLER is Professor of Slavic Languages and Literatures at Harvard University. Her most recent book *Commemorating Pushkin: Russia's Myth of a National Poet*, was published by Stanford University Press in 2003. Her current research is on contemporary Russian poetry.

EMMA WIDDIS is Lecturer in the Department of Slavonic Studies at the University of Cambridge. Her research focuses on Soviet culture of the 1920s and 30s, with a particular emphasis on cinema. Publications include *Visions Of A New Land: Soviet Film from the Revolution to the Second World War* (Yale, 2003), which examines representations of space and landscape in the culture of this period, and she has recently completed a book on the film director Aleksandr Medvedkin.

Preface

What is Russia? What is 'Russianness'? Who are Russians? For a thousand years these and similar questions have preoccupied Russian writers, artists, critics, musicians, film-makers, politicians and ideologists, theologians and philosophers, intellectuals and demagogues. Implicitly or explicitly, questions of national identity permeate Russian cultural self-expression, from the very first native literary and artistic endeavours of the 'Rus' (ancestors of Russians, Ukrainians, and Belorusians) in the eleventh and twelfth centuries, through to the intensified self-questioning in the 'new' Russia after the collapse of the Soviet Union in 1991. And implicitly or explicitly, the same questions permeate a great deal of writing about Russia by foreigners, whether academics or journalists or travel-diarists or intelligence analysts. What need, then, for yet another book on the subject? Why add to the cacophony of competing voices?

In the first place, there is the matter of scope and convenience. We hope that this book will be useful precisely because so much else has been written, for it is surprisingly hard to find an accessible overview, a broad and multi-faceted introductory account of this central theme in Russian cultural history. To state the obvious: Russia is a vast country with a huge population and a varied culture which has emerged and developed and changed over many hundreds of years. Few individuals can plausibly claim adequate expertise across the full range, and most studies tend understandably to reflect the particular partial interests of their authors. There is nothing wrong with this, and the results can be stimulating and admirable; but equally there can be clear benefits in pooling resources, in bringing together the combined experience of a number of scholars in distinct disciplines, specialists in different areas and periods of culture. No survey in a single, medium-sized volume can truly claim to be comprehensive, but we have tried to convey at least some sense of the amplitude and diversity of the problem: across time, across cultural forms, across types of expression and idea.

Secondly, there is the matter of approach. Much discussion of Russian identity is driven by the belief, or at least by the assumption, that the question has an answer, that Russianness is a 'thing' to be located, described, and explained. The assumption behind the present book is rather the opposite: that to seek an answer in such terms is, in a sense, to misrepresent the question. Identity is not a 'thing' to be objectively described. It is a field of cultural discourse. It is each person's perception of themselves: as an individual, in relation to a group or groups, and by contrast with other individuals and groups. Russian identity is and has been a topic of continual argument, of conflicting claims, competing images, contradictory criteria. And that is the point. There is no need to resolve the contradictions, to take sides, to adjudicate between contested notions of true Russianness. There is no separate 'reality' behind the cultural expressions of identity. Hence the somewhat pointed title of this book: national identity *in* Russian culture. The multiple cultural expressions and constructs *are* the identity, or the identities. Their reality, or their truth, is in their own existence as facts of culture, not in the extent to which they accurately reflect a set of external facts.

Third, there is the matter of organisation, both of the book as a whole and of the chapters within it. Taken together, the sections of the book, and their constituent chapters, are designed to form a kind of grid, a conceptual geography of the subject, a way of mapping the various categories of discourse on identity. The grid can be extended and applied beyond the confines of the specific surveys and analyses in this book. Within the sections, each chapter has a dual structure, starting with a very broad overview of the wider implications of its topic, and proceeding – by contrast – to some very specific readings or case studies. If the sections combine into a map, the case studies combine more as a mosaic. In each chapter, the case studies by themselves are merely illustrative fragments, but when put together and assembled over the course of the book they provide a fairly representative and nuanced picture of the diverse ways in which notions of national identity function in cultural practice. The book is intended to be accessible to those with little or no special knowledge of Russia and Russian culture. References to places, people, and events are, as far as possible, explained, and each section is prefaced by an introductory summary.

A note on the transliteration of Russian

There are several systems for rendering Russian words in English transliteration. Different systems may be appropriate for different purposes, even in
the context of a single publication. Thus in the present book our practice
varies as follows.

  (i) In most instances we use a modified version of the 'Library of Congress'
      system. This means, for example, using 'i' where some other sys-
      tems have 'y': hence Tolstoi and Maiakovskii, rather than Tolstoy
      and Mayakovsky. We stick to this system even when the name has
      become familiar in English in a different form: hence 'Chaikovskii',
      not 'Tchaikovsky'. Immigrants pose problems. We leave Stravinsky as
      he is, rather than converting him back to Stravinskii.

 (ii) We omit most diacritics (superscript marks). The only exception is
      the indication of the Russian 'soft sign' ('), which indicates that the
      preceding consonant is 'soft' or – to put it technically – palatalized.
      However, we only use this symbol in words which are clearly marked as
      'foreign' (through being set in italics) and in bibliographical references.
      Where Russian names appear as part of the normal English text, we
      omit the 'soft sign': hence Gogol, Gorkii and Prokofev rather than
      Gogol', Gor'kii, or Prokof'ev (or indeed Prokofiev).

(iii) In general Russian personal names are given in their Russian forms, not
      anglicised: thus Aleksandr Nevskii and Nikolai Leskov, not Alexander
      Nevskii or Nicholas Leskov. The exceptions, by oddly powerful con-
      vention, are the rulers of the Russian Empire from c.1700 to 1917: thus
      Peter the Great, Catherine the Great, Nicholas II, not Petr, Ekaterina,
      or Nikolai. Earlier rulers keep the Russian forms: Aleksei rather than
      Alexis; and of course Ivan the Terrible cannot be reduced to just plain
      John.

Map: The growth and contraction of Russia and its empire.

O C E A N

B E R I A

E R A T I O N

SAKHALIN

Lake
Baikal

Irkutsk●

Vladivostok

Scale
0   250   500   750   1000 km
0   250   500 miles

C H I N A

CHAPTER I

'All the Russias . . .'?

Simon Franklin and Emma Widdis

> The first rule which we have to follow is that of national character: every people has, or must have, a character: if it lacks one, we must start by endowing it with one.[1]
>
> Jean-Jacques Rousseau

In 1902, one Henry Norman (MP) published a book entitled *All the Russias: Travels and Studies in Contemporary European Russia, Finland, Siberia, the Caucasus, and Central Asia* – the result, he claimed, of some fifteen years' interest in Russian affairs, and four journeys in European and Asian Russia. 'Russia!' he wrote: 'What a flock of thoughts take wing as the word strikes the ear! Does any word in any language, except the dear name of one's own land, mean as much today?'[2]

'What *is* Russia?' Norman asked, in the introduction to his book; is it the Tsar, Orthodoxy, St. Petersburg, 'the vast and nearly roadless country', Siberia, Central Asia? It was, of course, all of those things. And in the end, Norman concluded with the intriguing assertion that 'it would be easier to say what is not Russia . . . In world affairs, wherever you turn you see Russia; wherever you listen you hear her. She moves in every path, she is mining in every claim. The "creeping murmur" of the world is her footfall – the "poring dark" is her veil. To the challenge of the nations, as they peer from their borders, comes the ever-same reply: "Who goes there?" . . . "*Russia!*"'

With allowances for the poetic flourish, Norman's words have lost little of their resonance over a century after they were published. His evocation of the power and threat of Russia can be traced in Western representations of the Russian Empire, the Soviet Union, and indeed of the Russian Federation in the early years of the twenty-first century. With the Empire that Norman described in 1902 dissolved, the Soviet Union disbanded, Russia today remains the largest country in the world, and exerts a power as much symbolic as practical. Norman's was one of many, many attempts, before and since, to encapsulate Russia for Western readers. Often they share Norman's sense of puzzlement, of mystery. Russia has seemed to be in a category of its own, a place and a culture that apparently fail to fit any habitual Western mental geography. Where, for example, is Russia? Is it 'Western' or 'Eastern'? It 'ought' to be Western in that – like 'the West' (which in such comparisons tends to be seen as a single cultural entity!) – it is heir to the traditions both of Christianity and of the Enlightenment, and has been a full and leading participant in 'Western' traditions of literature and music. Or perhaps it 'ought' to be Eastern: located predominantly in Asia, it is said to be mystical and authoritarian in its approach to religion, monolithic and despotic in its governance. Yet it is not quite 'the East' either: not India, Persia, or China (also lumped together as a single cultural entity in such comparisons). Russia's indeterminacy even leads to the invention of a special physical and conceptual space for it: 'Eurasia'.

Happily, the fictions and flaws of such definitions do not directly concern us here. In the first place, we are not concerned with Western perceptions of Russia but with Russians' perceptions of themselves. Western stereotypes are relevant only to the extent that (as is sometimes the case) they are filtered back into Russia and affect Russian habits of self-representation. And secondly, by contrast with Norman and others we are not attempting to define what Russia 'actually' is. The focus of this book is not any putative 'true' identity that might be traced amongst Russians present and past, nor any fixed definition of statehood or citizenship or national character. Rather, we are interested in Russia as what the influential historian and theorist Benedict Anderson might call an 'imagined community'.[3] Anderson's suggestion that national identity is constructed and sustained in cultural texts provides the theoretical justification for this volume, just as it has provided the basis for much recent theorization of 'the nation' and 'nationality'. The nation, as Homi Bhabha writes, is 'a system of cultural signification'.[4] It is located in its texts – in its flags, its anthems, its monuments, popular heroes and educational practices, in its fairy tales and literature. These texts embody and make real the abstract ideas of Russia and 'Russianness', making the collective identity visible for those who reckon themselves part of it. As such, in effect, they *create* identity. Or, more appropriately, they create *identities*, such that Russia and Russianness become constantly shifting and multiple forms. National identity is therefore a process rather than a result. Yet the suggestion that this is an 'imagined' Russia and Russianness should not imply that it is not *real*. To put it somewhat glibly: to note that such things are imagined is not to dismiss them as imaginary. Rather, these imagined Russian identities – *as they are written, discussed, pictured, or sung* – are the only ones there are. They are facts of culture, and culture is a fact. They are constructs, certainly, parts of a process of identity formation that is ongoing, fragile, and always incomplete; but they are also *lived*, and as such real.

This view of the nation as text, broadly understood, or as cultural discourse, raises inevitable questions both about agency and about consumption and community: who writes the texts of national identity? And who reads them or subscribes to them? If visions of Russian identity are located in cultural production, who produces them? And who shares, or is swayed by, or sees themselves reflected in, the vision? Clearly, the ideas of Russia and Russianness explored in this book are not solely the creations of the apparatus of state power. Nor are they the products of some kind of instinctive popular sentiment. They are created in a nexus between state and people, between policy and practice. But they are also – crucially – created by what might be called 'producers of culture' in the broadest sense (intellectuals, writers, film-makers, cartographers, historians, musicians, theologians, philosophers, artists, etc.). It is these culturally inscribed Russias that are our focus here. It would of course be nice to know what proportion of the wider population might have heard of or associated themselves with which aspects of which type of identity at which time. By and large, however, we try to steer clear of the trap of taking the populace for granted when attributing an identity to it, and such speculations are beyond our scope. Generally speaking, the discourses of national identity may spread as widely and as effectively as the relevant cultural technology, though we should beware of assuming that modern technologies, though massively quicker, are necessarily more inclusive than older technologies in the longer term.

Inclusivity is implied by the title of Henry Norman's book, *All the Russias*, which also happens to have been the working title for the present volume and which we retain as the heading for the present introductory chapter. It is not a claim to completeness. Its usefulness lies rather in the variety of cultural perspectives which it can evoke, for the expression 'All the Russias' may be read on at least three levels.

On one level, the expression 'All the Russias' cannot but carry echoes of its traditional English usage in imperial nomenclature, where the 'Tsar (or 'Autocrat') of All the Russias' ruled over a realm that included 'Great Russia', 'Little Russia' (Ukraine), and 'White Russia' (now Belarus).[5] Its usage here should *not*, of course, be taken to imply any suggestion that Ukraine and Belarus are 'really' part of Russia. The inclusiveness is nothing to do with modern politics. It simply reminds us that the limits of our subject are the historical limits of Russian cultural self-representation, and neither the modern political map, nor our or anybody else's preferred notion of what Russia should be or should have been, can impinge. Secondly, in similar vein, the phrase 'All the Russias' may be taken to allude to the apparent sequence of political embodiments of the land and people over the past millennium: the Land of the Rus in the Middle Ages, the Russian Empire, the Soviet Union, the Russian Federation. Again, the construct is questionable as 'fact', but again it is a proper topic of cultural discussion in the present context. Thirdly, and more revealingly, the inclusive phrase 'All the Russias' may be taken to imply the plurality and layering of identities that might constitute the field of 'Russianness'.

A great deal of Russian culture is – explicitly or implicitly, to a greater or lesser extent – self-referential, about Russia or indicative of 'Russianness'. But the 'self' turns out not to be a constant, clearly definable entity. Russian culture expresses a range of different types of 'myths' of Russia and Russianness (and here we understand 'myth' as a narrative which validates a community, a fact of culture regardless of its relationship to facts of history). Hence, even as its essence is asserted, Russia is continually represented as a question, a field of possibilities, a set of contradictions. This book does not seek to resolve the contradictions so as to explain what Russia and Russianness 'are'. Its purpose is to provide a guide to the many types of criteria and expressions of Russia and Russianness. In a sense, Russian national identity lies not in the resolution but in the nature of the discussion and argument. The flaw, therefore, in the notion of 'all the Russias' lies not in its appropriately programmatic sense of plurality, but in its further unrealisable implication of a kind of completeness, of totality, of potential closure.

Thus far we have used a sequence of terms without clear differentiation: Russia, Russian, Russians, Russianness; as if they are interchangeable in their relations to 'national identity'. The trouble is that they are not. In fact, they present a problem of theory, or at any rate of approach. Russia is often left out of Western European stories of 'nationalism' and 'nationhood'. Russia is not and has never been a 'nation state', where the geo-political boundaries and the ethno-cultural boundaries coincide. More or less from the start it has been a multi-ethnic, multi-lingual polity – an empire (even if its rulers have not always presented it as such) – but with a strongly dominant Slav (Rus, Russian) population and culture. Rus, the Russian Empire, the Soviet Union – all were expanding powers, continually enlarging their territorial boundaries and their spheres of influence through conquest and annexation. The creation of a 'Great Russian' identity became a political imperative, a process of cultural incorporation. Should Russia, then, be viewed through the prism of theories of empire, or theories of the nation state?

Perhaps part of the 'problem' of Russianness is its uncomfortable position between these two definitions. It lies, in a sense, on a fault line between imperial and national identities; or more precisely, between geo-political and ethno-cultural criteria of self-definition. In English this leaves an ambiguity even in language: are 'Russians' all the citizens of 'Russia', regardless of (for example) their mother tongue, religion, clothing, or political aspiration? It used to be common, even in reasonably sophisticated Western publications, to see 'Russian' used as a synonym for 'Soviet' (just as in Russia and elsewhere one will often find 'English' used as a synonym for 'British'). Or are 'Russians' a distinct nationality, regardless of where they live or where the lines are drawn on a map? The Russian language has developed the usage of two separate words (originally synonyms) to deal with this: *rossiiskii* and *russkii*. Both mean 'Russian', but *rossiiskii* refers to *Rossiia*, the geo-political entity (hence the imperial identity) while *russkii* is more narrowly ethnic and linguistic. These two terms make visible the coexistence of geo-political and ethno-cultural criteria of self-description. In Russia this coexistence has not always been easy.

Such conceptual uncertainties flow in both directions. Some of the Russian concepts may not migrate comfortably into English, but the Russian conceptual tools of self-identification have often themselves been imported and adapted. From the conversion to Christianity at the end of the tenth century, through the eighteenth-century Enlightenment to the ideas gleaned from Romanticism or Marxism and on to market capitalism and globalization: it is as if Russians have periodically sought to locate and re-locate themselves on conceptual maps originally devised by and for other people and other places. This can be true quite literally. In Russian, for example, Jerusalem is part of the 'Near East' despite being slightly to the west of Moscow: in this metaphorical geography it is as if the very language looks from Western Europe. In a sense, Russian discourses of identity have been formed in an implied dialogue with outsiders. It might be an overstatement to say, in the phrase of the literary theorist Harold Bloom, that Russian culture is marked by an 'anxiety of influence', but we can legitimately suggest a *negotiation* of influence, a relationship with an 'other', both real and imagined.

Our introduction to Russian identities in this book does not eliminate such ambiguities and tensions. We are not limited by theories of the nation state, or by visions of empire, or by any one of the successive or opposing sets of ideas, whether originally imported or indigenous. Rather we examine how such complexities have been negotiated. The flux between competing models and frameworks of identity is part of the cultural process that is Russianness.

The sections and chapters in this book represent points of orientation within the vast field of identity formation. They aim to equip the reader with the means of surveying the field, mapping the dimensions of Russian identity. The headings we have selected are by no means exhaustive. They represent key ideas, or areas, around which discussion of identity has focused, providing nodal points within the discourse(s). The 'grid' that we propose represents a framework through which to read identity as a field of signification. Each of the sections of the book explores a different type of identity, and the chapters within each section explore these broad conceptual categories in the Russian case. The grid is not a key to the secret essence of Russianness, but rather a structure through which to understand its articulations.

Section I – the first part of our 'grid' – is concerned with identities in time and space. It explores questions of orientation and location, attempts to construct or interpret Russia as a temporal or physical entity. Chapter 2 examines the importance of history in the narratives of identity. Shared histories create a shared sense of the present and future; but these histories are themselves unfixed. There are many possible narratives of Russia *in time*, and the negotiation of competing stories, various foundation myths, and alternative pasts is part of the discourse of Russianness. In Chapter 3, we examine the same problem of location *in space*. In order to conceptualize a country we first need some idea of where it is, of it shape and size, of what it looks like. We need, in other words, some kind of mental or physical map. Vast and diverse, often hostile and uninhabitable, the Russian territory poses problems not just of management, but also of symbolic definition. Where are the borders of the nation? As Henry Norman asked, what *is* the Russian landscape? Can there be a shared image of the territory?

With Russia thus located (or rather dis-located), our second section explores what we have called 'contrastive identities'. It shifts our attention from Russia to Russians, and examines how self-definition has been expressed and mediated in political and cultural terms. Who or what do the Russians think they are? Identity is often established in contrasts and comparisons. 'We' define ourselves not just through ourselves, but through how we believe we are similar to, or distinct from, 'them'. We can specify who we are by specifying who we are not. This raises questions of community and belonging, for visions of the national 'self' shift. Is national self-definition to be expressed in ethnic terms? Or in social terms? How can diverse strands of the population, separated by class, or by race, be integrated and united under the common heading of 'we'? How does Russia's status as Imperial power shape criteria of identity? Chapter 4 explores Russian ideologies of self, tracing official and unofficial constructs of the 'people'. Chapter 5, by contrast, examines representations of the 'other', showing how discussions and images of foreigners have provided a space in which Russian identities have been tested and refined.

Our third section is concerned with 'essentialist' conceptions of identity: the notion that what we *are* is innate and unique. The essentialist vision posits national identity in terms of inherent characteristics, creating an idea of the nation as a single entity or being, unchanging in time (and space). As such, the heterogeneity of a people is reduced to homogeneity, plurality to singularity. Such myths of identity might claim that Russians *do* view the world in a particular way, that they *are* all Orthodox, *are* melancholy and passionate, that they exhibit a particular relation to everyday life, etc. The widespread idea of 'the Russian soul' is a revealing example of such an essentialist myth of identity. The four chapters in this section trace four such hypotheses of Russianness, revealing how they have been constructed and functioned over Russia's long history. Chapter 6 explores the status of Orthodox Christianity as a symbol of identity, showing how the religion has been used to encode different categories and visions of Russia and Russianness. Chapter 7 investigates the myth of the 'soul', using the example of Russian music to trace the emergence of melancholy as a trope of identity. Chapter 8 considers the idea that the Russian language exhibits characteristics that are inherently 'Russian,' or that it *creates* an essentialist vision of Russianness. Chapter 9 turns to everyday life, revealing and unpacking essentialist myths of a specifically Russian 'way of living' or 'attitude to existence'.

The fourth and final section of the book explores 'symbolic' identities, examining how identities have been projected onto prominent visual or verbal emblems. How do particular buildings, monuments, or symbols assume significance in the discourse of identity? In Chapter 10, we discover the history of Russian monuments – the buildings, paintings, and sculptures that have been invested with significance over time, and their shifting prominence. The chapter explores, moreover, how the *idea* of the monument as a symbol of identity was constructed and promulgated in Russia, and its contemporary resonance. Finally – and surely fittingly – our last chapter turns to one of Russia's most famous children (and least successful exports): Aleksandr Sergeevich Pushkin. The concern here, though, is not Pushkin as a poet, or Pushkin as a historical figure, but rather Pushkin as an idea, a symbol of Russian identity. In the example of Pushkin, we can see how the discourse of identity shapes and alters its objects, rendering the reality of the poet and his work a vessel through which the shifting terms of Russianness can be projected.

The broad headings of our grid enable readers to track the discussion of Russia and Russianness across a millennium of relocations – historical, ideological, geographical, and cultural. They begin in the eleventh century and end in the early years of the twenty-first. As such, they offer a broad chronological framework, providing a perspective on Russian history which is not bounded by historical 'period'. They span the history of discourses of Russianness under the influence of diverse cultural and ideological influences and relocations, from Byzantine theology to postmodernism. To ensure coherence within such a broad frame of enquiry, each of the chapters in the book follows a common pattern. The first sections of each chapter outline their theme in general terms, across the larger time-span. They show how particular dimensions of identity have been discussed, represented, and contested. The later sections use focused case studies to illustrate how the issues can be played out at the level of the particular. This shift between the general and particular is vital. It is, after all, at the level of the particular, in the detail, that identity is located. Across the ten chapters, our contributors explore a vast range of cultural texts. Together, then, they reveal the *texture* of identity, the interwoven strands and multiple layers of imagined Russianness.

Identities in time and space

Before Russia can be described, it must first be circumscribed: found, located, identified – that is, defined as an entity – in time and space. Or so we might tend to think. A country, we are tempted to assume, is a distinct place with a distinct history: look at a map, and there is Russia, and its history is the important things that have happened in and to it over the course of time. Finding Russia is not, however, quite so straightforward. Russia in time is not a single, fixed narrative but a range of possible stories; and over that same time entities which we or their inhabitants might call Russia have appeared in radically different shapes and sizes, and even in different places.

Chapter 2 is concerned with the linear narratives of Russia, with the emergence and development of stories designed to create and sustain a sense of 'historical' coherence and significance: from chroniclers and sermonists in the eleventh and twelfth centuries right through to post-Soviet reflections on the shape of Russia's past. In the second part of the chapter, two 'case studies' illustrate how modern cultural products can play (both crudely and subtly) upon the accumulated narratives and thus make implicit – and sometimes polemical – claims about national identity.

Chapter 3 begins with a summary of shifting political borders and locations, from the early 'Rus Land', through Muscovy, the Empire with its capital in St Petersburg, the Soviet Union and eventually to the post-Soviet Russian Federation. The theme here is not just expansion, but expanse. Expansion is a geo-political process, expanse becomes a dominant image of Russia, a sphere of imagining, a metaphor which transfers from the physical to the spiritual, to representations not just of Russia but of Russianness. Yet it is also problematic, ambiguous. The case studies illustrate a constant slippage, or tension, between visions of chaos and order, conquest and freedom, openness and domestication.

Russia in time

Simon Franklin

In the late 1990s a book was published in Moscow with the same title as this chapter: *Russia in Time*. I quote from its conclusion: 'Across the vast Eurasian land mass . . . in the fourth to the second millennium BC' the written culture of the ancient Slavs, 'whose sounds are close to those of modern Russian . . . gave rise to the following civilisations: Sumerian, Babylonian, Proto-Indian, Cretan, Ancient Greek, Ancient Roman (and eventually European)'.[1] This kind of grandiose claim about a Russia spanning the millennia is a fairly typical product of the post-Soviet boom in amateur history. The shelves bulge with ever more ambitious assertions: that the ancient Etruscans were ancestors of the Russians; that Jerusalem was a Russian city, and that Christ was therefore a Russian prophet. Or, by complete contrast, according to one particularly fashionable theory: nothing in world history is more than about a thousand years old and Alexander the Great is a fiction invented around the time of Tsar Ivan IV (the Terrible) in the sixteenth century. In the chaotic freedom of post-Soviet popular publication, Russia in Time has become strangely elastic.

Historians wince. But the point, for present purposes, is not whether such schemes are true or false (in almost all cases they are utter claptrap), but the shared preoccupation with the shaping of time; the assumption that the way we shape time has significance for determining who 'we' are; the belief in linear narratives through time as the key, or a key, to something which might commonly be termed 'historical' identity. Such beliefs do not begin with the intellectual liberty – or anarchy – of the post-Soviet period. For as long as they have been able to write (and possibly longer), Russia's cultural opinion-formers have sought to define themselves and their status through control over the linear narratives, over the shaping and telling of time. The first part of this chapter therefore consists of a narrative of such narratives, an *overview* of some of the ways in which 'significant' time has been conceived in Russian cultural discourse. We subsequently look more closely at particular examples of how narratives of time may be embedded in and propagated through other forms of cultural production.

Two points of caution should be made in advance. First, this survey deals mainly with sources produced by the political or cultural elites. Although to varying degrees the privileged groups may have succeeded in persuading others, such that in some cases their narratives came to have very wide currency indeed, nevertheless I emphatically do not claim to be surveying what Russians 'in general' thought. Secondly, any such overview has to be highly schematic. One cannot skip through a thousand years in a few pages without a degree of over-simplification.

I. OVERVIEW: A BRIEF HISTORY OF HISTORIES

We begin at the beginning of recorded native historical thought, with the earliest surviving written narratives and explanations of self in the 'Land of the Rus'. The Land of the Rus is not – one should stress – modern Russia. It is not modern anywhere. It was, roughly, the area associated with the authority of a people, or at any rate a ruling dynasty, known as the Rus. The authority of the Rus, measured in terms of their capacity to extort money and goods from local populations (an activity quaintly known as gathering tribute), spread outwards from a relatively compact core along a north–south axis between the cities of Novgorod and Kiev, and at its peak extended to a substantial part of what is now European Russia, Belarus, and Ukraine. Greek writers called this land *Rhosia*. Latin writers knew it as *Russia*. Though remote chronologically, the first articulate Rus attempts to construct an identity for themselves in time are not mere distant curiosities, mere background to the 'real' and more up-to-date story. They established an agenda, a set of reference points, which turned out to be astonishingly durable and which continually re-emerge in subsequent narratives. In mythologies of identity, the remotest past can be perceived to be just as 'relevant' as this morning's newspaper.

The earliest self-explanations of the Rus come in the wake of their official conversion to Christianity, conventionally dated to the year 988.[2] Conversion could mean many things to many people. It could have political, economic, ethical, and aesthetic dimensions, besides at some level involving belief, faith. The aspect of Christianisation that needs to be highlighted here is what one can call its colonisation of time.

The imported religion sought to colonise every dimension of time, from the divisions of each day to the lifespan of the universe itself: the regular hours of church services, more suited to a Mediterranean regularity of day and night than to the seasonally changing northern cycle of light and dark; new names and lengths for the months; a new daily calendar, according to the fixed cycle of the commemoration of saints; the esoteric cycles of moveable feasts hinging on the date of Easter. These small-scale, cyclical chronologies are probably what impinged most directly on the lives of most people. But more important for present purposes are the grander visions of time: the very idea of a universal history, measurable precisely in a unified, linear sequence of years; and the significant thematic divisions of that history, the chapter headings in the book of the world.

The Rus took their Christianity from Byzantium, accepting the ecclesiastical jurisdiction of the patriarch of Constantinople. Byzantine chronology, by contrast with the chronology of the Western ('Latin') Church, counted years not from the birth of Christ, but in a continuous sequence from the creation of the universe. Hence the earliest native Rus historical narratives, the chronicles which start to be compiled from around the middle or late eleventh century, are organised according to an annalistic principle, noting events year by year as measured since the date of the Creation: in the year 6523 such-and-such a prince died; in the year 6524 such-and-such a battle was fought. The first task of self-location was to establish where the Rus fitted in the universal framework, in the sequence of the years of time. The chroniclers' conclusion was that the Rus enter into the picture around the middle of the fourth century of the seventh millennium since Creation which means, in our language, around AD 850–60.

But sequence alone is not enough. Some things happen earlier, some happen later: so what? Pure sequence needed other types of narrative to provide a sense of meaningful shape. The most potent significances are those created when different *types* of story can be made to coincide, to fuse together, reinforce one another, to produce an impression of purposeful coherence. In Byzantium this was a problem long solved. Although the Byzantines did not reckon the years since the birth of Christ, the event was nevertheless significant as a division between phases in the sequence. What else happened around the time of the birth of Christ? The birth of the Roman Empire, under Augustus, the first Emperor. This was a miraculous synchrony. Clearly, God chose the Roman Empire as His vessel: a universal Empire for the universal faith. So the Christianised Roman Empire – the Byzantine Empire, with its capital at Constantinople – was the fulfilment of the Divine Plan for mankind.

This might have suited the Byzantines, but what of the Rus? The main Byzantine map of time left room for the Rus as a fact on a bare chronological scale, but not yet as a meaningful fact, unless perhaps as an appendage to

Byzantium, and that would not do. So the early Rus chroniclers grafted other stories of self onto the bare chronology.

One strand was dynastic: tales of the great deeds of princely ancestors. Here, in a fusion of literate and pre-literate modes of shaping the past, the Byzantine chronological framework was filled out with local, probably oral, stories of the glorious traditions of the ruling family going back to Riurik, legendary founder of the dynasty. Riurik, the story went, had come from Scandinavia with his kin, by invitation rather than by conquest, to rule the local tribes who were unable to live harmoniously among themselves. The dynasty of Rus princes was thus legitimate, governing by the wish of the governed.

A second strand was ethnic. Though they were political latecomers, the chroniclers determined that the Slavs were ethnically ancient, descended from the peoples of the North allocated to the share of the third son of Noah in the division of lands after the Flood. The authority here was inherited Christian tradition: not the Bible itself, which unsurprisingly omits to mention the Slavs, but a range of apocryphal stories, amplifying the sparse narratives from the biblical book of Genesis, which were quite widely circulated and accepted in the medieval Christian world. Thus the Rus acquired for themselves the dignity of quasi-biblical antiquity.

Finally, there was the 'historical' lesson which Rus writers drew from the birth of Christ. Though they agreed with the Byzantines that the significance of Christ was universal, they were not remotely interested in the synchronicity of Christ and Augustus which sanctified and privileged the universal Roman Empire. Byzantine self-definition was based on the fusion of Imperial and sacred time. They called themselves Romans (*Rhomaioi*). The Rus' definition of the Byzantines was contemporary, based merely on language: they called them 'Greeks'. For the Rus the universality of the Christian faith implied inclusiveness, irrespective of imperial succession and of chronological priority. The Christian message was aimed at the Rus no less than at the 'Greeks'. The Rus were 'the new Christian people, chosen by God',[3] for 'it was meet that Grace and Truth should shine forth upon new people . . . and it has reached our nation of Rus'.[4] Indeed, not merely was 'newness' no impediment to equal dignity, but some even contrived to turn Byzantine sacred chronology on its head. If Byzantine imperial ideology made much of the fact that the Universal Empire was special because it was there first, bookmen from Rus discovered that they were special because they came last: for does not the Bible say that those who labour from the eleventh hour shall be rewarded as much as those who have laboured from the third hour, and indeed that 'the last shall be first and the first last'?[5] The

Rus found lines of narrative to demonstrate their ethnic antiquity; yet they could also accord themselves special status on account of their political and religious newness. Arriving late is turned into a virtue.

These constructions by the earliest Rus self-mythologists illustrate the processes of creating a coherent narrative identity from scratch, mixing and matching to create a distinct synthesis. The force of their invention lies in the way it creates a fusion, a meaningful coalescence, of different categories of narrative, different criteria for constructing time: a dynastic story of Scandinavian origins, an ethnic story of Slavonic origins, a conversion story of 'Greek' origins; a chronological framework of biblical origins, and a providential story justifying their own place in the overall scheme of time. These stories were astonishingly effective and durable. Devised and compiled by a handful of bookmen from the mid-eleventh to the early twelfth century, these tales of self-location and self-justification in time became *the* standard accounts of 'historical' identity. They were copied and re-copied and re-copied without fundamental alteration for the next half-millennium and more. And although they have since been joined or challenged by other types of story, they continue to resonate more powerfully than one might think, even today.

To find the first significant tinkering with this inherited story of 'historical' identity, we have to leap a long way in time and place: from the late eleventh century to the late fifteenth or early sixteenth century, and from Kiev to Moscow. In 1453, Constantinople, capital of the East Roman Empire for a thousand years, fell to the Turks. The writers and rulers of the growing Muscovite State came to view their own polity as a kind of replacement, as the divinely appointed successor, as the sole and true surviving – and flourishing – guardian of the True Faith. Hence they represented themselves in increasingly Byzantine terms. In ritual and ceremony this meant – eventually – adopting the formal Imperial title of *Tsar*, and displaying imperial paraphernalia allegedly received from Byzantium. In the construction of self in *time* it meant, in the first instance, compiling grand histories in which the tale of the Lands of the Rus was the continuation and culmination of universal history and not just one of its strands; and it meant looking with new eyes at the Imperial – that is, the 'Roman' – component of the Byzantine historical identity. If Constantinople had been the 'second Rome', Moscow was obviously the third. And miraculously it was discovered that the grand vision could be substantiated even in dynastic terms, for genealogists found that the ancestors of Riurik the Viking were actually descended from a relative of the Roman Emperor Augustus. It matters not a jot that the genealogical link – expounded in the *Tale of the*

Princes of Vladimir (Skazanie o kniaziakh vladimirskikh)[6] – is utter fantasy. The story served its contemporary purpose, and again we see the myth-making potency when more than one type of narrative can be aligned so as to point in the same direction.

The Muscovite invocation of a Roman heritage was purely abstract, ideological, quasi-theological. It did not imply any special interest in Rome as such. The more substantive re-orientation towards Western Europe is associated with the reforms of Tsar Peter the Great at the turn of the eighteenth century. Peter's 'westernising' project was ostentatious and pervasive. It was manifest in the style of his new urban environment (his new city of St Petersburg), in technology, in education, in language, in dress and personal appearance, and – the most relevant point in the context of the present survey – in chronology. Even before the founding of St Petersburg, by a decree dated 19 December 7208 (from the creation of the world), Peter ordered that henceforth the year should commence on 1 January, and be counted instead from the birth of Christ. The year 7208 from the Creation began in September 1699 from the Incarnation. On 1 January of that year – thus on 1 January 1700 – Russia formally adopted, with official celebrations, the new (for Russia) calendar. Peter's decree abandoned the essential framework for world history as inherited from Byzantium and formally placed Russia on a different map of time, a map which it now shared with Western Europe (though the reckoning of days and months was not changed until the Gregorian calendar was adopted in place of the Julian calendar by Soviet decree of November 1917).

Peter and his immediate successors were more concerned with re-shaping the present and the future than with reflecting on the shape of the past, but towards the end of the eighteenth century, and over the early decades of the nineteenth century, we find a significant re-emergence of interest in the more remote past of Russia (or Rus): early chronicles were copied from manuscript and published; historical genres appeared in literature, the monumental, stylish, twelve-volume (and unfinished) *History of the Russian State (Istoriia gosudarstva rossiiskogo)*, by the eminent writer Nikolai Karamzin (1766–1828) enjoyed huge prestige and informed the historical imagination for a generation and more. Peter himself was no longer the overwhelming present reality but became one of the narrative options in the native past. Or rather, writers began to perceive a potentially awkward disjunction between the Petrine narrative and the pre-Petrine narrative, which seem to imply quite different ways of constructing Russia in time, quite different criteria of 'historical' significance and authenticity. Here were two stories of self which did *not* easily coincide, which did *not* potently re-inforce one another.

Some merely noted the paradox and were prepared to accept it, to accept the tension between these stories of self, as part of identity. Others felt that a choice ought to be made. From the 1830s such debates gained fresh impetus and focus through the popularity (among the small intellectual elite, at any rate) of German Romantic philosophy, in which the shape and movement of universal time, and the place and fate of nations within it, were central concerns. Arguments raged as to which was the more 'authentic' Russia, the 'real' Russia, the more desirable Russia, and what was the 'true' story of Russia in time. Solutions appear in many variants, some crude, some subtle. They even included, at one extreme, the notion – propounded in the *Philosophical Letters* of Petr Chaadaev (1794–1856), published (in French) in 1836 – that Russia as yet had no proper history at all. But the characteristic, defining feature of the discourse lies not in any particular solution but in the preoccupation with the problem itself, in the specific dilemma of historical self-determination and the tensions generated thereby. The simple contrast between visions of Russia in time provided a narrative framework, if not the philosophical substance, for divisions and discussions between 'Slavophiles' (broadly speaking, those who felt that the proper course of Russian history was disrupted by the Petrine reforms) and 'Westernisers' (broadly speaking, those who felt that the proper course of Russian history only began with the Petrine reforms).[7] Though pushed out of the public domain for much of the twentieth century, the argument was revived in the late Soviet and post-Soviet era.

In the Soviet Union official ideology re-colonised time with a radical thoroughness reminiscent of the first Christian converts in ancient Rus. Cyclical time (the repetitive cycle of the days of the year) was appropriated to fit current values: the religious festivals and the daily calendar based on the commemoration of saints became displaced by annual commemoration of events in revolutionary and Soviet history and by a calendar of days designated to honour specified groups in modern society: Miners' Day, Navy Day, Railway Workers' Day, and so on. But more important was the new vision of linear time, of the criteria for constructing the shape of history as a whole, and hence for legitimising the present order. Gone were the dynastic stories, the annalistic stories based on pure chronology, the ethnic stories, the ethno-cultural stories of distinctive national destiny, the providential stories based on a Divine purpose. In their place came a new total vision, going back to the origins of human communities, and based on a universally applicable sequence of types of society, of socio-economic formations. All human societies were declared to develop according to a common pattern: from primitive communes, through slave-owning societies, to feudalism, capitalism, socialism, and eventually – in the inevitable future – communism. This was a new universalism, a total explanation of every phase of the life of mankind in and across time.

Where, in this scheme of time, was Russia? In a way, nowhere; or nowhere especially significant, not any longer, not now. The main point, the underlying principle, was that one scheme was valid for all, that *all* national histories were in essence, in fundamental structure, equivalent. The Russian Federation might continue to exist as a constituent part of the Soviet Union, but the formation of the Soviet Union rendered Russia irrelevant to the world-historical process, to current and future phases of time. The Russian Empire had been abolished on the political map, and Soviet ideology abolished any narrative which might legitimise its continuation on a temporal map. There was no role left for Russia in time. The best that could be done was to acknowledge Russia's role – noble, but past – in the preparation for and formation of the Soviet Union. Russia in time was a story of progress towards the abolition of itself as a distinct and autonomous geopolitical entity. This role was enshrined in the opening lines of the Soviet National Anthem, introduced in 1944.[8] The standard 'official' translation reads: 'Unbreakable Union of freeborn Republics, / Great Russia has welded forever to stand'. Yet the original actually has 'Rus', not 'Russia': sonorously vague, redolent of remote glories, untainted by grubby geo-politics.

This is not to say that national identities were thereby also abolished, or that national identities could no longer be set in terms of linear, temporal narratives. The relationship between national and supra-national stories in Soviet ideology was complex and not entirely consistent, but to overgeneralise again: the linear narrative of nation-states was concluded – even of a multinational state bearing a national name (such as Russia) – but ethnocultural narratives could to some extent continue. For the current phase of the story of Russia in time, the ethno-cultural was disentangled from the geopolitical, and the continuity of Russianness could be presented as a continuity of culture. For these purposes culture (which became ever more 'progressive') was construed largely in post-Petrine terms, with Pushkin as the pivotal figure.[9] Russian culture did nevertheless acquire a kind of meta-political status, through the imposition of the Russian language as the *lingua franca* of the Soviet Union.

The classic Soviet vision of time was not presented as a theory, but as demonstrable scientific fact. History had laws, and to recognise those laws was to acquire the freedom to pursue one's appointed purpose. But Soviet ideology also rediscovered the potency that is acquired when different types of story can be made to coincide. This was no place for paradox, but for a new miraculous harmony, and the objective laws of history turned out to have a moral dimension; they necessitated change for the better. In a kind of new Trinity of linked narratives, the *historically* inevitable (the triumph of communism) was represented as also *economically* the most efficient (a planned economy cutting out the wasteful duplication of resources in capitalist competition) as well as being *socially* the most just (catering for the needs of all members of society).

The reasons for the collapse of the Soviet Union are far beyond the scope of this survey, but long before the end in 1991 this cohesive vision, this Trinity (historical inevitability, economic efficiency, social justice) had lost much of its potency. Whatever one might think of the economic or social arguments, the core premise – that the triumph of communism was objectively inevitable – had lost much of its credibility. Late Soviet identity was more to do with the community of shared experience than with grand visions of the shape of human communities across time.

And so we arrive back at the beginning, browsing the shelves of a post-Soviet bookshop, noting the renewed post-Soviet search for (and discovery of) 'real' Russias in time. The choice has grown, as the status of the Soviet Union itself becomes one of the narrative questions. Was Soviet Russia 'real' or 'unreal' (in the somewhat surreal sense required by such constructions)? Does the story of 'authentic' Russia incorporate the Soviet experience, or was the Soviet Union a deviation from the 'true' path which is revealed when direct links to pre-Soviet Russia are restored? Old debates can be re-activated, new grand visions sought. Rarely have so many historic Russias been available.

2. CASE STUDIES: SIGNS OF THE TIMES

In order to illustrate how such narratives can function, both implicitly and explicitly, in real cultural production, we will consider two texts. Both of them are quite recent: transitional texts of the late-Soviet and early-post-Soviet period. Both are forms of official cultural discourse. I present them as no more than illustrative and perhaps instructive examples, since no two texts can come close to covering the full range of possibilities.

The first 'text' (using the word in the broad sense common in cultural studies) is (fig. 2.1) a series of five postage stamps. In fact what we have here is an oddly fussy composition: four parallel texts for the price – so to

2.1 Postage stamp series 'History of Russian Culture', 1991

speak – of one. Reading across the bottom line we discover the principal ostensible function of the objects: as postage stamps, with their various denominations. We can also locate the text: the stamps were issued in 1991, that is (and this is relevant) in the very last months of the existence of the Soviet Union. The second parallel text consists of a series of colour pictures, the central images; the third provides captions for the pictures, identifying the objects illustrated; and the fourth – the most peculiar and intriguing – consists of a secondary (smaller and fainter) series of words and images across the top of the stamps, line drawings with further captions which set the main colour illustration in a broader context. The images are in more or less chronological order, so that together they form a kind of linear narrative (or parallel linear narratives) spanning about 500 years in the case of the central pictures or, in the case of the upper captions, about 700 years.

What is suggested by a casual glance at these images? Most people are not likely to take more than a casual glance at the images on postage stamps, so that first impressions form one level of perfectly authentic reading. The general impression is perhaps that the series is meant to represent a theme such as 'icons' or 'early Russian (Christian) art'; something vaguely to do with the medieval heritage. And on one level that is enough: significant in itself to note this late Soviet popular official celebration of Russia's medieval Christian past. However, the series is also susceptible to – indeed it positively invites – more specific readings. In each case, the central image shows a made object, a piece of cultural production, which is identified and dated in the caption. And in each case the upper image shows and captions (but does not date) the person(s) or institution reckoned (sometimes by indirect means) to be responsible for the appearance of the main object. These parallel narratives are very carefully constructed, each provides its own commentary, together they form a composite interpretation of Russia in time.

The first central image reproduces a miniature of St Luke from the earliest surviving dated Slavonic manuscript book, the *Ostromir Gospel*, written out by the scribe Grigorii in 1056–57. The main caption gives the date, which thus locates the beginning of the series firmly in the Kievan period. The upper image is therefore somewhat surprising: two figures captioned 'Cyril' and 'Methodios'. Cyril and Methodios had nothing directly to do with Rus/Russia. They had been missionaries to quite different Slavs, in Moravia in the 860s, over a century before the conversion of the Rus and about two centuries before Grigorii produced the *Ostromir Gospel*. Yet in a sense Cyril and Methodios made the *Ostromir Gospel* possible, for they are credited with having devised the first system of writing for the Slavs, and with having first translated the Gospels into the Slavonic language. The manuscript Slavonic Gospel book from Rus is thus represented not just in its own temporal context ('1056–57' in the main caption) but in an implied narrative of the wider Slavonic legacy of Cyril and Methodios.

The second central image is another manuscript page, but now with writing alone. The caption identifies it '*Russkaia pravda*. XI–XIIIc.'. *Russkaia pravda* is the earliest Rus code of written law. This is custom law, emphatically *not* derived from Christianity, but an achievement emblematic of the emergence of a State. Again the upper caption provides the didactic context: 'Iaroslav the Wise'. Iaroslav was prince of Kiev in the mid-eleventh century (he died in 1054, in the same decade as the writing of the *Ostromir Gospel*). He was a son of Vladimir, Converter of the Rus, and is widely associated with an ambitious programme of Christian cultural production including Kiev's main and most magnificent monument, the church of St Sophia. Though these are visible in the background in the upper image, here Iaroslav is most prominently linked to his secular, administrative initiative: to the institution of written law, one of the chief implements and attributes of the State. This is an image of political origins, again based firmly in the 'Kievan' age.

The central image on the third stamp in the series shows an embroidered portrait, labelled 'Sergii of Radonezh. Embroidery. 1424'. Sergii of Radonezh (d.1392; 1424 is the date of the embroidery itself) is viewed as the father of Muscovite and subsequent monasticism, and his major monument is displayed in the upper image: 'The Trinity-Sergii Monastery', a little way to the northwest of Moscow, the most prestigious of Russian monasteries to this day. Here the relationship of main to upper image is curiously reversed: the main image shows the achiever and the upper image shows the achievement, rather than the reverse. More significantly, Sergii's legacy is expressly represented in the impressive buildings, in the grand walled monastery, perhaps the most typical and distinctive feature of the early (pre-Petrine) Russian urban landscape.

The fourth central image shows the most frequently reproduced of all Russian icons. The caption identifies it as 'The Trinity. Icon. c.1411'. The 'Trinity' here is the so-called 'Old Testament Trinity': the three youths who visited Abraham at his tent in Mamre,[10] interpreted as angels, and as prefiguring the New Testament Trinity. The rather quaintly drawn upper image shows the painter, labelled 'Andrei Rublev'. Icon-painting was an almost entirely anonymous form of devotional representation, but modern conceptions of the artist require brand-recognition, the individual genius, and Andrei Rublev – one of very few icon-painters whose names we happen to know – is the acknowledged genius of early Russian art: a familiar name even to those who might otherwise have no interest in icons; an emblematic, evocative name, guarantor of the status and dignity of the old Russian artistic heritage.[11]

The central image on the fifth stamp – the last – shows a printed portrait of St Luke, at the start of (as the main caption states) the '*Acts and Epistles*, 1564', printed by (upper images and caption) 'Ivan Fedorov and Petr Mstislavets'. Ivan Fedorov's reputation is as the first known, named Moscow printer, and his *Acts and Epistles* is the earliest dated Moscow printed book. The image here is associated with progress in the technologies of culture: the adoption of printing. Coming at the end of the series it therefore neatly balances, both visually and thematically, the opening image in the series – also of St Luke – from the earliest known dated Slav manuscript book, representing the adoption of writing.

The set of stamps thus displays an emblematic sequence of official images, produced in the final months of the Soviet Union, presenting Russia in time through a set of parallel verbal and visual narratives. The origins are located firmly in Kiev, with an assumed continuity between Kiev and Moscow. The surprising feature, in Soviet official discourse, is the apparent religious content. Before the late 1980s it would have been very odd to find this sequence of images in this type of public context. The catalyst for change was the celebration of the millennium of 'Russian' Christianity in 1988, which became a kind of test for President Mikhail Gorbachev's declared policy of openness (*glasnost'*). Initially the anniversary was planned as a private occasion for the Church; eventually it became a major, public, national event. Read on this level the series of stamps is a product of the new (from the late 1980s) attitude to Russia's Christian past.[12]

On another level, however, a closer reading also shows the extent to which the text is still bound to conventional Soviet habits. Although the images are principally religious in origin, every effort is made to contextualise the images as 'culture': as culture conceived in a Soviet manner, as a sequence of 'progressive' phenomena, linked to wider advances in politics, technology, and construction. There is a museum-like quality, a fussiness in the design reflecting a certain didacticism in the production as a whole: the careful mixture of media (one manuscript miniature, one manuscript text, one textile, one panel icon, one printed image); the prominence of dates in all the main captions; the telling absence of the word 'saint' in at least three places where it might be applied in unselfconsciously Christian discourse (Sts Cyril and Methodios; St Sergii of Radonezh; and St Luke); and above all the addition of the secondary images and captions which serve as commentaries on the central images. The upper images and captions focus the narrative, give it a specificity: the emergence of writing; the establishment of law and governance; the formation of impressive architectural monuments; the creation of Great Art; the emergence of printing. This is what lies behind the peculiar design.

Finally, the series reinforces a geo-political narrative of the formation of Russia in time: a tale of Slav origins, of the foundation of a native State in Kiev, and of Muscovy as its successor. The text can be read on all three levels: as an evocation of the story of early Russian Christianity, as a representation of cultural and technological progress, and as an affirmation of national continuity from Kievan origins. The designers were presumably aware that in practice most users are unlikely to read postage stamps quite so rigorously. Perhaps they deliberately colluded in the dissemination of a religious-based narrative of identity while inserting the secondary images and captions as a vestigial fig-leaf of Soviet decorum. Whatever their assumptions about how the stamps might be perceived, their design clearly prevents the series from standing as a straightforward, unmodified assertion of Christian continuity as a defining component of Russia in time. In 1991 the genie was almost out of the bottle, but still just about held by the tail. The official title of this set of Soviet stamps is 'Russia's Cultural Heritage'. The Russian, post-Soviet postal services today would have no qualms whatever about labelling such a sequence 'The Heritage of Russian Christianity'.

The second 'text' is a set of Ukrainian banknotes (fig. 2.2). This selection may appear perverse in a study of aspects of Russian national identity: Ukraine is no longer part of the Russian Empire, no longer part of the Russia-dominated Soviet Union. However, narratives of identity extend beyond the current map. Ukraine is not Russia, but in a sense it is at least partly *Russia* in the old Latin sense, since part of Ukraine, like part of Russia, fills part of the space once covered by the Lands of the Rus. Thus, as we shall see, a story of Ukraine in time overlaps with – and in some versions directly challenges – a story of Russia in time, and in their interrelationships something of the nature of each is clarified.

By contrast with the late Soviet stamps, the Ukrainian banknotes were not issued simultaneously as an integral set. They were produced over time, in changing circumstances. They therefore present a doubly dynamic narrative, as the tale told by the objects runs alongside the tale of its telling. The series begins with one of the first banknotes issued by independent Ukraine: a 'coupon' for one 'karbovanets', dated 1991. The note shows a rather dramatic young lady, instantly recognisable to a Kievan as Lybed, a figure on one of the well-known local monuments. Her picture thus

2.2 Ukrainian bank notes, 1991–96

provides some local colour for the local currency. It is used as an emblem of Ukraine, rather as elsewhere one might use Britannia (for Britain), or the Statue of Liberty (for New York or America), or Marianne (for France). As the series develops, however, so the language of emblems becomes more focused, more specific, more pointed in its narrative implications. By 1992, on the 1,000-karbovanets note (inflation is an all-too-obvious sub-theme here), the lone maiden is revealed as the figurehead, who is now joined by three other figures in a representation of the full monument, which turns out to be a longboat. The effect is to underscore the historical allusion, for the three figures in the boat are Kii, Shchek, and Khoriv, the legendary founders of the city of Kiev, while Lybed herself is moved into closer proximity to the word *Ukraina* (Ukraine), towards which the boat seems to be sailing. Thus the notion of 'Ukraine' is associated not just with local landmarks, but with the ancient foundation of its current capital city, and with a sense of historical dynamism, the beginnings of a story of time.

In the third note in our series, the 5,000-karbovanets note from 1993, an additional emblem has appeared: a trident-like sign to the left of the boat, where previously there had been a blank circle. In common language and perception this is the 'Ukrainian trident', symbol of Ukrainian statehood. But where does it come from? One answer is that it picks up pre-Soviet emblems, emblems of an earlier period of twentieth-century independence movements in Ukraine.[13] In fact, however, the emblem is much older. It was a dynastic emblem used by the ruling princes of Kiev from the late tenth century, and this particular variant of it is a copy of the version used by Prince Vladimir, converter of the Rus to Christianity. There is even precedent for its use on currency: Vladimir did not issue banknotes, but the trident emblem does appear on his silver coins.[14] Hence in the next phase of development of this visual narrative (the 10,000-karbovanets note) the link is made explicit, as Lybed and her brethren are replaced by Vladimir himself, holding the Cross, alongside his own emblem. Having started with a bit of local colour, the series of banknotes thus turns by clear stages into a statement about the ancient roots of Ukrainian statehood, a declaration about the place of Ukraine in time. The declaration is polemical, since this story of Ukraine in time is in direct opposition to the familiar story of Russia in time – with its statehood also traced to Kievan origins – as represented on the almost contemporary late-Soviet postage stamps. The two visual narratives promote competing perceptions of 'historical' identity and legitimation.

The text continues. In 1996, Ukraine introduced a new currency, the hryvnia (the last in the sequence illustrated in fig. 2.2). Apart from providing

2.3 Ukrainian bank notes: reverse

an opportunity to knock several noughts off the denomination of the highly inflated karbovanets (the value of one hryvnia was set at 100,000 of the old units), the new currency represents a further refinement of the implied narrative of Ukraine in time. What is a hryvnia? The name of the currency unit is allusive and evocative. Again it echoes the currency of a previous twentieth-century period of independence, but again it also echoes early Kievan statehood: a grivna (the same word as hryvnia in a different articulation and transliteration) was the main unit of currency in the Kievan period, the value of a standard silver ingot. Moreover, the earliest substantial text to mention grivnas turns out to be *Russkaia pravda*, the very work illustrated as part of the Russian heritage on the late-Soviet series of stamps. The claim to the disputed time-line becomes ever more insistent. Let us consider again the picture of Vladimir on the hryvnia note. This is no longer Vladimir the Converter, robed and bearded, bearing his Cross. This is Volodymyr[15] with the drooping moustache of a Ukrainian hetman, not as a spiritual figure, but as a fully nationalised head of State.

Volodymyr is not yet the beginning of the temporal story. Compare the pictures on the reverse of an old-currency 1,000-karbovanets note and on the reverse of the new hryvnia (fig. 2.3). The karbovanets note – like all karbovanets notes – bears a picture of the church of St Sophia and its surrounding buildings in Kiev. Again this suggests eleventh-century Christianity, although the image is also readable simply as one of the most prominent local landmarks. The hryvnia note is altogether more ambitious and complex. The image hints at Christianity with its outline shape, which might be taken to suggest a multi-domed church, but within this frame it depicts, perhaps unexpectedly, the ruins of the ancient Greek city of Chersonesos in the Crimea. The inclusion of Chersonesos on the national currency may be read in a number of ways. Most pointedly, for example, it may be read as a polemical visual declaration of the Ukrainian-ness of a highly disputed territory on the modern map, which many Russians would claim as rightfully, 'historically' their own. Or, on a more sophisticated level of allusion for the knowing reader, the image calls to mind the early chronicle story which places Volodymyr's baptism in Chersonesos ('Korsun') – which in turn either implies a thousand-year-old pedigree for the claim to the Crimea, or, more gently, again serves as an emblem of a thousand-year-old tradition of Ukrainian statehood. Alternatively, on a still grander conceptual scale, this picture of classical ruins implies an association of the idea of 'Ukraine' with the heritage of all civilisations currently found on Ukrainian territory; and if the idea of 'Ukraine' is somehow associated with the ancient Greek ruins, then the resonances of 'Ukraine in time' extend not just over the previous decade, or the previous eighty years, or the previous thousand years, but over nearly two and a half thousand years.

The progression of implied visual narratives – from local Kievan landmarks to a fully articulated representation of national statehood going back one or two millennia or more – is not accidental. The hryvnia was introduced as the official Ukrainian currency in 1996, yet the date on the reverse of the note is 1992. The notes had actually been printed (in Canada) four years in advance. This was a conscious programme for the appropriation of time, prepared well in advance of the timetable for the introduction of the currency. In a period of conscious 'state-formation' following post-Soviet independence, the Ukrainian banknotes reflect a dynamic process of the re-modelling of a story of All Rus, precisely to distinguish it from a Russia-based story of 'All the Russias'.

These two visual texts – the late-Soviet series of postage stamps and the Ukrainian succession of banknotes – are as tiny droplets in a vast ocean. They cannot come close to 'covering' the subject of cultural representations of Russia (or of *Russia* in the older sense) in time. Yet they are, to an extent, indicative. In particular, they exemplify ways in which cultural visions of Russia in time can be reaffirmed and reinvented, supported and subverted, upheld and undermined, in one and the same process. Both texts are 'official', and mass-produced. Both texts function through assuming a widely shared visual vocabulary, a shared set of emblems implying shared narratives of nationhood, yet both also seek to exploit the recognition of these emblems in order to shape their own distinctive and didactic representations of the narrative. Both texts can be read – and were probably designed to be readable – on several levels: at one extreme, as reassuring sets of general cultural reference points; at the other extreme, as highly specific, pointed challenges to common assumption. Both texts play on a communal sense of tradition, yet in their manipulation of tradition both are firmly situated in their own local and temporal milieu. They illustrate graphically (in all senses) ways in which the discourse of national identity may reflect a continuing struggle for ownership of the shape of time, ways in which ingredients from the accumulated menu of stories can be selected and blended so as to concoct whichever imagined flavour of the past best appeals to the taste-buds of the present.

CHAPTER 3

Russia as space

Emma Widdis

Walking in Moscow in 1927, ten years after the Bolshevik revolution of 1917, the German philosopher and critic Walter Benjamin (1892–1940) was struck by a peculiar thing – everywhere he looked in the city he saw piles of maps for sale. As he recalled in his 'Moscow Diary': 'Russia is beginning to take shape for the man of the people. On the street, in the snow, lie maps of the [R]SFSR, piled up by street vendors who offer them for sale . . . The map is almost as close to becoming the centre of the new Russian iconic cult as Lenin's portrait.'[1] Sixty years later, in Moscow in the late 1980s and early 1990s, it might have seemed that nothing had changed. At metro stations and in street kiosks, maps were once again a product of choice, piled up on makeshift tables for the consumer's perusal. As the Soviet Union collapsed in 1991, so there were new atlases of the new Russian Federation, and of the CIS (Commonwealth of Independent States). As Moscow's streets were renamed, shaking off their Soviet heritage, so new maps of the city itself were needed. Russia once again, and in a quite different context, was 'taking shape for the man of the people'.

The obsession with maps and mapping in the 1990s was understandable. Just as the openness sanctioned by Mikhail Gorbachev's policies of *perestroika* (re-building) and *glasnost'* (openness) meant a rewriting of history (filling in the 'blank' spots of official history), so it meant a rewriting – or re-drawing – of geography. In the course of 1989, the Soviet-influenced 'Eastern bloc' disintegrated: the Berlin Wall (in place since 1961) was dismantled in November. Two years later, in 1991, the Soviet Union was dealt final and shattering blows. The Warsaw pact (between the Soviet Union and Eastern European states) was dissolved in July, and the fragmentation did not stop there. At its height, the Union of Soviet Socialist Republics (USSR) was a union of fifteen Republics (including the three Baltic states, Lithuania, Latvia, and Estonia that were annexed to the Soviet Union in 1940). Between January and April of 1991, Lithuania, Estonia, and the southern republic of Georgia, declared their independence. By the end of the year, they had been followed by the twelve remaining republics, creating a plethora of newly independent states: Armenia, Latvia, Moldova, Ukraine, Azerbaijan, Turkmenistan, Uzbekistan, Tajikistan, Kyrgyzstan, Kazakhstan, and Belarus. On 21 December 1991, in Alma Ata (now Almaty), the Union of Soviet Socialist Republics was formally dissolved, and replaced by the Commonwealth of Independent States (CIS). The fifteenth republic, the RSFSR (Russian Soviet Federative Socialist Republic), formally the governing centre of that vast Union, found itself abandoned at that centre, forced into an independence that it had not sought, and positioned within a transformed geo-political sphere.

This repositioning was accompanied by a curious, and traumatic, rediscovery of the space of the Russian Federation itself. As Gorbachev came to power in 1986, calling for openness (*glasnost'*) about the Soviet Union's traumatic history, a decade-long process of 'uncovering' the details of the country's history of oppression, of deportation, and of terror, began. Across the territory, formerly 'secret' cities (generally linked to the military-industrial complex, and frequently the sites of nuclear research), which had been left off official maps of the Soviet Union, and to and from which travel had been forbidden, were reopened, becoming marks on the developing map of the transformed space. In addition, the spaces of former labour camps were uncovered, many of them situated in virtually inaccessible and uninhabitable northern regions. The spaces of labour camps had long been inhabited, under duress, but had remained officially 'unmapped', hidden by inaccessibility and secrecy.

All these changes brought about a fundamental dislocation in what one might call the shared national map – the real and imaginary geography of Russianness. It took place at a micro level too: within cities, street names were changed, as Soviet versions were rejected in favour of a return to pre-revolutionary nomenclature. Monuments were dismantled, often destabilizing common points of orientation within the urban space. In the early 1990s, when you asked for directions, even in central Moscow, you got the following kind of reply: 'Go past Derzhinskii – or at least, the empty pedestal where Derzhinskii used to be, up the old Marx Avenue, past the new parliament, turn right onto Gorkii Street – sorry, Tverskaia; continue until you come to Maiakovskii Square . . . though it's called Triumphalnaia now . . .' Moscow, renamed and remapped, was suddenly an unfamiliar place for those who lived there. Like history, space itself could not be trusted.

During the *perestroika* period, then, change – social and political change – was echoed in a change of map. Those maps for sale had a significance that was as much symbolic as practical. Perhaps they were an attempt to resist the spatial fragmentation of Russian identity, to retain a shared conception of the homeland, to 'know' a space that threatened to become unknowable? Or just a means of tracking rapid and destabilizing change? In any case, they are evidence of the ideological and symbolic significance of space. And this, of course, is linked to what Benjamin observed in Moscow in the late 1920s: those piles of maps in the snow were part of a vast process of map-making which took place in Soviet Russia in the first two decades after the Bolshevik revolution in 1917. Producing and disseminating images of the territory was a crucial task for the new regime, marking the boundaries of power, creating a coherent, shared notion of Soviet space. It was a form of social incorporation. In 1931, for example, an article in the adventure journal for adolescents entitled *All Around the World* (*Vokrug sveta*) boasted that one Leningrad factory had produced only 800 maps of the territory per annum before the revolution; now by contrast, the article claimed, the same factory produced 125,000 globes and 28,000 geographical maps of the territory, although, the author conceded, 'for our boundless [*neob"iatnyi*] Union' even '125,000 [globes] is too few.'[2] From 1925 until 1947, a special cartography committee worked on the creation of what was to be the largest and most detailed map of the Soviet Union. Its scale was intended to echo the vast scale of the territory itself (and, according to urban legend, it was constantly increased, so that the final map was on a scale of 1cm:1km, making a map some fifty metres in breadth). The significance – ideological, social, and cultural – of map-making in Stalin's Russia is made clear by the fact that in 1935, control of national cartography was assumed by the NKVD (Peoples Commissariat for Internal Affairs). But the map-making process was not limited to cartography. All the resources of Soviet propaganda (films, visual arts, literature) were enlisted in the project of creating a new imagined geography for the young regime.

In the final section of this chapter, I will return to the specific 'taking shape' of the Soviet Union. First, however, I will suggest that this obsession with mapping is part of a problem that is recurrent in Russian culture. As the title of a 1926 documentary film proclaimed, the Soviet Union in 1926 occupied 'a sixth of the world' – of its total land surface. Even now, after the break-up of the Soviet Union, the Russian Federation itself remains the largest country in the world, stretching from the 'European' Russia of Moscow, across the vast plains of Siberia, to the east coast, towards Japan and Alaska. And the construction of coherent narratives of identity flounders on the intransigent planes of the vast territory. It has long been tempting to link territory and nation, to view the gigantic unwieldiness of the space as both cause and symbol of Russia's similarly unwieldy history. In the nineteenth century, the philosopher and social theorist Aleksandr Herzen (1812–70) claimed that Russia was 'more subject to geographical than to historical authority.'[3] In the words of the poet Aleksandr Blok (1880–1921), writing in 1908, on the brink of a new era: 'Our spaces are fated to play an elemental role in our history.'[4] Blok's statement of the 'historical' and fateful role of space seamlessly blends the apparently practical with the clearly symbolic – a mix characteristic of descriptions of the Russian territory. The *neob"iatnyi prostor* (boundless territory) offers a powerful symbol of Russian national identity.

In this chapter, we will explore the problems that the vast unwieldiness of the territory causes, and has caused, and the different ways in which the space, indefinable or otherwise, does function as a metaphor for, and expression of, something that is perceived to be fundamentally Russian. To do that, we need to go backwards, to submit to a race through time – or more appropriately, through space. I will briefly, and inevitably schematically, look at different ways in which the territory has been variously represented and contested, across a large time-scale, before returning to some images from Stalinist culture of the 1930s and 1940s for closer analysis. My focus throughout is not the real geography of Russia, the Russian Empire, and the Soviet Union, or indeed their maps, but rather how images of the territory were culturally inscribed – which images of the space were produced, and what they expressed. The purpose is to show different ways in which the metaphor and reality of the space intersect in the shifting imaginary geography of the nation.

I. THE REAL LANDSCAPE: SHIFTING BORDERS

What, then, is the Russian 'space'? The answer depends partly on the time (borders move, seats of power move) and partly on the criteria by which this space is defined. Russia has been a flexible concept. Perhaps its only clear feature is that, by virtually any criteria, it has expanded massively. The earliest *Rhosia* was literally boundless, in that it was a conceived as an approximate sphere of influence (the influence of people known as the *Rhos*, or Rus)[5] rather than as a territory with fixed borders, but it was tiny by comparison with later versions. Its backbone lay on a north–south axis formed by the river-roads between the Baltic Sea and the Black Sea. The Rus were predominantly Vikings, drawn southwards from Scandinavia, probably beginning in the late ninth century, by the prospect of trade with Constantinople, heart of the Byzantine Empire and the richest city in Europe. The journey took them through lands inhabited by Finnic tribes in the north, Slavs in the centre, and Turkic nomads in the southern prairies, or steppes: quite distinct geographic and ethno-cultural zones, with numerous distinct and diverse local identities, none of them initially 'Russian'. The Rus sustained this trade route by establishing themselves in settlements along the way, and the settlers gradually extended their regular contacts with the local tribes and began to become linguistically assimilated to the Slavs. By the mid-tenth century (earlier political history is obscure and disputed) their principal northern and southern bases, at Novgorod and Kiev respectively, had grown into prosperous and populous towns, both under the control of the Kievan ruling family. For contemporary Byzantine writers *Rhosia* was the area in which these *Rhos* (i.e. Rus) rulers and their associates operated.

The official conversion to Christianity towards the end of the tenth century helped provide the tools for the conceptual integration of dynasty's growing and diverse territories and populations. Kievan writers begin to identify and justify a 'Land of the Rus' (*russkaia zemlia*). The preamble to the *Primary Chronicle*, a compilation from the early twelfth century, states that one of its main aims is to tell 'whence the Land of the Rus came into being'.[6] For the chronicler who tries to construct a story of coherence and homogeneity (that is, an identity), the creation of a narrative of nationhood was inextricably linked to the creation of an imaginary geography of that nation.

Despite having apparently 'come into being', however, the *russkaia zemlia* remained very much in a process of 'becoming'. The eleventh-century polity was firmly based on Kiev because of its position on the north–south trade route, but by the second half of the twelfth century the rapidly proliferating members of the dynasty had significantly expanded their zones of activity, pushing outwards in both directions from the central axis and establishing strong regional centres as far apart as Vladimir in the northeast (beyond Moscow, which is first mentioned as a fortified outpost in 1147) and Galich in the southwest (in what is now Western Ukraine). Thus through continual dynastic (and cultural) colonization the *russkaia zemlia* grew, both spatially and conceptually.

Regional growth generated problems, since in practice the dynastic 'land' now consisted of distinct competing 'lands'. The terminology of space and territory splits accordingly. On the one hand, sources often use the term 'Rus' in a narrow sense, with reference just to the areas around or controlled from Kiev, *as distinct from*, say, the 'Suzdal land', or the 'Smolensk land'. On the other hand we also find *russkaia zemlia* used with a wider, pan-dynastic meaning. The label had been devised to promote a sense of integration around the rulers of Kiev; but the profusion of strong and increasingly autonomous regional principalities, while broadly a sign of the dynasty's continuing success, could also give an impression of *dis*integration when measured against the earlier comparative compactness. Already by the thirteenth century we hear laments over the decline of the *russkaia zemlia*. In origin a synthetic label for what 'was', for an emerging geo-political entity, for what 'had come into being', the *russkaia zemlia* – in its expanded sense – had turned into a more overtly abstract notion, a metapolitical notion of what should be, an explicitly ideal geography of nationhood. This was the time when the idea of '*All* Rus' (*vsia Rus'*) was invented: 'All Rus' meaning all the lands that the users of the term wished, by whatever criteria (initially it was to do with the jurisdiction of the Church), to associate with the idea of Rus, regardless of current political structures.

The metapolitical *russkaia zemlia*, could withstand more than merely dynastic divisions. In the fourteenth century, when the eastern lands were tributary to the Mongols, and the western lands (including Kiev) had been absorbed into Lithuania (and eventually into the Polish-Lithuanian Commonwealth), 'All Rus' remained a standard feature of ecclesiastical geography and hence in the ideology of the ethno-cultural (if not of the geo-political). Moscow's expansion in the fifteenth century, as the Mongol grip slackened (tribute-payments ceased in 1480), is often described as the 'gathering' of the Rus lands. 'All Rus' re-entered the language of political aspiration, and in 1547 became enshrined in official political terminology as Ivan IV ('the Terrible') was crowned 'Tsar of All Rus' (*vseia Rusi*); or, as a tradition of English mis-translation would have it, 'of All the Russias'.[7]

In its origins, then, Russia was a space fought for and contested. It was increasingly 'imperial' in ambition, its borders fraught and changeable. There were three principal directions for expansion: west, south, and east. To the west lay the heavily populated spaces of Poland, Lithuania, and Sweden, but also the Baltic Sea, and invaluable potential access to the navigable oceans of the north, unavailable to Russia because of her largely frozen northern coast. To the south lay the Black Sea, and its access through the Dardanelles to the Mediterranean. To the east, across the Ural mountains, lay the vast, rich, and unexploited tracts of Siberia and – eventually – the Far East. Expansion to the west and south, into heavily populated spaces, was fraught with difficulty, and those borders were contested and shifting from the sixteenth century until the Second World War. To the east, by contrast, expansion was relatively unimpeded. The history of Russian expansionism, and the myths of its space, are underpinned by such historical pragmatics: Siberia, 'beyond the Urals', was its principal 'conquest', and remains a key metaphor for power.

The most significant expansion of Muscovy took place in the seventeenth century, and in both directions: to the west, the annexation of much of Ukraine, including Kiev itself (and, in the Muscovite view, the reunification of the *russkaia zemlia*, the realization of an ideal of All Rus); and to the east – Siberia. Expansion was not without battle, however: the Empire itself underwent invasion by both Poland and Sweden. Tsar Mikhail Romanov (1613–45) drove the invaders back from his cities, but they continued to occupy large sections of the territory until Peter the Great (1689–1725) successfully repelled the Swedes and secured access to the Baltic. Thereafter, Peter's reign was one of expansion – in particular into Siberia. By 1710, there were some 200,000 settlers east of the Ural Mountains, and Peter made Siberia one of his first administrative Provinces, thus incorporating it within the governmental structure of his Empire. From the late seventeenth century on, Siberia was at once a space for adventurers and heroes, and a space of exile, as criminal and political prisoners were deported to its furthest depths.

For all his success as conqueror, however, Peter was unable to reach the Black Sea, and over the hundred-year period between 1735 and 1829, when she obtained the right of passage, Russia underwent long wars with Turkey, as both states fought for sovereignty over the Black Sea. Under Catherine the Great (1762–96), parts of the Crimea and Kuban region were 'annexed', securing part of the coastline. This policy of annexation – the assertion of political might, and the subjugation of resistance – was characteristic of Catherine's reign. The first 'Partition' of Poland in 1795, meant that Russia took over large swathes of Poland, and continued to annex further tracts of land until the end of the eighteenth century, when Russian sovereignty reached as far as the border with the Austro-Hungarian Empire. Through the nineteenth century, the Empire continued to expand its boundaries towards the west and east, so that by the beginning of the First World War in 1914, Russian territory included the Polish capital of Warsaw and the three Baltic states of Estonia, Lithuania, and Latvia.

It was, broadly speaking, this space that the Bolsheviks inherited in 1917, but they did not do so without struggle. Indeed, the collapse of the monarchy, and the chaos engendered first by the World War and then by the Civil War, seemed to offer an opportunity for freedom to many of those annexed by Tsarist armies in the preceding centuries. Between 1917 and 1920, Bolshevik armies fought for Azerbaijan, Armenia, and Georgia, in addition to fighting on the contested border with Poland. They did so under the banner of World Revolution – a vision of an international workers' uprising that would render such national boundaries obsolete. In the meantime, pragmatically speaking, there were borders to defend, and a new space to map.

The space inherited by the new regime was not, of course, entirely unmapped. Indeed, the first *chertezhy* (sketches, or 'maps' without degree grid) of the *russkaia zemlia* had been produced during the sixteenth and seventeenth centuries, marking rivers, lakes, wells, and adjacent towns. The first 'atlas' of Siberia was produced in 1701. In 1745, an official 'atlas' of the Imperial space, produced by the Academy of Sciences on Imperial command, was issued, comprising 'nineteen special maps, presenting the All-Russian Empire and its Neighbouring Territories'. During the nineteenth century in particular, in association with Imperial expansion, the project of mapping took place at a number of levels: in the literal sense of cartography, in the construction of infrastructure and networks of communication (the St Petersburg–Moscow railway was built between 1842 and 1851), and in the development of related disciplines such as ethnography. The scale of the territory was apparently insurmountable, however, and in the apparently authoritative discourse of an encyclopedia of 1895, it was still possible to write that 'vast tracts of the territory of the empire remain technically unmeasured'.[8]

The geo-political history of Russia and the Soviet Union, then, was one of expansion, and this has certain key effects on the conception of the Russian space. First, the very foundation of any idea of the Russian 'nation' was based on a perpetually shifting idea of what the territory was. The earliest *russkaia zemlia* had its symbolic focus in Kiev. Moscow subsequently claimed to inherit the status and authority of Kiev, despite being in a quite different place, a long way to the northeast. Peter the Great shifted the centre of his nation once more, this time to the northern Gulf of Finland. The construction of St Petersburg as a 'window' to the West marked a reorientation – both practical and symbolic – of Russian space. Ideology was mapped onto geography – the so-called modernization of the nation was to be achieved by a spatial re-mapping. Similarly, the decision of the Soviet leadership, in 1918, to shift their Socialist capital back to Moscow, was a rejection of the Imperialist space of St Petersburg, with its associations of workers' oppression, and an attempt to appropriate a new capital – but one which nevertheless offered the symbolic armature of history as support. Kiev, Moscow, St Petersburg: all three cities offer different symbolic narratives, different strategies of national self-identification. One of them – Kiev – is now the capital of Ukraine, not even a part of modern-day Russia, yet it is Vladimir's capital, the site of the official conversion to Christianity, and as such a founding space in one of the principal narratives of Russianness. Where, then, is the symbolic locus of Russian identity?

Secondly, it might be suggested that this history of conquest constructs a particular relationship with the territory – its nature and its people. From the first *bogatyri* (heroes) who populate Russia's epic folklore, to the early heroics of Ermak (d. 1585), first explorer of Siberia, through to the adventurers of Stalin's Russia, and the romantic wanderers of the 1960s 'Thaw' period, the territory has offered a series of adventure spaces, images of which recur in folklore, literature, and film. In representations of the territory, we can trace an attitude that might be described as the desire to conquer, or to tame, the natural world. A whole series of terms to describe conquest – *osvoenie* (assimilation, annexation), *zavoevanie* (conquest through battle), *pokorenie* (subjugation) – are consistently used in relation to the territory itself.

2. THE SYMBOLIC LANDSCAPE: UNBOUNDED

The imperative to conquer focused on nature, as much as on peoples. For the 'problem', if we may call it that, with the Russian space, was not just quantitative. It was also qualitative. The sheer vastness of the territory incorporates an enormous diversity of terrains, from the dramatic mountain ranges and deserts of the south, to the birch forests of the central region, the icy plains (taiga) of Siberia. To further complicate matters, vast quantities of the territory are uninhabitable. Despite enormous reserves of natural resources, at least two-thirds of the territory are considered unusable from an agricultural point of view. Large sections of Siberia and the far north are covered in permafrost (permanently frozen soil). All of the main Russian seas are frozen for parts of the year (only Murmansk, near the border with Norway, is kept unfrozen by a peculiarity of the Gulf Stream). For practical and historical reasons, most settlement is concentrated far to the west. Moscow is twenty times closer to the western frontier than it is to the eastern one. Relations between centre and periphery are thus complex: the sheer breadth of the territory means that it encompasses some eight different time zones, such that when it is noon by 'central' Moscow time it is 3pm in Novosibirsk and 7pm in Magadan in the Far East. Different spaces create different times, rendering problematic the practicalities of centralization (the coordination of train timetables, of religious festivals, etc.) and the pragmatics of governance.

Aside from these problems of governance and of habitation, there is another problem – that of symbols. What is or can be the 'symbol' of the Russian landscape? Is it a birch forest? The Siberian taiga? The vast rivers of the Don and the Volga? The frozen North? What, in any case, is the status of any national symbol of landscape in an Empire which incorporates so many diverse peoples? After all, the Soviet Union proudly proclaimed 150 different nationalities within its borders at one point. And that same article in the magazine *All around the World* boasted of the production of maps and globes in twenty-nine of the languages of the peoples of the Soviet Union.

Despite this extraordinary diversity, however – or perhaps because of it, because of the need for strategies of incorporation – there are common threads which run through descriptions of the territory in Russian cultural texts. These can be seen particularly clearly in the verbal and visual texts of the nineteenth century, when questions of identity and nationalness assumed particular urgency. A French traveller, the Marquis de Custine (1790–1857), who travelled in Russia in 1839 offers one of the most damning accounts of the landscape, describing Russia as a 'country without landscapes', but with endless empty space: 'What a country! [. . .] It's an endless, flat, plain – flat like the palm of your hand, without colour, and without shape; an eternal bog, with intermittent, rare, wheat fields.' After a few weeks, he concludes, 'the traveller's heart is overtaken with horror', and he wants to 'run from this graveyard, which seems to have no end, and no edge'.[9] This account, by a foreigner, can be compared with a curiously similar description from a Russian – from Vasilii Kliuchevskii (1841–1911), whose multi-volume account of Russian history was completed in the early twentieth century. Kliuchevksii begins his history with a description of the uniqueness of the Russian space, recounting how an imaginary Russian traveller, arriving in the West, feels restricted and hemmed in, recalling his native land. In his dreams of Russia, Kliuchevskii says, the Russian 'sees the level, empty fields, which seems to curve around the horizon, like a sea, with rare settlements.'[10] In these two quotations, a hundred years apart, one by a foreigner, and one by a Russian, we find some key things in common, but given very different emphasis. First, both writers comment on flatness, and emptiness. Secondly, both evoke the horizon, or lack of it. De Custine writes in horror of a land with no end and no edge; Kliuchevskii describes a flatness which seems to curve *around* the horizon, which seems to deny the very existence of an edge to the space – of the horizon. This denial of limits is characteristic of descriptions of the territory. The Russian space is frequently described as something that appears endless – it seems to have no edge. As such, it is unknowable and implicitly uncontrolled.

For Kliuchevskii, then, the 'empty' Russian plain, with its lack of distinguishing features, provides a kind of definition of Russian identity. Its power lies precisely in its emptiness – as both symbol and reality. This Russian emptiness can, implicitly, be invested with whatever signficance you choose, and its distinctiveness is apprehended through comparison: De Custine, the foreigner in Russia, sees only chaos. Kliuchevskii's imaginary Russian abroad recollects – by contrast – openness and freedom: a kind of freedom and lack of claustrophobia that more conventionally 'national' (and by this we understand West European) landscapes do not offer. In parallel, Russian identity, we infer, has a freedom and purity all of its own. This process of turning disadvantage into advantage is one that we can trace through many of the many 'discourses on national identity' that this volume explores. Just as the 'lateness' of Russia's conversion to Christianity was transmuted into a virtue of uniqueness,[11] so the 'specialness' of being the most mysterious, unknown, and difficult to know or to map could be configured as a virtue. The Russian space is consistently defined in terms of its mystery – in terms, in fact, of all the things that make Russian identity problematic. In recalling the vast emptiness of the territory, for example, Kliuchevskii evoked Russia's refusal to be 'enclosed', either physically, by borders, or metaphorically, by definition. In a much-quoted short poem by Fedor Tiutchev (1803–73), Russia 'cannot be measured by common *arshin* [term of measurement]', just as she cannot be understood by mere rationality. Her spirit, like her space, defies limitation: 'in Russia one can only believe.'[12]

The term *neob"iatnost'* expressed precisely this slipperiness of definition; it is not just 'ungraspability', and can shade easily into 'unboundedness'. The *prostor* is both unbounded (free), and boundless (it cannot be restricted). That is, it offers a unique apprehension of freedom, an ability to breathe deeply. This is clearly expressed in the words of the 'The Song of the Motherland', composed by Isaak Dunaevskii (1900–55) with words by the popular poet Lebedev-Kumach (1898–1949), for Grigorii Aleksandrov's (1903–84) musical comedy, *The Circus* (*Tsirk*), of 1936, 'Wide is my native land . . . In her there are many forests, fields and rivers . . . I know no other country . . . Where man can breathe so freely.' The song was so popular that it quickly became an unofficial national anthem. In Stalinist culture, then, we see an appropriation of the very same symbols of the territory – the vastness of the space is appropriated as a cipher for an openness and freedom in the Russian (Soviet) psyche.

This vision of Russia as unlimited open space is common to many descriptions of the national space. It can also be traced through the vocabulary through which the territory is described. I have shown how this works in the familiar *neob"iatnyi prostor*. But there are other terms, more clearly laden with symbolic meaning, which are consistently used to evoke the space. *Volia*, for example, can be translated as freedom, but the translation is inadequate, for *volia* is not just freedom from restriction, for which Russian has another term, *svoboda*. It is also 'will', or 'volition.' According to the critic Dmitrii Likhachev, the difference between the terms is that *volia* describes *svoboda* plus the *prostor*, the wide open, *unlimited* space so characteristic of Russia.[13] It is freedom *in space*. The loosely defined *russkaia zemlia* of early texts coexisted in folklore with an adventure space which was explicitly not mapped, but was marked by its rivers and its vast plains. One folk epic (*bylina*), for example, opens with the lines: 'From the most distant distance, from the open field (*iz chista polia*) / Come two brave young youths.' This blend of youth, bravery, and open space demonstrates the slippage between the territory as space and the territory as symbol. We should note also the phrase *chistoe pole*, which can be translated as open field, but the meaning of which in fact is far more multi-valent. *Chistoe* refers to purity, thus evoking the value of open, pure, empty space – of those very planes, the *ravnina* or steppe, that de Custine described with such horror, and Kliuchevskii with such nostalgia. The term retained its resonance: at the beginning of the twentieth century, the writer Ivan Bunin (1870–1953) wrote 'I was born, and grew up, in the open field (*v chistom pole*), which a European can't even imagine.'[14]

Thus the lack of definition becomes a form of definition in itself. Like the space, Russia itself is characterised by open-ness, which becomes a symbol of freedom, bravery, and open-ness of heart. But the symbolism of unboundedness has a further important dimension. In the epic accounts of folk heroes moving through the *chistoe pole*, we also see the emergence of a characteristic response to the territory, and one which has a long history. The sheer size of Russia seems to demand movement through it, to encourage a focus on the experience of travel. The folkloric adventure is structured around an exploit, a journey, through the adventure space that is the *chistoe pole*. In parallel, the wanderer, or *strannik*, emerges as a kind of spiritual wiseman of Russian religious lore, whose freedom from materialist burdens is symbolised by his perpetual wandering. And the vast territory, of course, provides the space for this.

Often, then, images of the landscape in nineteenth-century landscape painting were marked by a focus on a path, or *put'*, heading off into

3.1 Isaak Levitan, 'Vladimirka', 1892

the distance (fig. 3.1). So-called songs of the coachman or troika driver
(*iamshchik*), or the highwayman (the *razboinik)* emerged in musical folklore, all praising the experience of travel as an embodiment of the metaphor
of freedom. In the words of Nikolai Gogol (1809–52), 'Is there any Russian
who does not like fast travel?'[15] The Empress Catherine the Great herself,
after all, was famed for her love of speedy troika rides across the countryside.
This emphasis on travel developed, in turn, into a metaphor of the historical path of the nation. The *put',* or journey, of Russia's history, is as chaotic,
adventurous, and fraught with challenges as the real *put'* through her landscape. This is encapsulated in Gogol's vision, at the end of Book One of his
novel *Dead Souls* (*Mertvye dushi*; 1842), of Russia as a bird-troika, career-
ing through her own limitless landscape.[16] In another example, Aleksandr
Blok's 1908 poem, 'On Kulikovo Field' (*Na pole Kulikovom*), which cel-
ebrates a Muscovite victory over the Mongol horde in 1380, we find a
description of Russia's destiny which explicitly blends space and time: 'Our
journey is one of the steppe (*nash put' - stepnoi*).'[17] The flat, monotonous,
and vast territory is thus transformed into a symbol of endless potential.
It is a symbol of the long road that Russia has to travel, and of all that she
has to endure, but it is also a symbol of possibility. In the same way, in
the early years of the Soviet Union, the fast moving train steaming across
the territory was a symbol of Russia's headlong rush into a dynamic and
better future. In the image of the *put',* visions of time – progress, history –
are conceived in images of the national territory, its vast distances, and the
journey across them.

3. PROJECTING SOVIET SPACES

There is a not accidental contradiction emerging here. First, I have emphasised the desire to conquer and subdue the space. Second, I have focused on the freedom offered and symbolised by the mysterious expanse of an *unconquered* space. This opposition, between the symbolism of open space and the urge to enclose that space, runs through representations of the territory. Signs of settlement, and of domestication, play an important role in those same evocations of the *prostor* and the *dal'* (distance). Mikhail Lermontov (1814–41), in his poem 'The Motherland' (*Rodina*; 1841), speaks of his joy in coming across the 'trembling lights' of a village, as he travels by night across the vast steppe – a sign of the courage and resilience of habitation in the wild territory.[18] This ambiguity is central to any discussion of Russia 'as' space. Images of the territory are defined by a constant slippage between visions of chaos and order, freedom and restriction. The desire to conquer the space sits in perpetual tension with the desire to emphasise its resistance to conquest. This finds a kind of resolution in these images of fragile settlement. They offer a vision of a space that is always contested.

To demonstrate this paradox in action, I will focus now on two visions of space that were produced and disseminated during the Stalinist period, showing how popular culture drew on familiar images and associations of the Russian landscape in order to build a vision of a Great Soviet Identity. The first 'text' is in fact a film: *Tale of the Siberian Land* (*Skazanie o zemle sibirskoi*) made in 1947 by the very successful director Ivan Pyrev, responsible for producing many of the most popular films of the 1930s and 40s. Pyrev specialised in a kind of Soviet feel-good movie, which drew on the narrative techniques of Hollywood musicals, complete with dancing spectaculars, but which used them to tell the politically correct stories that Socialist Realist culture demanded. *Tale of the Siberian Land* is a romantic tale of a pianist, wounded in the Second World ('Great Fatherland') War, who loses his faith in music and its role in the new Soviet world, and disappears off to Siberia, where he works on the construction of a paper-processing plant. While there, and engaged in the honest labour that he seeks, he begins to sing in the evenings in a local café. He encounters an old friend, a singer from Moscow, with whom he was long in love, and who loves him, but their first encounter is ultimately unsuccessful. Devastated, Andrei disappears even further into the *prostor* – heading to the far north where he is so carried away by the heroism of Soviet construction projects that he writes a choral symphony, the 'Tale of the Siberian Land'. His

3.2 Ermak and his troops: from *Tale of the Siberian Land*, dir. Ivan Pyrev, 1947

beloved tracks him down, they are reunited, and the piece is performed, to great acclaim, in the Conservatory in Moscow.

As the Moscow audience watches, enthralled, Andrei's story unfolds – a performance of the Russian space. As the music begins Andrei, in a narrative voice-over that continues throughout the symphony, introduces the 'mysterious, wild, silver grey' expanse that is Siberia. In this first description, as we watch the orchestra play, he evokes images that we have seen to be familiar to descriptions of the Russian territory more generally. Siberia disappears 'beyond the Urals, into the silver expanse'. The expanse is apparently endless – 'Maybe it has no end?' The power and freedom of the landscape are evoked simultaneously: the *prostor*'s lack of limits is evoked as a symbol of power. These foundations are essential for what is to come, for the extreme heroism of the Russian and Soviet conquest of Siberia depends upon the extreme might of the land that it challenged. 'But . . .', Andrei goes on: 'desperate Russian hearts' were striving towards Siberia, towards her offer of freedom (*volia*), and he describes, in epic tones, to the accompanying clash of percussion, how the mighty Ermak made his way through fog and mist, to do battle with Siberia.

At this point the film offers an extraordinary visual montage, which implicitly transports Siberia to Moscow, and to the film's audience. In this sequence of images, we can trace key features of the representation of the Russian landscape. First, we see it as witness of history – an almost pantomime hero, Ermak, commanding his forces in battle (fig. 3.2). Here, the director taps into the folk imagination, and the landscape that he evokes is plainly the landscape of the epic. As the battle ends, the natural world

3.3 The fire of conquest: from *Tale of the Siberian Land*

3.4 Nature subdued: from *Tale of the Siberian Land*

itself expresses the majesty of Ermak's achievement (fig. 3.3). Fire shades into lightning, and then the rain begins: the conquest of the elements is complete, as nature bows down in the face of Russian strength, and Siberia is conquered. At this point, the visual evocation of Siberia departs somewhat from the aural text. As Andrei describes the continuation of the process of conquest, as Ermak's ancestors, he says, made their way across the Siberia, the visual track assumes a more gentle tone, and we see first mountains, then sky, and then simply flatness (fig. 3.4). Nature emerges here as a softer force, until: 'Great Russia saw before her the great ocean,' Russia has penetrated across Siberia to the ocean – Siberia has been, in the words of Stalinist

3.5–6 . . . and Siberia inhabited: from *Tale of the Siberian Land*

propaganda, 'opened up', providing access to the Pacific ocean. And as the
great ocean meets Great Russia, so throughout the sequence, the might of
nature echoes the might of her conqueror. As the choral symphony comes
to its end, the *prostor* is inhabited – factories are built, towns populated
(figs. 3.5, 3.6). The huge natural strength of Siberia meets its match in the
huge courage of the Soviet Union, and we return to Moscow, where it all,
implicitly, began.

This film, then, demonstrates how images produced during the Stalin
period papered over the diversity of the Soviet space, to produce a single,
Great Russian territory. The final sequences are a collage not of Siberia
specifically, but of Siberia as a cipher for a more generalised Russian space.

The audience is taken through diverse landscapes. In places, the imagery is pastoral – we witness the domestication of the landscape, and its use for agriculture, as corn sways in the wind and flowers bloom. We see the space inhabited by both animals and people. In other places, it remains wild and remote. In the course of this montage, then, Siberia becomes an incorporative term that describes the 'boundless territory' more generally. This is an image of Siberia as transformed by Soviet power, but it also demonstrates, and relies on, a historical continuity in relation to the territory. The landscape is evoked as guardian of continuity between Stalinism and the great conquerors of early history.

The 'tale' of Siberia both begins and ends, moreover, in Moscow. Just before the performance begins, we see two of Andrei's simple, local friends, who have come to Moscow to watch the performance, and who stand proudly in front of the Conservatory, pleased that they have been invited to Moscow to see something that is, in their words, 'all about them'. Symbolically, the wild periphery has its identity confirmed by the centre. This highly centralised structure, which places Moscow firmly as the symbolic centre of the space, was fundamental to the imaginary geography of Stalinist culture, underpinning the need to 'conquer' and subdue the territory. Channeling images of Siberia through Moscow, the structure of the film itself re-enacts the process of subjugation that it narrates. It grounds the *neob"iatnyi prostor*, locating it in relation to a controlling centre. This performance of the space carries the implicit message that 'Siberia is for everyone' – it is a shared national pride. At the same time, however, the interplay between control and wildness is fundamental. Siberia is conquered, but remains at some level ungraspable and all-powerful, and as such is evoked as a metaphoric equivalent of the strength of the Russian psyche. Caught between domestication and wildness, control and freedom, the image of Siberia expresses the paradoxes of the discourse of Russian identity.

My final 'text' is a map of the Soviet Union (fig. 3.7), produced in 1935 as the frontispiece for a volume that was made to celebrate the opening of one of Stalin's great projects: the building of a canal from the Baltic Sea to the White Sea, which was part of the utopian project of making Moscow a 'port of five seas'.[19] This map is a document of conquest. It is not, of course, a map in any useful sense at all. But as a symbolic representation of the imaginary geography of Stalinism, it is very useful indeed. We see Moscow, the red star firmly at the symbolic (although not actual) centre of the map, with Stalin pictured within the star. From here, lines of influence

3.7 Map of the USSR: from M. Gor'kii, L. Averbakh, and S. Finn (eds.),
Belomorsko-Baltiiskii kanal imeni Stalina: istoriia stroitel'stva (Moscow, 1934), insert

extend radially. The space is firmly bounded – its borders clearly marked
and, implicitly, protected. Within them, the wild, ungraspable territory
sits domesticated. 'Here', in the depths of Siberia, for example, the text
proclaims that 'it turns out the wheat can grow'. On the northern coast,
'ice-breakers are making the sea navigable'. Benign Soviet influence extends
into the furthest, darkest corners of the territory, on a map that, as it
proudly declares, 'is not the same as old maps'. This map, then, locates
itself firmly outside the discourse of *ungraspability* and *unboundedness* that
we have identified in relation to the space. It domesticates and encloses the
territory, viewing it as the benign provider of resources for the centre, from
which Stalin, at his podium, is implicitly watching.

In these two texts, then, we can trace some of the ingredients of 'Russia
as space', modified by Stalinist culture. In both, we can trace a discourse of
conquest, an emphasis on subjugating and domesticating the wild, intransigent *prostor*. In both, this is linked explicitly with heroism – the might
of the Russian people is in direct proportion to the might of her landscape, the forces of nature. Both texts are ideological documents, designed
to communicate political truths to a vast audience. Yet both – and the
film especially – communicate on several levels, refering to a historical
context and a symbolic repertoire that reaches far beyond the immediacies
of the Soviet period. In *Tale of the Siberian Land*, the discourse of conquest is accompanied by an emphasis on resistance to conquest, on the
ultimate 'unknowability' of the territory, which act, in turn, as a cipher for

a more generalised mystery of Russianness itself. The space itself becomes a symbol for the impossibility of self-definition. It is *neob"iatnyi*: it can't be grasped, or summed up. It can't, indeed, even be properly bordered. As such, like Russian identity, it is open to endless manipulation, to imaginary 're-mapping' according to shifting political and social imperatives. In contemporary Russia, in a quite different political context, that project of mapping continues.

SECTION II

Contrastive identities: 'Us' and 'Them'

If the chapters in Section I began with the questions 'when are we?' and 'where are we?', then this second section proceeds from the question 'who are we?' In other words, the focus moves from ideas about Russia to ideas about Russians: not, of course, about Russians individually, as people, but about Russians collectively, as *a* people; or indeed about the masses, conceived as *the* people. Self-definition may be both affirmative and contrastive: we are we because of what we are; and we are we because of what we are not. There is a close relationship, sometimes amounting to interdependency, between representations of the self and representations of 'the other'.

Chapter 4 starts with a broad survey of Russian ideologies of self, of Russianness, from the eighteenth century onwards. These are official and elite ideologies of the nation, devised and propagated from above: by rulers and their agents, by writers, critics, and intellectuals. Such elites were quite capable of producing radically different constructs of the nation while invoking the imagined 'people'. But how – if at all – did the 'people' themselves conceive or represent Russianness? The second part of the chapter looks at examples from 'popular' culture, at emerging forms such as posters and postcards and popular music, to reveal another dimension and dynamic in the production of ideas, or ideals, of Russianness.

Self-definition is sharpened through contrasts with 'the other', with foreigners. Stereotypes of foreigners are as common as stereotypes of self, but they are not always as stable as we might imagine them to be. For example, in Pushkin's verse novel *Eugene Onegin* (1824–32), or in the novel *What is to be Done?* (*Kto vinovat?*; 1845–46) by Aleksandr Herzen (1812–70), a German education produces misty-eyed idealism, whereas in the 1859 novel *Oblomov* by Ivan Goncharov (1812–91) we already see the complete opposite: the Germanic as a source of practicality and efficiency. Chapter 5 traces the development of Russian cultural attitudes to foreigners, beginning with the language itself and including such questions as the actual status of foreigners in Russia, Russian responses to foreign descriptions of Russia, and the fictional representation of foreigners. The case study here is a survey of Russian attitudes to the English. Such attitudes were complex and often paradoxical as the desire to emulate jostled with the desire to be different. Thus statements about Englishness can often be read as coded statements about the self.

CHAPTER 4

'Us': Russians on Russianness

Hubertus F. Jahn

In the middle of the Caucasus mountains, not too far from the northern slopes of the Cross Pass, where the Georgian Military Highway reaches its highest point, the traveller comes into a wide high-mountain valley, which suddenly opens up after a long stretch of narrow gorges and canyons. Its barren landscape is quite typical for this part of the mountains, which is usually battered by heavy snowstorms and avalanches in winter and scorched by the sun during summer time. Yet in the middle of this valley, next to the few houses that make up the village of Kazbegi, a few trees have managed to survive under these rough conditions. Surrounded by the rock-strewn sandbanks of the river Terek, they provide the backdrop for a monument, which one would hardly have expected in this wild and inhospitable location: the poet Aleksandr Pushkin (1799–1837) sitting on a bench (fig. 4.1).

Pushkin statues abound in the former Soviet Union. Usually they can be found on central squares, in parks, or on streets named after the famous poet. The remarkable monument in the Caucasian wilderness, however, has a quite specific reference. It recalls Pushkin's journey to Arzrum in eastern Turkey, which he undertook during the war between the Russian and the Ottoman Empires in 1829. During this trip, he travelled along the banks of the Terek, crossed the Caucasus, and, for the first time in his life, set foot on foreign soil. As he confessed a few years later in his famous travel account *Journey to Arzrum during the Campaign of 1829* (*Puteshestvie v Arzrum vo vremia pokhoda 1829 goda*): it was with an 'inexplicable feeling' that he left Russia and saw a foreign country. The border in particular puzzled him; he experienced it as something very mysterious. For despite having entered a foreign country, he reasoned, he nevertheless still remained in Russia. After all, this stretch of land had already been conquered by the Tsar's armies.[1]

Pushkin's sophistic remarks about his whereabouts, his 'inexplicable feeling' before a border, which obviously meant more to him than simply a

53

4.1 Pushkin monument, Kazbegi

state boundary, point to an old problem of Russian history: what is the essence of being Russian? What, consequently, is the content of Russian patriotism? The nature of Russian national identity? It may be impossible in good faith to answer this question with any claim to scientific certainty – after all, there are about as many national and other identities as there are individual human beings, and probably even more. Yet this chapter will at least try to approach the problem by first presenting a general overview of the more or less well-known intellectual debates about Russian national identity from the eighteenth to the twentieth centuries. This will then be followed by a brief and more specific investigation of mass culture in order to identify popular perceptions of Russianness.

I. THE VIEW FROM THE TOP

In his travel account of 1835, Pushkin highlighted two notions of Russian national identity. On the one hand, he explicitly referred to the Caucasus and to the newly conquered territories as Russia. In other words, he depicted Russia as a multinational empire. On the other hand, he constantly described the Caucasus as foreign and exotic and clearly as a part of the so-called Orient. The people living there were consequently characterised as primitive and dangerous, but also as noble savages, to whom civilisation should be exported from Russia in the form of the samovar and the Gospel. By highlighting the foreignness and the backwardness of his surroundings, Pushkin implicitly revealed another, quite different understanding of Russia. According to this second notion, Russia meant only the Slav heartland of the Empire, an Orthodox nation, which had developed a high level of culture and was inhabited by ethnic Russians.

Pushkin's two differing perceptions of national identity, the imperial and the ethno-cultural, as one might call them, have their own history. Their roots go back to the eighteenth century and in particular to the reforms of Peter the Great (1689–1725). At that time, Western European ideas and ideologies as well as absolutist forms of government were introduced *en masse* into Russia, accompanied by the symbols and the language of imperial power in its Western, classical form. Peter and his successors, in particular Catherine the Great (1762–96), thought of themselves as absolutist monarchs. Their rule was characterised first and foremost by military glory, territorial expansion, and a government based on the principles of the well-ordered police-state, rather than on Orthodox piety and Byzantine tradition, as had been the case in old Muscovy. Consequently, the representations of their power, or, as Richard Wortman called it, their 'scenarios of power'[2] were heavily geared towards the creation of an imperial myth, which had little to do with Kievan Rus or Muscovite Russia, but a lot in common with ancient Rome. Thus Peter adopted the Latin title of emperor (*Imperator*) and had himself portrayed with a laurel wreath around his head. For her part, Catherine appeared on allegorical pictures and coins as an ancient goddess, whose empire resembled the Roman Empire both in its ethnic diversity and in its geographical dimensions.

State institutions and classical-imperial forms were not the only imports from Western Europe into Russia. With them came ideas of the

Enlightenment, artistic styles, cultural trends, and European ways of life and behaviour. They were first absorbed by a small group of educated people among the elite, who were soon inspired by all these new and foreign theories and practices to reflect on themselves, to search for their own, specifically Russian culture and identity. The emergence of a national consciousness in Russia was thus both a result of and a reaction against Western influences. Closely related to this development was the appearance of a national culture. This national culture did not differ much from its counterparts in Western Europe. In other words, just as in other countries, it relied heavily on the discovery of a glorious historical past and on the creation of a national language, literature, and music. Furthermore, under the auspices first of Sentimentalism and then of Romanticism, educated Russians, just as other Europeans, also believed that they could find peculiar national characteristics of their own country among the ordinary people, the *narod*.

In the journals and the literature of the Catherinean era, for example, a simple and innocent rural life was often praised as virtuous and typically Russian. Idealised villages and their inhabitants were set against the corruption and decadence – the badly imitated French fashions and the luxurious lifestyle – of the Westernised aristocracy in the capitals St Petersburg and Moscow. Outspoken sceptics such as the journalist and publisher Nikolai Novikov (1744–1818) and the writer and social critic Aleksandr Radishchev (1749–1802) emphasised the virtues of the common people in their various condemnations of serfdom. Particularly famous is Radishchev's *Journey from St Petersburg to Moscow* (*Puteshestvie iz Peterburga v Moskvu*; 1790), which, in some of its most captivating moments, brings to life people from the lower orders. The peasant girl Aniuta, for example, is portrayed as an archetype of rural modesty and morality, quite unlike the posh St Petersburg ladies to whom she is compared by the author. Likewise, a blind man singing an old beggar's song in the town of Klin is praised for his poor but virtuous way of life; his plain Russian song is said to have been many times more beautiful than the songs sung by the Italian opera singers in the capital.

While peasants were discovered by sentimentally inclined intellectuals as the carriers of typical Russian virtues, other members of the upper classes seemed to have had quite a different understanding of national character. For them it was simply associated with pastoral idylls and folkloristic kitsch, as one might now call it. Catherine the Great's friend, Princess Ekaterina Dashkova (1743/4–1810), for example, once entertained an English visitor by putting on a typical country feast. In order to show her visitor the 'real

Russia', as she understood it, she had a village built on one of her estates, which was settled by some of her serfs. For the feast, these people were made to wear their Sunday dresses and to sing and dance on the grass, 'according to our country's fashion'. Russian food and drinks were served at the occasion, and the foreign guest is said to have been 'no less charmed with the nationality of the scene and beauty of the dresses than with the picturesque effect of the groups which sang and danced before her'.[3] Clearly, this show of happy Russian peasants did not aspire to any social criticism or moral statement. It rather was an early version of the balalaika ensembles, folk choirs, and richly costumed dancing troupes, which became standard features of mass entertainment in the late nineteenth century and which continue to attract large audiences both in Russia and abroad to this day.

If peasants were the embodiments of high moral standards and of an allegedly true national character, their songs and tales were believed to contain the very essence of Russianness and to offer direct access to the soul of the people,[4] the *Volksseele*, as Johann Gottfried Herder (1744–1803) put it. Consequently, they also attracted the interest of numerous collectors. In 1826, for example, a report by the infamous Third Section, the secret police created under Nicholas I (1825–55), noted with a certain surprise that Aleksandr Pushkin, who at that time was exiled to the provinces, had been seen in peasant outfit in villages and on rural fairgrounds. Pushkin was understood to be gathering fairytales, songs, and proverbs. He was probably the most famous collector of such art works. However, folk music had already been collected more or less systematically since the mid-eighteenth century and published in several anthologies. The most famous of them by Nikolai Lvov (1751–1803) and Jan Práč (d. 1818) appeared in 1790 and became highly influential among composers of serious music, including such foreign celebrities as Rossini and Beethoven. By the late eighteenth century, folk melodies and peasants had also entered the Russian opera stage, where they remain very popular. Peasant and folk choirs are a staple of many Russian operas, and it is hardly surprising that the hero of Russia's quintessentially national opera, *A Life for the Tsar* (*Zhizn' za tsaria*) by Mikhail Glinka (1804–57), is a peasant by the name of Ivan Susanin. Incidentally, his feat, the rescue of the young tsar Mikhail Romanov (1613–45), took place in a period which has later been interpreted as one of the key moments of Russian nationhood – the expulsion of the Polish invaders and the establishment of the Romanov dynasty at the end of the 'Time of Troubles' in the early seventeenth century.

Glinka's opera, which premiered in 1836, was, however, not the first one to exploit the story of this famous patriotic peasant. In 1815, Catterino

Cavos (1775–1840), a Venetian composer in Russian service, had already written an opera, which he named *Ivan Susanin* and which was praised for its historic quality and its use of folk tunes. Cavos's opera was part of a wave of patriotic music triggered by another invasion, that of Napoleon and the Grande Armeé in 1812. The ensuing war, later suitably called the 'Fatherland War', fundamentally changed the quality of national consciousness in Russia. It was indeed won with the help of ordinary people, like Ivan Susanin. Although little is known about the kind of patriotism that motivated ordinary Russians to fight against the invaders, it is nevertheless a historical fact that they did so and that they expelled Napoleon and his armies from Russia. All of this happened after Tsar Alexander I (1801–25) himself had appealed to the Russian population for help to defend the country. By putting national defence into the hands of the people, albeit for a short period, Alexander implicitly weakened the myth of an omnipotent and divine emperor, promulgated by his predecessors, and recognised a political role for the *narod*, something with which he was not at all comfortable. Right after the war, therefore, he proclaimed Russia's victory and the expulsion of Napoleon from Central Europe to have been an act of divine providence, exerted through him, the all-powerful Orthodox tsar. Nevertheless, the paradox remains: his appeal had helped to raise the spectre of popular sovereignty. As a result, discussion of Russian national identity started to come of age after 1812. It turned from a literary and cultural obsession with the national soul into an increasingly politicised issue.

Another discovery of the folk, a quite literal one, supplemented and accelerated this process. It also occurred during the war of 1812, when a large number of young noble guard officers and their troops were encamped and slowly retreating along the Smolensk highway between Russia's western border and Moscow. Under the prevailing conditions, officers and soldiers necessarily came into close contact; they had to rely on each other for survival and at times even had to share accommodation. The young officers were thus able to learn first-hand about the way of life and the daily problems of ordinary Russian people. With Napoleon advancing not too quickly, they also had plenty of opportunity to think, to write diaries and letters, to visit friends in other army units and to talk with them about what they saw and experienced. The fate of Russia in general and that of its oppressed people in particular was top of the list of these conversations. It was then that a new generation began to emerge in Russia, the 'people of 1812', as the literary and cultural historian Iurii Lotman has called them. These people soon chased Napoleon all the way back to France. On their way, they were welcomed into the salons of Warsaw, Berlin, Paris, and many other cities, where they picked up the latest philosophical ideas and political theories of Western Europe. Once they came back to Russia around 1815, they inevitably began to compare these ideas and their personal experiences in the war with the realities of their own country. The contrasts could not have been more imposing. While the rest of Europe was discussing the rights of the individual, celebrating the freedom of nations, and implementing constitutional reforms, Russia remained an autocratic empire, marked by police despotism, strict censorship, the institution of serfdom, and a tsar who increasingly succumbed to a rather obsessive mysticism.

If, a few years later, one could have asked the returning guard officers what it meant to them to be Russian, they would most likely have said that they felt ashamed at the conditions existing in their country, yet they would also have spoken about a patriotic duty to change them. The moment for such a change seemed to have arrived in December 1825, when young nobles and officers of the imperial guards used an unforeseen succession crisis after the death of Alexander I to stage a *coup d'état* in St Petersburg's Senate Square. The revolt failed miserably, and the Decembrists, as the insurgents were later called after the month of their attempted coup, were prosecuted, sentenced to death, or sent to Siberia. Yet in their view and in the opinion of many educated Russians, they had acted in pure patriotic spirit. Patriotism obviously meant something quite distinct to these men. It certainly had nothing to do with official notions of patriotism, that is the classical myth of empire promoted by the monarchy. It also was different from the purely cultural discovery of a national soul deeply rooted in the *narod*. Instead, it had a strong philanthropic connotation and it focused on a modern Russian nation, which was to consist of free citizens and to be distinguished by the rule of law. The specific characteristics of such a nation and particularly of its constitution had been discussed over several years before 1825 in a number of secret societies and literary circles. They had also been the subjects of numerous treatises and poems, and eventually they had been written down in two major constitutional drafts, which, interestingly, also reflected to some extent the two main concepts of national identity – that of a multinational and that of an ethnically Russian state. At the centre of many of these writings, however, was the abolition of serfdom and the liberation of the people, which were clearly seen as the main national tasks. But there were also plenty of references to alternative patriotic traditions in Russian history, which contradicted the official imperial myth. These were traditions of freedom and popular rule thought to be particularly evident in the institutions of the medieval city-republic of Novgorod. Finally, there was a good dose of plain animosity against Tsar Alexander I in these writings, who on several occasions had violated the patriotic feelings and national pride of his officers and who suspiciously often travelled abroad, prompting Pushkin once to call him a 'nomadic despot'.[5]

Some of the Decembrists not only discussed and wrote about the fate of Russia in the years before 1825; they also began to apply their patriotism in everyday life, that is, they tried to take on the identity of ordinary Russian people and to live up to what they thought were typical Russian traditions. Every Monday, for example, the poet Kondratii Ryleev (1795–1826) used to invite his like-minded friends to so-called Russian suppers. Conspicuously absent from these occasions were the fine food and the expensive wines usually available at upper-class Petersburg tables. In their place, simple rye bread and sour cabbage were served together with a carafe of vodka. While the participants at the meals were in a sense attempting to russify themselves through their diet, they also tended to smoke cigars after they had eaten, apparently impervious to the fact that by doing so they were succumbing to a typically Western habit which was hardly known among and certainly not practised by Russian peasants. This episode clearly shows how europeanised the champions of a modern nation and of popular sovereignty were and how European and therefore elitist the phenomenon of patriotism was in early nineteenth-century Russia.

The person who was put in charge of inventing a new, official national ideology for the empire some years after the Decembrists' revolt did not even bother to write in Russian, let alone to eat cabbage and rye bread. Sergei Uvarov (1785–1855), education minister under Nicholas I, despised Russian culture and corresponded usually in German or French. Yet in 1833 he created what could be called 'imperial nationalism', which effectively replaced the classical imperial myth of previous decades. This was a late acknowledgement of the threat posed by the Decembrists' liberal brand of patriotism and at the same time a concession to the revolutionary *Zeitgeist* of Western Europe, which, despite censorship, secret police, and travel restrictions, was finding its way into Russia. However, Uvarov's attempt to integrate a national element into an ideology, which was basically concocted to save and consolidate the dynastic legitimacy of the emperor, produced a rather strange hybrid. The formula of 'Orthodoxy, Autocracy, Nationality' (*Pravoslavie, samoderzhavie, narodnost'*) soon became the main ideological framework for Russian statehood. Known in the historical literature as 'official nationality', this slogan only confused contemporaries. While its first two components were clear, the third caused serious problems. It was generally understood and accepted that Russia's fate remained, as always, closely linked with the Orthodox church and the monarchy, but it was not at all clear what the term *narodnost'* actually meant. At its root is the word *narod* (people). But was this word to be interpreted in an imperial sense: that is, should it denote a closer connection between the monarch and the people from all the different nationalities of the empire? Or did *narodnost'* refer to an ethnic Russian national consciousness and thus lay the groundwork for Russian hegemony in the empire? Both interpretations were hotly contested right from the start, and they even led to serious divisions in the highest ranks of the state bureaucracy. No wonder, then, that Pushkin was also confused and that he vacillated, in his *Journey to Arzrum*, between the two notions of national identity, the imperial–multinational and the ethno-cultural one. Incidentally, but perhaps not coincidentally, he was writing his travel account at the very time when Uvarov promulgated his controversial ideology.

The two opposing concepts of national identity continued to live on in different forms through the nineteenth and the twentieth centuries. By the end of the 1830s, they were, however, pushed into the background by another question, which went right to the heart of Russian national identity. It was raised by the famous first *Philosophical Letter* of Petr Chaadaev (1794–1856), an eminent thinker who was admired by Pushkin and had been in close contact with the Decembrists. In his letter, which appeared with some delay in 1836, the author claimed that Russia had not contributed anything important to the history of mankind. According to him, Russia belonged neither to the West nor to the East, she was without a historical continuity, and lacked a moral personality. Her culture was based wholly on borrowing and imitation, while her people were like illegitimate children or nomads who had come to the world without patrimony and without a connection to universal ideas. In particular they lacked knowledge of the moral atmosphere prevalent in the Roman-Catholic West, that is the ideas of duty, justice, right, and order.

Once this indictment of Russia's national character was out, it acted like a wake-up call in intellectual circles. Chaadaev himself became a sought-after guest in literary salons, while Tsar Nicholas I had him declared insane and put under medical observation. Of the issues raised in the letter, Russia's relation to the West and her role in history triggered a particularly heated debate, which eventually led to the emergence of two opposing groups of thinkers – the Slavophiles and the Westernisers. Both groups consisted of highly educated people who were deeply rooted in European culture and particularly influenced by German idealism. Their mutual concern was the future of Russia; their arguments therefore tended to draw heavily on the country's historical past. They revolved around the question of what Russia should be, how Russia should develop. In their search for an ideal Russia, they also re-discovered the *narod*. The Slavophiles believed that most of Russia's problems began with the imperial state created by Peter the Great, when a Westernised elite lost contact with age-old Russian traditions and fell prey to Western notions of rationalism, Roman law, and private property. In their opinion, however, the real, pre-Petrine Russia was still preserved in the communal principles of Orthodox religion, which they saw embodied in the traditions and institutions of the *narod*, in particular the patriarchal family and the village commune. Russians as a whole should revert to these principles and in a way russify themselves again by becoming more like the *narod*. One of the leading Slavophiles, Konstantin Aksakov (1817–60), who tried this out quite practically by donning what he thought was peasant dress, was, however, mistaken for a Persian by the very people he allegedly emulated.

In the ideas of the Westernisers, the *narod* played quite a different role. They wanted Russia to proceed along the path entered upon by Peter the Great and emulate Western European social and political models. Correspondingly variegated were the opinions and viewpoints that one could find among the Westernisers. Over time, they ranged from liberalism to socialism and anarchism. Despite such obvious differences in political outlook, all these ideologies had in common a strong pedagogical impetus. Educated society and the elites should not become like the *narod*, as the Slavophiles wished, but they should rather lift up the *narod* from its allegedly primitive and pre-modern state through knowledge, enlightenment, and, later in the century, also through revolutionary action. According to this reasoning, peasants should be turned into citizens, the *narod* should become the nation, and national identity should be based on political consciousness rather than a murky tradition of community.

The ideas of the Slavophiles and the Westernisers took many different forms in the nineteenth century, and in modified versions they are still relevant today in the discussions about post-Soviet Russia's role as a nation. Eventually they also came to influence official notions of national identity in the nineteenth century. When some influential publishers and politicians began in the 1860s and 70s to extend Slavophile concepts of community onto an international level in order to promote Russia's role as a protector of all Slav peoples against suspected German and other threats, the government in St Petersburg soon picked up these ideas. Although 'pan-Slavism' did not become an important force in foreign policy, it nevertheless helped to change the meaning of the term *narodnost'* in Uvarov's old formula. Instead of an ethnically neutral populism of the monarchy, this word now came to denote a purely Russian nationalism with imperial aspirations. In real life, this equation of the empire with Russia proper resulted in the Russification policies of Alexander III (1881–94), which, ironically enough, affected not just Baltic Germans, Jews, and Finns, but also fellow Slavs such as Poles and Ukrainians.

Russification was not only restricted to the non-Russian nationalities of the empire. It extended to the monarchy itself, albeit without any need for coercion. Alexander III was an ardent Russian nationalist, who, before his ascension to the throne, had been an enthusiastic supporter of the pan-Slav cause during the war with Turkey in 1877–78. He even went so far as to change his outer appearance. That is, he grew a beard. As is well known, beards had been cut off by Peter the Great, both literally and metaphorically, because they were perceived as signs of Russia's backwardness and lack of civilisation. During the war with Turkey, however, soldiers were allowed to go without shaving, probably for practical reasons. In order to show his patriotic loyalty to these men, but also to eventually present himself in the mould of a medieval Russian knight (*bogatyr'*), Alexander stopped shaving as well. His beard was soon seen as a symbol of national strength and old Muscovite virility and authority. Likewise, the representations of monarchical power also changed once Alexander III came to the throne. Gone were the times when classical antiquity and Western European imperial forms dominated the scene. Instead, a quite literal resurrection of Muscovy took place in the building of numerous old Russian churches and the revival of authoritarian rule. Nicholas II (1894–1917) continued to invent Muscovite traditions. He and his (German) wife loved to appear in costumes of the times of Tsar Aleksei Mikhailovich (1645–76), and they liked to believe in the old myth of a sacred union between tsar and people. Hence their predilection for folk music and folkloristic evenings, and hence their inclination to surround themselves with allegedly ordinary Russian people such as the infamous monk Grigorii Rasputin (1871–1916).

Ordinary people, though now without allusion to a Muscovite past, became the focal point of officially propagated identity after the Bolshevik revolution of 1917. In line with the Communist Manifesto's dictum that workers have no fatherland, proletarian internationalism was meant to replace national and ethnic loyalties. As a result of Russification policies, the latter had become increasingly contested issues in the Tsarist Empire before its demise and had manifested themselves violently during the Civil War in the early 1920s. For the Bolsheviks, what really mattered was social class, not national identity. However, with the rise to power of Iosif Stalin (1879–1953) and his rejection of revolutionary experimentalism, conservative values, including national ones, took centre stage again in the early 1930s. This does not mean of course that nationalism was fostered among the many ethnic minorities in the Soviet Union. Indeed, their national aspirations were suppressed until Mikhail Gorbachev's reforms in the 1980s, and they eventually played a major role in the collapse of the Soviet state. Instead, Soviet Patriotism, as it became known, was launched in 1934 in connection with the celebrations of a successful air rescue operation of shipwrecked sailors from an ice floe. The 'arctic flyers' were soon joined by other heroes, such as the shock worker Aleksei Stakhanov (1906–77), and by other extraordinary feats of Soviet power, such as the Moscow Metro, to form a pantheon of patriotic motifs which encompassed all Soviet citizens, regardless of their nationality. State-controlled mass media and the newly introduced precept of Socialist Realism in the arts propagated this image of the Soviet Union as a land of abundance and happiness, led by an omniscient and benevolent leader and populated by enthusiastic factory workers and cheerful collective farm labourers. Just as Uvarov's Official Nationality one hundred years earlier, however, Soviet Patriotism was an ideological construct, providing a hybrid national identity for a multinational empire, without a specific historical tradition or a particular ethnic aspect.

The German invasion of the Soviet Union in 1941 fundamentally changed the character of Soviet Patriotism. Almost overnight, Russian history became the main point of reference in nationalist propaganda. The Russian people were portrayed as the older brothers of the other Soviet nationalities; military heroes and saints from Kievan Rus, the Muscovite state and the Tsarist Empire were called upon to fight the enemy,[6] just as they had been in the First World War. It seemed as if this new, 'Great Fatherland War', as it was soon called in reference to the war of 1812, was not a conflict between the many nationalities of the Soviet Union and the Nazi regime, but rather a final showdown between Russians and Germans. This kind of ethnic Russian nationalism continued to shape official Soviet national identity throughout the post-war period and may well have been a reason for the confusion of the term 'Soviet' with 'Russian', which was so widespread in the West during the Cold War.

The end of the USSR brought not only the independence of many Soviet nationalities; it also allowed Russia to dissociate herself from the Soviet legacy. In today's capitalist Russia, the business of creating identity flourishes everywhere. The revival and increasing popularity of the Orthodox Church attest to a widespread reassertion of a specifically Russian religious identity, qualified only by the simultaneous appearance of countless sects and esoteric groups. On the political level, a joint five-year programme of the Ministry of Education and the Ministry of Defence announced in 2001 aimed to 'arouse feelings of pride in Russians for their country by increasing pro-Russian programming on television and selling patriotic souvenirs'.[7] The intention of the programme was to draw on memories of the 'Great Fatherland War' and on Slav folklore. This type of official neo-Slavophilism was counterbalanced by President Vladimir Putin's foreign policy, seeking to present Russia as a Western country and as part of a common European heritage. Meanwhile in the streets of Russian towns and cities, numerous groups offer answers to what Russia is or should be. Anything between anarchy, monarchy, and right-wing dictatorship is on offer. Many cities themselves experience an unprecedented rise of local self-esteem and, in some instances, even urban regeneration. In the absence of a clear and consistent national identity, regional patriotism in towns and districts of the Russian Federation manifests itself, among others, in a widespread enthusiasm for local history, the restoration of old buildings and churches, and the separatist policies of individual provincial governors. Ordinary Russian people, finally, are increasingly concerned with their own identity, national or otherwise, in these transitory times. Some archives have begun to offer genealogical research services for those studying their family history, while countless sources related specifically to people's experiences and sufferings in the Stalin period have been collected by the human-rights organisation *Memorial*.

2. THE VIEW FROM BELOW

It was in the immediate aftermath of the war with Turkey in 1878, that some ordinary Russian people, apparently peasants from nearby villages, attacked three porters of Tatar origin in Apraksin Pereulok, a Petersburg street famous for its slums and filthy taverns. The attack quickly turned into a serious fight, in which a mob of several hundred mostly drunken people participated. When a police officer arrived at the scene, he was told: 'Your Honour, the Turks didn't spare our guys, so we now want to cut the throats of the Tatars'.[8]

It is impossible to establish with any degree of certainty whether patriotic motifs were indeed behind this attack, whether the Tatars were knowingly or unknowingly associated with the Turkish enemies because of their appearance or their accents, or whether the attackers just made up a convenient excuse for their assault. Yet this episode of foreigner-bashing raises a much wider question, which until recently has received only little attention in historical research, but which has serious implications for the interpretation of Russian history in the nineteenth and twentieth centuries. How in fact did people from the lower orders see themselves in the Tsarist Empire, the Soviet Union, and post-Soviet Russia? Did they have some kind of national identity, some feeling of patriotism? Or were their loyalties purely local and social? The village, for example? An urban neighbourhood? A specific factory? Or the working class?

This chapter has so far concentrated exclusively on the perceptions of national identity among poets and composers, tsars and ministers, philosophers and intellectuals. To a large extent this is due to the sheer abundance of written sources left by and about these people. Pushkin's experience of the Caucasian wilderness, Catherine's imperial scenarios, the patriotic ideas of the Decembrists or the Slavophiles, Uvarov's national doctrines, the tenets of Soviet Patriotism – these are all easily accessible and have long been part of the standard repertoire of Russian history. But can these sources explain why some kind of popular patriotism erupted in 1812? Can they help to understand a decreasing veneration of the tsar among Russian peasants in the nineteenth century? Can they shed light on the emergence of a lower middle class in a provincial town, whose members may have perceived themselves as Russian citizens, as urban residents, or simply as belonging to a certain neighbourhood or milieu? Finally, can these sources help to evaluate the kind of patriotism asserted by the thugs of Apraksin Pereulok as an excuse for their outrageous behaviour?

Questions like these have in recent years prompted historians and slavists to look for new or under-used types of sources and to investigate such unconventional materials as broadsheets, posters, popular literature, schoolbooks, fairground culture, film, and the tabloid press. All these materials convey meaning in the broadest sense, and since they were part of a fastgrowing, market-regulated consumer culture, they can be interpreted as reflecting the dreams, ideas, and imaginations of their clientele. While this kind of analysis cannot provide clear-cut answers on the level of historical causality, it nevertheless shows that the world of the lower orders in Russia was much more complex than often assumed, that there was a high degree of social mobility and cultural adaptation, that loyalties could be diverse, and that identities were much more multi-layered than official categories (estate and nationality) or ideological concepts (*narod* and class) suggest.

Regarding the development of a national identity among ordinary Russians, it is safe to assume that the same conditions apply as in other countries. As Eugen Weber has shown for France, these were above all an increasing rate of urbanisation as well as a country-wide dissemination of schools, state institutions, transport, communication, and especially mass media.⁹ In the Russian case, visual media in particular, but also some performing genres played a predominant role, as the vast majority of the population was still illiterate by the end of the nineteenth century. The most popular of these media early in the century were broadsheets, so called *lubki*, and fairground attractions like the *petrushka* or puppet theatre and the *raëk*, a kind of peep-show. These genres offered an entertaining alternative to the religious imagery of the Orthodox church and also conveyed ideas about what it meant to be Russian and what distinguished Russians from other people, usually the Germans. Oftentimes these were simple personal characteristics like, for example, courage, openness, and peasant wit, as opposed to German pedantry, dullness, and small-mindedness. But over time, historical, geographic, and ethnographic peculiarities were added as well.

The *raëk* was particularly instrumental in creating a popular stock of patriotic iconography. *Lubki* were put in a box with magnifying glasses, illuminated by a candle or oil lamp, and then explained verbosely and in a sensationalist manner by the *raëshnik*, who ran the show (fig. 4.2). Incidentally, many of these men were veterans of the war of 1812, who had 'seen the world', as they themselves would proudly proclaim. One could even call them a 'folk version' of the elite generation of 1812: people who had shared all kinds of experiences abroad in Europe, which they then used to enlighten their peers at home. Among the classic images on display were, for example, a view of the 'big city of Paris', with or without Russian troops, or Napoleon's crossing of the Berezina river. Other pictures included views of Constantinople, a city of potential conquest and of a legendary past, which apparently held as much fascination for ordinary Russians as it did for Petersburg politicians and pan-Slavic ideologues. Last but not least, views of the Moscow Kremlin were also popular, suggesting that for most common people the heart of the country was still the old capital, not the new one.

The genres of Russian popular culture proliferated especially in the second half of the nineteenth century, when censorship was less stringent. With new printing techniques available, *lubki* were soon produced in striking colours and in huge numbers. Commercial and charitable posters as well as picture postcards appeared, as did numerous illustrated journals. A growing railway network helped to disseminate these media all over the country, while at the same time bringing more and more people into rapidly developing cities. There they would find many new, typically urban types of entertainment, from show wrestling to people's theatres, from music halls and cinemas to public amusement parks and ice-skating rinks. If they

4.2 'Raëk' picture show

saved a little money, they might even be able to purchase a gramophone or a music box and listen to a recording of Glinka's *Life for the Tsar*.

Works from elite culture had been popularised for quite some time, allowing people from the lower classes to participate in the national heritage and putting into question traditional perceptions of a clear division between elite and popular cultures. *The Last Days of Pompeii*, for example, the most famous picture by Karl Briullov (1799–1852), who later became professor at the St Petersburg Academy of Arts, was made into a rather elaborate *lubok* in 1834, only one year after its first exhibition. From the 1870s, the classics of Russian literature began to be issued in popular editions, promoting both literacy and a common set of narratives which transcended social divides. History was likewise popularised and became a standard feature in commercial advertising. One example is a poster of the famous sixteenth-century conqueror of Siberia, Ermak (d. 1585), surrounded by the latest agricultural machinery (fig. 4.3). The poster came out at a time when a campaign to colonise Siberia was in full swing. Its content, therefore, is quite suggestive, as Ermak, standing in a pristine forest, points to the plough both to be bought but also to be used in breaking up new soil. Advertisements such as this have once again become very popular in today's Russia. There is hardly an insurance company or an investment trust that is promoting its services on Russian television without the support of old Muscovite boyars or legendary folk heroes.[10]

One indication of more and more ordinary Russians developing a common sense of national identity in the late nineteenth century is the large proportion of village-related themes in popular culture. This phenomenon might be called a discovery of the *narod* by the ordinary people, similar to that by the elites a few decades earlier. While peasants were clearly interested in 'the big city of Paris' or the Moscow Kremlin displayed in a fairground *raëk*, they probably had rather little use for a *lubok* depicting a village dance and the lyrics of a village song (fig. 4.4). Such material was likely to be sold predominantly in cities, where it catered to the nostalgia of people who had recently moved there from the country and who were now struggling for a new identity in a different and quite hostile environment. Defining oneself and categorising the other were the two constituent elements of this process. Hence an obsession in all kinds of popular media with classifying people, with ordering the social environment according to types and certain standard behaviours. Typecasting was particularly evident in popular literature and the penny press. But it was also a regular feature in advertising. The Moscow chocolate factory Einem, for example, issued two series of bonus

4.3 Ermak: advertisement poster for Randrup Company in Omsk (1909)

4.4 'Village Song': popular print (*lubok*), lithographic studio of Efim Iakovlev, 1871

card pictures called 'Views and Types of Old Moscow' and 'Scenes from Russian Life' (fig. 4.5). Clearly, these do not depict authentic situations, nor do they openly promote any particular political agenda. They rather form an ideal image of Russianness, a sentimental picture of reality, not unlike that produced in Princess Dashkova's park back in the eighteenth century. An important part of the picture then were happy peasants singing and dancing. By the late nineteenth century, countless folk music ensembles had taken over this role. The peasant choir of Mitrofan Piatnitskii (1864–1927) and the 'great-Russian' balalaika orchestra of the 'musician-patriot' Vasilii Andreev (1861–1918), for example, were highly successful and always attracted huge audiences from all walks of urban life. The latter still exists today and has become an export hit of Russian folk culture all over the world. It goes without saying that the repertoire of these two ensembles had more in common with fakelore than with authentic village music. If one were thus to identify the most widespread national self-stereotype, the

4.5 'Scenes from Russian Life'; artist unknown: chocolate factory advertising card

most potent patriotic motif in Russian popular culture, one would certainly have to propose some kind of sanitised village idyll.

Defining oneself played an essential role in the formation of national identity. Categorising the other was equally important. While the Germans had long been the standard adversary against whom the Russians measured themselves, various 'Asians' or 'Orientals' became the new opponent by the second half of the nineteenth century and in many ways still are today. Caucasians in particular populated the imagination, as shown, for example, in a fairground panorama depicting the wars with rebellious mountain tribes under the leadership of Imam Shamil (1797–1871). They were the heroes or villains in numerous popular adventure novels, a genre which was only just emerging and which was closely linked to an increase in literacy among new urbanites. In the Caucasus mountains, the self and the other became entangled for ordinary Russian readers, imperial pride and ethnic self-consciousness came together. And while most Russians never visited the place in reality, the Caucasus nevertheless confronted them with borders, albeit in their imagination, borders which were more than just state boundaries. It confronted them with their identity as Russians, once they crossed 'the rapid and terrible river Terek', as one of the novels put it.[11] There, in the middle of rocks and mountains, along the banks of the Terek, this chapter began. There, next to Pushkin's monument, it also concludes.

CHAPTER 5

'Them': Russians on foreigners

Anthony Cross

I

The Greeks, as they invariably did, had a word for it, or in this case, for 'them'. The word was *barbaros*, and it meant a person who did not speak Greek and, by extension, was not open to the benefits of Greek culture and civilization. The Romans, who took so many things from the Greeks, also took the word with analogous application to the non-Latin speakers and the unenlightened mob. It was their invaders from the North, the Huns and the Goths, who became the very incarnation of Barbarians, writ large, for the havoc they wrought in the very epicentre of the civilized world. The negative cultural implications of the word thereafter took precedence over the linguistic. In the post-medieval world, countries vied to call each other names, among which 'barbarian' was particularly prominent. The French became especially generous in applying the word to everyone and anyone who did not subscribe to the glories of French civilization and, by inference, to the majesty of the French language. They were never slow to brand the English 'barbarians', attributing the defect to the Roman legacy or Germanic ancestry of the English, and finding, for instance, a splendid condemnation of 'barbares Anglois' whose 'cruels couteaux / Coupent la tête aux rois, et la queue aux chevaux'.[1] By the eighteenth century, however, Britain, France, Germany, Holland, and Italy, whatever they had called each other in the past and continued to do *sotto voce*, were at least united in viewing the countries further north or, by an increasingly common re-alignment of the map, to the east as lands of darkness populated by barbarians and awaiting the sun of the Enlightenment. They were also prepared, by and large, to recognize that in Peter the Great Russia had found, whether it liked it or not, its own Sun King (i.e., a barbaric version of one).

By the time of Peter, the Russians themselves had already long acquired the vocabulary to deal with all whom they perceived as barbarians, foreigners, and the like. Barbarians, rendered as *barberi*, *barberiany*, *varvarin*, but most often as *varvar*, make their appearance in various sources from the twelfth century but particularly in the seventeenth, and the word had inevitably much the same associations as in other languages, although the main emphasis was from the beginning *religious*, denoting pagans, non-Christians, people of a different faith or creed. Most often it was the Mongols who were so named – 'the godless and malicious tsar Batyi, the evil barbarian (*varvarin zloi*)' – and the land they inhabited in one seventeenth-century source is termed *Varvariia*: 'Varvariia, that is to say the land of the Tatars,[2] whose faith and language are basurman'. *Varvar* was on occasion used to designate foreigners in general, but there were other words that were more widely used, such as *inostranets*, *inostrannik*, *inozemets* ('from another land'), all of which carried the connotation of different faith (seen literally in the form *inoverets*). However, it was *nemets* above all others that related to foreigners of mainly Western European extraction during this same period. It shared with the Greek *barbaros* an indication of the inability to speak the language of the host country, the 'dumb ones', but was used primarily but far from exclusively before the eighteenth century for people from the German lands. *Nemets* appeared in what now seem to us often amusing combinations (I use 'German' as the translation to heighten the effect): 'visiting Germans from various states' (*priezzhie nemtsy roznykh gosudarstv*); 'her father was a German from the Scots, who observed the German faith' (*otets byl shkotskikh nemets, derzhal veru nemetskuiu*); or 'Italy is a Latin country, near Rome, and there live in it wise Germans' (*Italiia – strana latinska, bliz Rima, a zhivut v nei mudrii nemtsy*).[3]

Foreigners were ever a problem for the Russians; it was not simply a matter of what you called them so much as how you treated them.[4] For Patriarch Ioakim, writing at the end of the seventeenth century, it was all very simple:

> May our sovereigns never allow any Orthodox Christians in their realm to entertain any close friendly relations with heretics and dissenters – with the Latins, Lutherans, Calvinists and godless Tatars (whom our Lord abominates and the church of God damns for their God-abhorred guile); but let them be avoided as enemies of God and defamers of the church.[5]

Those who professed the Orthodox faith were 'us'; those who did not were 'them'. Russia, or rather, Muscovy, was no different from other early societies in seeking its identity in its religion. It was always the bastion which protected against the invader, and the invader who came not in war but in peace was no less an insidious threat. The foreigners, however, had been there from the very beginning, even before the religion. The *Primary Chronicle* tells us that the Varangians (i.e. the Scandinavian Rus) were invited to Novgorod in 862 'to rule and to govern' since the natives were making a hash of things; and even the religion came from outside, when Prince Vladimir saw the light through the eyes of his bride, the Byzantine emperor's sister Anna. But once accepted, it was Orthodoxy which made a Muscovite and let him accept as 'us' those who professed the same faith and with a touch more reluctance those who converted to the faith, but he, or rather his rulers, could not do without the heretics, particularly those who came from the West. This has remained the central dilemma, if not paradox, of the Russian state in its various transformations down the centuries. However, Kievan Rus did not seem to have the same problems as Muscovy, enjoying relatively easy and multiple contacts with its neighbours, as too did Novgorod in its great centuries. It was essentially after the lifting of the 'Mongol Yoke' in the fifteenth century and the emergence of the independent state of Muscovy that the foreigner problem took on the *actualité* it has never lost. Moscow in its self-appointed role as the New Rome and New Constantinople[6] could blame the Mongols for all the past evils visited on the land without acknowledging their cultural legacy and at the same time steadfastly look down both on the Turks and on the West, hoping to remain ideologically pure and untarnished.

The sixteenth and seventeenth centuries nevertheless brought the West into Muscovy's heartland; it was in the reign of Ivan the Terrible (1547–84) that the first German or Foreigners' Quarter (*Nemetskaia sloboda*) was founded in Moscow and 2003 marked 450 years of Anglo–Russian contacts following the so-called English 'discovery' of Russia in 1553 that led to the founding of the Muscovy Company and the invasion by British merchants. Muscovy suffered during the 'Time of Troubles' invasions of a different sort from the heretic Poles which gave rise to a not unexpected hostility towards foreigners in general. The seventeenth century presents us with a picture of increasing foreign presence in Muscovy in the form of soldiers of fortune, experts in all aspects of waging war, specialists of many kinds, prominent among whom are physicians, and merchants; the creation of a new German Quarter in 1652 and, perhaps surprisingly, the building of Protestant churches in and outside Moscow, and it also gave rise to more denunciations from churchmen for the evil the foreigners allegedly brought. In the latter part of the seventeenth century, protests against the influence of foreigners are scarcely attributable to any inborn xenophobia in Muscovites as such who were as ever wax in the hands of the media, i.e. the clergy in the seventeenth century. Foreign visitors, most often diplomats, naturally highlighted Muscovite antipathy towards foreigners in their generally damning accounts of Russia, but there was much evidence of official, i.e. ecclesiastical and governmental, moves against westerners and western ways, including the cursed sot weed (i.e. tobacco), dress, shaving of beards, music and dance, and other devilish entertainments.

The British merchants, the '*angliiskie nemtsy*', became a particular target after the 'barbaric' execution of King Charles (we recall the earlier quoted French condemnation) and were expelled from Moscow to distant Archangel. A few years later, foreigners were probably as happy as the Orthodox priests to see themselves corralled behind the walls of the new German Quarter. What the Muscovites were being sheltered from, however, was not always what you might expect:

Let us not imitate too much the curious and painstaking cleanliness of the Germans, who so often wash the floors of their houses, and where a guest may not spit or spew on to the floor. And if by chance he does so, straightway a servant wipes it up. Such men in their voluptuousness and carnal cleanliness, attempt to make a heaven out of a mere earthly home.[7]

As Archpriest Avvakum (1620/1–82), the arch Old Believer, said in a different context: 'Oh, oh, you poor things! Russia, why did you want German ways and habits?'[8]

One who not only wanted but adopted many of the ways of the accursed foreigners was Peter the Great. Four walls do not a prison make, indeed, they often enclose a *hortus inclusus*, a secret garden of heavenly delights, and the delights of which the young Peter partook in the German Quarter were manifold and their effects long and lasting. The debate continues whether Peter was a reformer or a revolutionary, but there can be no doubt that in terms of imposing his view of the West on his often protesting people he was, as the phrase has it, a man not for turning. Peter sallied forth not only into the German Quarter but into foreign lands, not as head of his 'Great Embassy' (1698–99) but as a humble member of the ambassadors' entourage, to see and to learn from foreigners. Unlike his tsarist predecessors, who ostentatiously washed their hands after contact with visiting envoys, Peter enjoyed close contact with foreigners of every station and, in the case of the London actress Letitia Cross, very close contact indeed. Peter's father, Aleksei, in 1675 had decreed that 'courtiers are forbidden to adopt foreign and German and other customs, to cut the hair on their heads and to wear robes, caftans and hats of foreign design';[9] Peter encouraged the opposite, by decree, by personal example, and by 'gentle' persuasion. He also encouraged into Russian service countless specialists

from all the nations of Europe to establish his new navy, to train and
command his army, to teach mathematics and navigation, to construct
canals and docks, and to build his new city of St Petersburg. He brought
foreigners out from the compound of the German Quarter and allowed
them to work and trade throughout Russia.

Most provocatively for his people, the tsar who in London, for instance,
had witnessed at Lambeth Palace the inauguration of an Anglican priest,
Christopher Clarke, and attended meetings of the Quakers, decreed in 1702
that 'each Christian' be allowed 'to work for his own salvation at his own
risk'.[10] The last words had an ominous ring about them and in that very
same year the Rev. John Urmston, chaplain to the British congregation in
Archangel, whose high opinion of the Russians he expressed as 'the Russians
stile themselves Christians, but indeed are too worthy of the Character some
of our Country-men have given them, viz. ye Scum and dregs of Xtianty;
they pretend to be of the Greek church, but strangely ignorant, yet great
Bigots', feared that 'if his Ma^{ty} should die in the Minority of his Son who is
but 14 years old we must expect all to be murdered' because of the perceived
Russian hatred of foreigners.[11]

Anti-foreign sentiments were part and parcel of every popular protest
from the *strel'tsy* ('musketeers') rebellions of 1682 and 1698, via the revolt of
Kondratii Bulavin in 1708, to that of Emelian Pugachev in 1773–74 during
the reign of Catherine the Great. Peter, the hero of the Enlightenment in
western eyes, was himself seen as a foreigner, a German substituted for the
real tsar, a man who had betrayed his religion and his people, who indeed
was the Antichrist, whose 'cows' hooves' were the German stockings and
boots he wore. And it was inevitable that the city that Peter created in the
northeastern corner of the country, far from the heart, not to say the soul, of
Mother Russia, should be seen as the abode of the devil and of his supporters, the foreigners. Petersburg, its history and its myths, form a very important part in the complex story of Russian attitudes to foreigners, of love and
hatred. The hatred took the form, within years of Peter's death, of Moscow's
restoration as the capital during the short reign of Peter II (1727–30), but the
Empress Anna Ivanovna (1730–40) brought the court back to St Petersburg
and there it remained until the Bolshevik revolution in 1917.

Anna, daughter of Peter's half-brother Ivan and erstwhile Duchess of
Courland by the Baltic, from which she brought her German friends and
advisers, also instituted what has been called the 'dark era' of foreign rule,
otherwise known as *Bironovshchina* (after the empress's favourite Ernst
Bühren or Biron), and ending with the accession to the throne of Peter's
own daughter and the alleged restoration of Russian rule. Interestingly,

Peter the Great now emerged in popular consciousness as the truly Russian hero, and Catherine the Great in selecting as the dedication to Falconet's Bronze Horseman '*Petro Primo Caterina Secunda*' ('Catherine the Second to Peter the First'), wished to emphasize continuity and hide, as it were, her own German origins in a display of Russianness. However, an opposite, if obviously unintended, reading is possible – the acknowledgement that it was Peter who was responsible for introducing 'the Germans up at the Palace', as Princess Diana once remarked about the British royals, beginning with the marriage of his son, the Tsarevich Aleksei to Princess Charlotte of Brunswick-Wolfenbüttel in 1711. It was Peter the Great who is reputed to have said that 'we need Europe for a few decades before we turn our backside to it', but things, of course, never worked out like that. Foreigners remained indispensable and occupied probably as many important posi-tions in government and the forces under Peter and Elizabeth (1741–62) as they did under Anna, but national perceptions of the situation varied according to the moment. Catherine the Great was nevertheless in many ways more Russian than the Russians, ostentatiously opting for Russian dress, appointing Russians, and encouraging Russian culture, while openly declaring in her *Instruction* to the Legislative Commission (*Nakaz*) that Russia was 'a European country'.

Russia shared or attempted to share the cosmopolitanism of the age and the effects were both enlightening and strange. St Petersburg in the reign of Catherine was an astonishing city, not least for its multinational mix and character. A British visitor in 1789 wrote:

I feel myself here as in another world, the dress, the manners, and customs of the people are so different from those of other nations in Europe.

Besides the variety of nations which compose the Russian Empire, in my daily walk through the city I meet with English, Danes, French, Swedes, Italians, Spaniards, Portuguese, Venetians, Poles, Germans, Persians, and Turks; the latter are arrived here prisoners from Oczakow. This assembly is a natural masquerade, and no city upon earth presents any amusement of this kind in such perfection as Petersburg. In other great cities the variety of strangers are not so distinguishable as here, owing to their accommodating themselves to the dress of the country in which they reside, or sojourn, in order to prevent the mob from staring at them.

In Petersburg there is no need of this compliance: let foreigners be dressed ever so oddly, they will find, in every lane, subjects of the Russian Empire to keep them in countenance. She brings into this ball her various swarms, from the snowy mountains of Kamschatka, to the fertile plains of the Ukraine – a space of 4,000 miles! Siberians, Tongusians, Calmucs, and an endless train of Tartar nations, the Fins, the Cossacs, &c. Petersburg is a strange city, even to the Russians: it increases daily, with new recruits from every corner of the empire.[12]

Petersburg from the very beginning had been multinational and international. Areas of the young city, *slobody*, were named after the dominant population – thus the Greek, the Finn, the French, the German, the Tatar, and streets bore names indicating the presence of the Dutch, the Swedes – and the British: the English Embankment was the name officially recognised by the beginning of the nineteenth century for the thoroughfare on the left bank of the Neva where the wealthiest members of the British community had rented or owned imposing homes since at least the 1740s. The city was also famed for its religious toleration and it was during Catherine's reign that Nevskii Prospekt became known as the street of toleration with the construction of impressive churches, Lutheran, Catholic, Armenian, and Orthodox, on the stretch from the Admiralty to the Catherine Canal. The empress also instituted *dîners de tolérance*, which the clergy of the various churches were expected to attend, if some of the Orthodox did so with ill grace. There was, however, no recognition for the Tatars/Muslims; the first mosque in St Petersburg was to be built only in the twentieth century, between 1910 and 1920.

Mention of the Tatars again at this juncture reminds us that while Tatars from Astrakhan and Kazan (regions conquered by the Russians back in the sixteenth century), many of whom had been persuaded to be baptised as Christians, were among the first workers drafted in large numbers to begin the construction of St Petersburg, it was Catherine's reign that brought the annexation of the Crimea and the inclusion in the Russian empire of further Tatar people, descended from the Horde and regarded very much by the empress as barbarians and 'them'. It was also in Catherine's reign that the 'them' question was further complicated not merely by great expansion of the empire by conquest and also by attempts to increase the population by invitation, by colonisation. There was an influx of foreigners from all of the European and Mediterranean countries, which led, for example, to the setting up of German colonies along the lower reaches of the Volga and to populating the Crimea itself. There was, incidentally, a proposal to bring in British convicts – Crimeans would have been an apt name for them – but they were sent to Botany Bay instead. Catherine's Russia was thus a huge melting-pot of nations, aiming to create subjects out of its multiple nationalities, making 'us' out of 'them' (and of course in this not basically different from other countries with empires or from 'new' countries). Napoleon is notorious for allegedly saying: 'Scratch a Russian and you'll find a Tatar', but it was increasingly likely that you would find a Scot or a Finn or a German, as incomers and Russians intermarried.

Nevertheless, the nineteenth century polarized nations as never before as statehood and identity and nationalism and some other malodorous -isms reared their heads and passports became the norm. Wars at least made it clear who your external enemy was and Russians like other combatant nations were urged by state and church to fight the good fight. The enemy within was often looked for in such times and at others when scapegoats were needed. The anti-German demonstrations in Petersburg (soon to become slavonized as Petro*grad*) before the First World War embraced Russified Germans of several generations. But such demonstrations pale against the fantastic variations played during the Soviet period against enemies of the people within and without, wreckers, traitors, and spies. *Pogrom* is a Russian word; and the following excerpt from a recent speech by President Putin:

Our country's spiritual revival is unthinkable without the understanding that Russian culture is a combination of the traditions of all the people who have lived in Russia for centuries. Every person and every ethnic group has been adding the colours of their own discoveries, energy, and talent to the palette of our common culture.[13]

was spoken next to the burned-out synagogue at Marina Roshcha in September 2000. In 1989, the deputy Mikhail Tolstoi, who was president of the sub-committee for cultural links with foreign countries, was posed a question by a reporter of *Moscow News* (about a momentous forthcoming International Congress of 'Fellow-Countrymen'): 'Who do you consider fellow-countrymen? Not only Russians but also Jews, Germans, Armenians left and are leaving Russia.' Tolstoi replied: 'True, and on the marble plaques in the St George's Hall in the Kremlin every fourth person is a Frenchman, a German, an Englishman, an Italian . . . The glory of Russian history was achieved also by those people who according to their passports were not Russian.'[14] From September 1997 the Russian Federation finally began to issue passports which no longer had citizenship and nationality as separate categories:[15] all are Russians in the civic sense (citizens of the Russian Federation) whether or not they would also reckon themselves Russians in the ethno-cultural sense.

II

The Russians have perhaps never possessed the strong faith in their country's cultural and social traditions and institutions, the general sense of superiority which has distinguished the English and the French in particular and generally, if not always, immunised them against foreign opinion.

They, and of course, I have in mind mainly the government, the guardian of Russia's image, have always been particularly tetchy about what foreigners have written about their country, its rulers, people, religion, and customs. Curiously enough, however, the first chapter in what has been more or less an unending book was occasioned not by the Russians themselves but by the English merchants of the Muscovy Company, alarmed at Giles Fletcher's *Of the Russe Commonwealth* and petitioning with success in London that unless all copies of the original edition of 1591 were called in, the book would 'turn the Companie to some great displeasure with the Russe Emperour'. They had a point, for Fletcher, a fierce Protestant, did not mince his words, attacking the tsar, clergy, and Russian national character and believing the Russians were so anxious to keep foreigners from 'the inland parts of the realm for fear of infection with better manners and qualities than they have of their own'.[16] It is highly unlikely that Tsar Fedor (1584–98) ever knew of the existence of Fletcher's work, but when over two hundred and fifty years later, in 1848, a Russian scholar attempted to publish a translation, the Minister of National Enlightenment, S. S. Uvarov (1786–1855), was quick to inform Nicholas I of Fletcher's venomous attack on the autocracy and the church, the journal was confiscated, and new pages substituted.

The eighteenth century produced several examples of Russian sensitivity to western criticism. Peter the Great took strong exception to the secretary of the Austrian legation Johan-Georg Korb's harrowing description of the execution of the *strel'tsy* and of his own sadistic participation and ordered his agents in Europe to do all they could to buy up copies and suppress the book. During the reign of Anna Ivanovna, the Italian adventurer Francesco Locatelli, unhappy about his experiences in Russia, vented his indignation in his *Lettres moscovites* (1736). The Russian ambassador in England, Antiokh Kantemir (1709–44), was moved not only to commission a German version of the work with a point-for-point denunciation of its author but also to suggest that he should hire men to beat up the unfortunate Italian when he appeared in England in 1738 – a strategy which recommended itself to a later ambassador who wished to deal with a similar problem during Catherine the Great's reign.

Catherine's early years on the throne were fraught with a whole range of similar problems of dealing with troublesome foreigners. In one notorious case, she moved to suppress, through the good offices of Voltaire, Diderot, and Mme Geoffrin, the publication of Claude Carloman de Rulhière's *Anecdotes sur la révolution de Russie en l'année 1762*, which was circulating in manuscript in 1763 but was printed only in 1797, after the empress's death.

In another, she resorted to her pen to write under the guise of a 'Lover of Truth' a rebuttal of the French astronomer Jean Chappe d'Auteroche's *Voyage en Sibérie* (1768).

Things did not get any better under Alexander I (1801–25). When Robert Lyall, a Scottish doctor in Russian service, dedicated his monumental *Character of the Russians, and a Detailed History of Moscow* (1823) to the emperor, Russian reaction was immediate and extreme. The Russian vice-consul in London wrote to *The Times*, protesting that the dedication was unauthorized and soon the newspapers were carrying reports of an imperial decree, according to which

no foreign writer shall be authorized to dedicate any work to his Majesty, without having previously solicited permission from the Minister for Foreign Affairs, through the Russian ambassador resident in the country in which the author resides. The prohibition has been caused by the inconceivable audacity of an Englishman, who has, with great effrontery, dedicated to his Majesty a book written against his government, and the entire Russian nation.

This was followed by general denunciations of British travellers and the expulsion of 'a Blind spy, a Methodistical one, and a Quaker'.[17] Lyall, the blind James Holman, who was the author of *Travels through Russia, Siberia, Poland . . .* (1825), and many other authors, who down the decades incurred Russian wrath for their descriptions of exile, prisons, rebellions, atrocities, or unfavourable depictions of Russian moral turpitude or backwardness, undoubtedly relished the *succès de scandale* that ensured their publications received far more notice and discussion that they warranted. Examples could be multiplied, let one suffice which has a degree of topicality. Just before the First World War, the Russian ambassador in London even sought a ban on George Bernard Shaw's farce, *The Great Catherine*, which he saw as an attack on the dignity of the Russian autocracy. The Lord Chamberlain's office apparently recommended that 'Potemkin appear in the play as a mere captain and a teetotaller, and Catherine as a monogamist so as to avoid giving offence to Grand Duke Vladimir of Russia, a friend of the British Royal family'.

The Russians of course have had their ways of getting their own back, and this opens up another fascinating alleyway. Increasingly and particularly after 1762, when the gentry was freed from obligatory state service and had new opportunities to travel, Russians gained firsthand knowledge of Europe; many found it wanting in many respects and wrote accounts that were their counterblast to what foreigners wrote about Russia. Denis Fonvizin's letters from the late eighteenth century and Fedor Dostoevskii's

Winter Notes on Summer Impressions (*Zimnie zametki o letnikh vpechatleni-iakh*) from 1862 are but two prominent examples from a considerable number up to the Bolshevik revolution, whereafter damning accounts of the capitalist West were written to order.

Another, indeed a more successful method of influencing one's compatriots' ideas about foreigners, and one of which both Fonvizin and Dostoevskii also made conspicuous use, was the creation of literary characters whose names became a sort of shorthand reference to the qualities, more often the deficiencies, of a foreign nation. A very early text of this type is the seventeenth-century satirical *A Book of Cures for Foreigners* (*Lechebnik, vydan ot russkikh liudei, kak lechit' inozemtsev i ikh zemel' liudei*), reflecting that hostility to foreigners we have noted earlier in its offering of mocking, impossible prescriptions to cure, i.e. to intensify, foreigners' maladies.[18] It is, however, only in the eighteenth century that we encounter both vivid examples of Russians who have been corrupted by foreign ways and glimpses of the sort of foreigners held responsible. From the satires of Antiokh Kantemir from the first decades of the century to the satirical journals, comedies, and comic operas of Catherine's reign, Russian *petits-maîtres* or Frenchified monkeys are endlessly ridiculed. In Fonvizin's comedy *The Brigadier* (*Brigadir*; 1770) the young Ivanushka parades his absurdity with such statements as 'my body was born in Russia it is true, however my spirit belongs to the crown of France',[19] while Nikolai Novikov's journal, *The Drone* (*Truten'*; 1769) features in a mock news item 'a young Russian piglet, who has been travelling in foreign parts for the enlightenment of his mind and who having duly profited, has returned a perfect swine, may be seen free of charge on many streets in this city'.[20] The foreign tutor was a particular target for Russian satirists: Catherine the Great in her comedy *The Deceiver* (*Obmanshchik*; 1785) includes a French tutor Roti, who had 'spent a year making his living in taverns' before his appointment, and an absurd French governess, Mme Grybuzh, while Fonvizin has an eloquently named German tutor Vral'mann ('Liemann', 'Fibmann') in his *The Minor* (*Nedorosl'*; 1781) and a preposterous M. Pelikan in his unfinished *Choice of a Tutor* (*Vybor guvernera*).

The foreigner in Russian fiction does not, however, begin to appear with any regularity before the 1820s. Pushkin has a whole gallery of foreign types, who as a rule flash by and are accordingly characterized in a few sentences. In the case of the Englishman who attended the funeral of the old countess in *The Queen of Spades* (*Pikovaia dama*; 1833) it is a matter of a couple of words: on being told that Hermann was her illegitimate child, he 'replied with a dry "Oh?"'. There is a wonderful pen portrait of an English governess, Miss Jackson in *The Lady Peasant Girl* (*Baryshnia-krest'ianka*; 1830), 'a prim forty-year-old spinster, who whitened her face and blackened her eyebrows, re-read *Pamela* twice a year, and was dying of boredom *in this barbarous Russia*' and the tutor/governess figures in other works (Evgenii Onegin, for instance, was put into the hands of 'monsieur l'abbé, a wretched Frenchman'). After Pushkin, a list of foreigners in Russian literature would be vast, ranging from virtually all the major novelists and poets through to attacks on foreign wreckers and spies in officially approved Soviet works.

III

For a more detailed look at a specific problem area within our general theme, let us now return to the late eighteenth century and Anglo–Russian relations, which offer interesting variations on Russian attitudes towards foreigners, not least within the context of travel and literature.

In the latter decades of the eighteenth century, Russia (and the Russia I am referring to here and subsequently is, of course, a tiny literate elite, and then only a tiny part of it, and I am making no reference to the masses, slumbering or revolting) was gripped by Gallomania. Russia was in no way unique in its excessive love of all things French, including ways of dress and manners, language and literature. All the countries of Europe suffered to a greater or lesser extent from the epidemic, although in Russia it was virulent and persistent, perhaps not least because of the hegemony of the French language, into the first decades of the nineteenth century. It was also not unlike the rest of Europe in finding a potentially counter-productive antidote to Gallomania in an enthusiasm for England, a tendency given its initial impetus, somewhat paradoxically, in France. In 1763 the renowned English historian Edward Gibbon wrote that 'Our opinions, our fashions, even our games were adopted in France: a ray of national glory illuminated each individual, and every Englishman was supposed to be a patriot and a philosopher';[21] a decade later, the great Russian publisher, journalist, and committed freemason Nikolai Novikov suggested in one of his journals:

We have become accustomed to adopting greedily everything from foreigners, but unfortunately we frequently adopt only their vices. For instance, when the French were in fashion, our intercourse with them left us only with flippancy, inconstancy, foppery, freedom in manner which exceeded all bounds of decency, as well as many other vices. The French have been replaced by the English: now men and women are falling over themselves to adopt something from the English; everything English now seems to us good, charming, and everything enchants us.[22]

The word *angloman* appeared for the first time in a Russian dictionary in 1803 where it is defined as 'a person who is astonished by, and imitates to a ludicrous excess, everything that is done in England'.[23] By that time there were many examples in life, if not in literature – the literary Anglomaniacs really start to make their appearance in the short fiction of Pushkin and his contemporaries in the 1830s – but what one might call the early stage of Russian enthusiasm for England was in fact characterised not so much by excess and mindless acceptance as by a discriminating and enquiring attitude, which is better termed 'anglophilia' than 'anglomania', and which had as much to do with discourses on Russian identity as with England itself.

Generally influential in establishing a persuasive positive image of England and the English was literature, historical, descriptive – and imaginative. Indeed, the reign of Catherine witnessed a vogue for the so-called 'English novel', stimulated not merely by translations (into Russian and French) of the works of such as Fielding, Richardson, Smollett, and Sterne but also by numerous French and German works masquerading as 'English compositions', in which reverence for the English was immense. Nikolai Karamzin was to recall that:

There was a time when having met almost no Englishmen, I was enraptured by them and imagined England to be the country most attractive to my heart. It seemed to me that to be brave was to be English, magnanimous also, a real man also. Novels, if I'm not mistaken, were the main source for such an opinion.[24]

Seen from afar, England was perceived generally with more than a degree of idealism. Princess Ekaterina Dashkova, who played a major role by her own assessment in the palace coup which brought Catherine to the throne, was wont to exclaim, prior to her travels which were to take her to the four corners of Britain: 'Why was I not born an Englishwoman? How I adore the freedom and spirit of that Nation!';[25] In 1789, Vasilii Malinovskii requested a post at the London embassy, 'wishing to know a state famed for the wisdom and happiness of its government and people';[26] while Karamzin also wrote of the land 'which in my childhood I loved with such passion and which for the character of its inhabitants and the degree of national enlightenment is certainly one of the first states in Europe'.[27]

Seen at close quarters, England for many Russians only confirmed its promise. First impressions were of cleanliness and order, of abundance and contentment, of industry and activity, of neat homes and gardens and fine country estates, of excellent roads and street lighting and well-stocked shops, of well-dressed people at all levels of society, prostitutes and beggars notwithstanding. London itself brought a chorus of delight and astonishment for its beauty and its thousand attractions. Russian visitors willingly partook of the entertainments, but were also intensely interested in more serious aspects of English life and government. At the centre of attention was the working of the English constitution and the general practice of law. Russians visited Parliament, witnessed elections, were present at trials at the Old Bailey and at county assizes. Amidst a chorus of general approval, Karamzin alone was anxious to sound a cautionary note: 'The laws are good, but it is necessary to carry them out faithfully for people to be happy'; his observations led him to suggest that the laws could be bent, but that the enlightened English would always discern where their true advantage lies, and therefore 'not the Constitution but the enlightenment of the English is their true Palladium. All civil institutions must be in harmony with the character of a people; what is good in England will be bad in another country'.[28] Nevertheless, the possible relevance for Russia of the various English legal institutions they were describing was uppermost in the mind of many Russians.

The preservation of the family was seen as basic to the English way of life and the Englishman's undisputed claim to be enlightened. Russians waxed lyrical in their descriptions of family life, particularly as exemplified in the middle class and in the country rather than in the city; they admired the role of the housewife and mother and the decorum and harmony they confessed to see in family relationships; they were charmed by the English Sunday, by the edifying sermons preached in the country churches. Outside the family, there was ample evidence to confirm that the English were the most enlightened nation in the world. Englishmen at all levels were well-informed; merchants could talk about politics and history, even servant-girls read the latest novels. The English set great store by education. Nikolai Korsakov, a canal engineer travelling extensively through Britain in the late 1770s, believed that the English had 'more geniuses and more true savants than any other European country'.[29] He also suggested that the working classes, although without formal education, showed great application and specialization which resulted in excellent workmanship. He continually highlighted the lack of opportunities and facilities in Russia, and in almost the final entry in his diary of 1777 he pleaded the case for more universities in Russia, impressed by what he had seen at Oxford and in Scotland. Other visitors found much to commend in both public schools and the new Sunday schools, which helped to spread literacy among the humblest of the people. Institutions of all kinds were lauded: the British Museum, the Royal Society, the Penny Post, the Society of Arts, Greenwich Hospital.

After a visit to the last of these in 1789, Karamzin observed that 'there is much that is good in England: and best of all are the social institutions which show the virtuous wisdom of the government. *Salus publica* is truly its device. Englishmen should love their country'.[30]

If praise for English institutions, funded by state or individuals, was unstinting, reaction to the English themselves was predictably mixed. Englishwomen were universally admired for their beauty, elegance, intelligence, and the role they played within society and the family. The absence of powder and paint on their faces pleasantly impressed a number of travellers, disgusted at their abuse by Russian ladies, although an English reviewer of Karamzin's letters suggested that the traveller could not distinguish between natural colour and a dye skilfully applied.[31] Englishmen did not elicit the same enthusiasm. The sentimental Vasilii Zinovev, brother-in-law of the Russian ambassador in London in the 1780s, complained that Englishmen were loath to confess their love to their wives, and added: 'I greatly respect Englishmen for the good use they make of their reason – the soul's principal quality – but I do not like the lack of tenderness in their hearts'.[32] It was the Englishman's coldness and egoism that repelled Karamzin: 'Now I have seen Englishmen at close quarters, I do justice to them, I praise them – but my praise is as cold as they are themselves'.[33] The Englishman possessed undoubted qualities – he was seen as honest and reliable in business and public life, a good friend, when you broke down his reserve, resourceful, inventive, independent. But it was the dark side of his nature that exercised the greatest fascination and England was perceived as the home of an astonishing gallery of eccentrics, splenetics, melancholics, and suicidal maniacs, spurred to their excesses by climate (the eternal fog), eating habits (undercooked roast beef), and drink (port and porter). Karamzin allegedly saw amazing characters everywhere and suggested that Fielding had merely to copy and not to invent in order to people his novels; he discerned bestiality as the dominant feature on English faces and realized that Hogarth, too, had merely 'painted from nature'.[34] Karamzin probably did more than any other contemporary Russian to promote these aspects of the English character – by his descriptions in *Letters of a Russian Traveller* (*Pis' ma russkogo puteshestvennika*) and by the numerous anecdotes he contributed to journals over the period 1791–1803. But if his personal experiences inclined him to prefer the French, others were prepared to accept the English, warts and all, as their 'favourite nation'.

What I have done so far is largely to examine Russian attitudes to England and the English, Russians speaking about one particular foreign nation, and over a restricted period of time (with only the occasional hint that something seen or described may perhaps have been found relevant to Russia. However, 'us' and 'them', as we have recognised from the outset, are but two sides of a single coin and I now wish to concentrate on further aspects in Russians' perceptions of the English which were central to their (the Russians') perceptions of themselves or of what they themselves should be, i.e. their own identity.

One particular trait of the English which was unfailingly remarked upon was their patriotism. It frequently manifested itself in arrogant assertions of superiority and unconcealed hostility towards foreigners. A visitor in the 1790s suggested that: 'Not to be born an Englishman and to be an honest man seems to them an incomprehensible contradiction. Thinking in this fashion, they receive a foreigner coldly, with a look of contempt, with an obvious desire to avoid getting to know him'.[35] This is a companion piece to Karamzin's description of foreigners as 'some sort of imperfect, piti-ful people. "Don't touch him", they say in the street, "he's a foreigner" – which means "He's a poor man or an infant".'[36] But Russian visitors were quick to note the positive aspects in English attitudes. 'In the whole of Europe the English alone excel us in generosity; but their generosity is not limited to mere amusements as it is with us: it extends most of all to everything that serves the general good.'[37] The English were proud of their nation's history and of their great men: Westminster Abbey was a magnet for Russians, who were duly impressed by the monuments erected by a grateful nation to its poets, scientists, and statesmen. When England was under threat, Englishmen rallied to the flag. In 1803, when war with France was imminent, both Karamzin and Malinovskii independently voiced their concern and marvelled at English patriotism. Malinovskii wrote:

From amidst our peace and security we look at the state of England, but not with indifference! . . . The English are a grateful and magnanimous people, they feel themselves abandoned and rejected by all, and therefore the more earnest is their love for their homeland.[38]

In even more moving terms Karamzin wrote in his influential journal *The Messenger of Europe* (*Vestnik Evropy*):

In England the homeland is not a word but a thing, and love for it is not a figure of speech but a feeling. We as yet do not know what will happen in France, but we have seen for a long time what is in England, and we must desire, for the happiness of the world and posterity, for the progress of civic life and all that is truly human in people, that the Genius of Albion long, long will preserve the prosperity of this wonderful island.[39]

Karamzin and Malinovskii were writing at a time when Russian discussions of patriotism, of what makes 'a true son of the fatherland' were much to the fore and the particular stimulus afforded by English example was very apparent.

In 1796, Malinovskii had begun to publish anonymously extracts from his travel diaries in Britain under the title 'A Russian in England'. Deeply impressed by almost everything he saw in England, he confided nevertheless that 'living among Englishmen, I think most of all about Russians',[40] and launched himself into an essay entitled 'History'. He called for a true history of Russia, which would 'inspire love and respect for our fatherland not only among ourselves but also among other nations'. For 'of all sentiments, of all passions, love of country is the most noble. Love for oneself, innate in all men, is the prime source of love for country'. After enumerating several historical events and personages capable of inspiring pride in Russians, he appealed to Russians with 'a spark of patriotism in them' to donate money for a fitting history – the sort of action that he and many others noted as commonplace among Englishmen.[41]

Karamzin, who with his *History of the Russian State* (*Istoriia Gosudarstva Rossiiskogo*; 1818–29) was ultimately to provide Russians with just the sort of history that Malinovskii wanted, was throughout his career conscious of the connection between history and patriotism, and never more so than in the early years of Alexander's reign, when the English section of his *Letters of a Russian Traveller* was published for the first time and he edited the influential *Messenger of Europe*, which included such essays as 'On the Incidents and Characters in Russian History Which May Provide Subjects for the Arts' (*O sluchaiakh i kharakterakh v Rossiiskoi Istorii kotorye mogut byt' predmetom khudozhestv*; 1802) and 'On Love for the Fatherland and National Pride' (*O liubvi k otechestvu i narodnoi gordosti*; 1802). He defined patriotism as 'the love for the good and glory of the fatherland and the desire to serve them in all respects. It demands reflection – and therefore not everyone is capable of it'. In terms close to those used by Malinovskii he connected love of oneself with love of country and citing the Greeks and the Romans as outstanding examples from past ages, he suggested that 'the English, who in recent times are famed for their patriotism more than other nations, think more than others about themselves'.[42]

A more thoroughgoing parallel between England and Russia was made by Nikolai Muravev, who had served in the British navy in the 1790s and whose 'Essay on Great Britain and Subsequent Reflections' (*Opyt o Velikobritanii i posledstvennye rassuzhdeniia*), dedicated to 'the beneficent Father and the true sons of the Fatherland', was published in 1805. At the centre of Muravev's attention in the first half of his essay was the nature of English patriotism, which was founded on the belief of the English in their superiority and their determination that it should continue. Parading both the just and the less attractive reasons for English national pride, Muravev called for Russian emulation:

I wish that the reader, even though roused to indignation by the alleged haughtiness, boorishness and rudeness of the British, would consider the subsequent reflection: is this accusation just and does it not perhaps put upon us ourselves the sacred obligation to attempt to revive in ourselves and to pass on to future generations such a distinctive national morality as animates the fortunate British?[43]

However, rather than rejoicing in what Russians already had, he was highly critical on almost every count. Instead of simply taking pride in Russia's past heroes, he imagined them as groaning at the present state of Russia, where the gentry enjoyed too many privileges, agriculture and the arts were not encouraged, and adequate laws had not been framed. In his attack on the hold that everything foreign had on Russian society, Muravev manifests that blend of Slavophilism and admiration for England which was characteristic of a certain type of Russian at this period.

English patriotism had one further vital ingredient of which all the authors mentioned were very aware. The English attitude towards their native language was one of unquestioning pride and complete confidence in its richness and power. Prince Aleksandr Kurakin, visiting England with two other young aristocrats in 1772, praised Englishwomen, not least because 'few of them know French and even when they understand it, they prefer to keep to the language of their own country'.[44] Karamzin, attempting at a dinner in London to speak French with the lady next to him and rewarded with a 'oui' and two 'non's, reflected that 'all well-educated Englishmen know French but do not wish to speak it'.[45] In a later essay he expressed his admiration for the English attitude, for 'language is important to the Patriot; and I love Englishmen for the fact that they prefer to *whistle* and *hiss* in English with their beloveds rather than speak a foreign language which they all know'.[46] Muravev wrote that the Englishman 'prides himself on his knowledge of French, German and Italian literatures, considers a knowledge of Latin and Greek very important, but he recognizes the necessary obligation to speak lucidly and intelligibly in his own native language, to write it elegantly and correctly, and also to speak it and write it when communicating with his own countrymen'.[47] Such statements are invariably accompanied by reflections on the very different situation in Russia and by exhortations to Russians to speak their own language.

'What a difference in our country!' Karamzin exclaimed after describing the English attitude. 'Anyone who is able only to say: *comment vous portez-vous?* needlessly distorts the French language simply to avoid speaking Russian to a Russian; and in our so-called *fine society* without French you are deaf and dumb'.[48]

Was this in fact the final degradation? A Russian rendered dumb, indeed a *nemets*, in his own country without a knowledge of French: it was other foreigners, the English, who offered a solution. It was necessary to look at 'them' to learn how to be 'us'. Karamzin, who all his life loved the play of paradox, would not have demurred.

SECTION III

'Essential' identities

In this book, we apply the word 'essentialist' to the idea that national identity is innate, timeless, intrinsic to the age-old character of the people. And where, according to the essentialist supposition, does one find signs of this deeply embedded, pristine and perfect Russianness? In the most basic and fundamental spheres of human expression and activity: in the songs and words and spiritual beliefs of the people, in the habits and patterns of daily life. Whether explicitly or implicitly, many types of discourse on Russian identity are founded on such essentialist assumptions. Each of the four chapters in this Section – on religion, music, language, and everyday life – begins by explaining the essentialist position, and then proceeds to illustrate some of the issues and problems (different in each case) that arise from it.

Religious identity has already been, and will again be, mentioned in several chapters. Russia, it is said, has traditionally been a Christian country, a land of Orthodoxy. The generalization can hide extreme contrasts of opinion: from the view that Russian culture emerged in a Christian context which it thankfully escaped on encountering the Enlightenment, to the prescriptive view that a 'true' Russian must be a practising and believing Orthodox Christian. Chapter 6 surveys the relations between Christian identity and the dominant culture from the Middle Ages to the present day, and then looks in more detail at a specific question: that of the tensions and accommodations between, on the one hand, a sense of religious identity – or at least of religious emblems as signs of the national identity – and, on the other hand, the predominantly 'secular' forms of modern culture.

Music enters the discourse of national identity in two ways. On the one hand, musical works may be created specifically to serve as official emblems of identity. On the other hand, music may come to be perceived as an innate, spontaneous expression of qualities peculiar to the nation. Chapter 7 considers both aspects of the theme: the official sounds of national identity

93

through the composition and promotion of national anthems, and the Romantic idea that Russian folk music is an expression of the spirit or soul of Russia. The main purpose is to reveal and strip away the layers of mythologizing: to show how the 'Russianness' of music has been selectively construed, how it is not a source for but a product of discourses of national identity.

One simple ethno-cultural definition of Russians might be linguistic: Russians are people whose native language is Russian. Yet the status of the Russian language has varied even among its own speakers and it has by no means always been a prime marker of community and esteem. For nearly three quarters of a millennium, until the eighteenth century, the prestigious language of culture was Church Slavonic; and well into the nineteenth century the polite language of polite society was French. With Romanticism, however, came the notion that the character of the language itself embodies the character of its users: that Russianness is shaped and encoded in the very grammar and/or vocabulary of the Russian language. The notion of language as a reflection of – or as a factor in the creation of – national identity has remained quite popular to the present day. This is the starting-point for Chapter 8, where some of the subtleties of the issue are explored: although linguistic forms have no intrinsic meaning (hence the pure Romantic idea is an illusion) they can acquire functional meaning through their cultural and contextual associations (hence the perception that they are bearers of a particular 'character').

In the Soviet Union, few Russians were unaware of the officially approved and propagated aphorism that 'being determines consciousness'. This is, of course, a thoroughly anti-essentialist statement: identity cannot be intrinsic, it is forged by life itself; change the conditions of life and you change the person; the conditions of life must be of the utmost importance to any definition or explanation of identity. On the one hand, the slogan was a challenge to a common essentialist view of the Russian character: the idea that Russians are peculiarly impervious to – even dismissive of – the constraints of the everyday. And on the other hand it encapsulated the justification for social policies which were designed to change the conditions of life and thereby to create a new and pre-planned consciousness, a Soviet identity. In neither case, as Chapter 9 shows, was the equation quite as straightforward as its proponents might have wished.

CHAPTER 6

Identity and religion

Simon Franklin

Russia is unthinkable without Orthodoxy. The spirit of Russia rose
from Byzantium. Constantinople, the Imperial City . . . passed on to
Moscow the honour of being the capital of the Orthodox Kingdom . . .
(enjoining) us to preserve this Kingdom as God's gift, as a barrier in
the path of the spread of evil in the Universe.[1]

Archbishop Iuvenalii of Kursk and Rylsk

This chapter is *not* about the nature of Russian faith or Russian spirituality
or the 'Russian soul', nor even about the place of religion in Russian culture.
The aim is much narrower. We are not concerned with belief, but with identity (in a sense, with beliefs about beliefs, or at least with declarations about
beliefs). Nor are we even concerned with the 'actual' role of religion in Russian national identity, but merely with the roles which have been ascribed
to it, with its representations, whether explicit in ideology and thought and
propaganda, or implicit in other forms of cultural production. We start with
a broad survey over the course of a millennium, before looking more closely
at some of the ways in which the issue is reflected in specific materials.

I. OVERVIEW: BELIEFS ABOUT BELIEFS

Towards the end of the tenth century – the conventional date is 988 –
Prince Vladimir Sviatoslavich of Kiev 'officially' converted his people, the
Rus (*Russia* was originally a Latin word meaning the Land of the Rus) to
Christianity. Over the previous few years, Vladimir had been seeking ways
to consolidate and legitimize his rule over a large and culturally diverse set
of territories. One of his projects was religious integration: to replace the
diversity of local pagan cults with a single focus of spiritual authority closely
associated with himself. Christianity – specifically, Byzantine, or Eastern
Christianity, under the jurisdiction of the Patriarch of Constantinople –
was his eventual choice. Vladimir was building the state, and Christianity
could help him establish a sense of nation.

From a twenty-first-century perspective the whole idea of an 'official' conversion of a people seems very odd. What about individual conscience? How can one officially make people believers? Or deem them to be so? Or persuade them to accept such a designation? Surely this was really just the conversion of Vladimir, and the rest was wishful thinking? Not at all. There had been individual conversions before. Vladimir's grandmother Olga had become Christian, but the identity of the people was unaffected (according to the chronicler, for Olga's son Sviatoslav refused to convert because – he said – his soldiers would laugh at him!).[2] Vladimir's choice was for everybody, whether they liked it or not. None of the sources glosses over the fact that 'official' conversion involved compulsory mass baptism. To become a Christian was to be baptised. Some may embrace the faith willingly; but if not, then forced baptism was equally valid, to the greater glory of God. Baptism defined status and identity; beliefs could be nurtured later, like love in an arranged marriage.

Christianity came with the tools for the job. Vladimir's envoys are said to have been especially affected by its devotional rituals (visiting St Sophia in Constantinople they 'did not know whether [they] were in heaven or on earth'). It had huge organisational experience and a trained personnel. It brought with it the technology and skill to transform the public space, with grand masonry churches amid the local wooden dwellings; to transform the visual environment with its devotional images; to transform the verbal environment through exploiting its mastery of writing (an information technology barely known to the Rus at the time) to disseminate its own texts. Granted the scope, it sought also to reach out beyond the church, beyond the public, into homes and daily lives: to regulate on food and clothing, on sex and marriage, on proper observance from birth to burial. The Church could also provide intermediaries (saints) who might be called upon to help in healing the sick, punishing the guilty, and defeating enemies in war. Baptism also changed one's legal status, since Christians and non-Christians were accorded different protections and privileges. Of course a prime task for churchmen was also to teach the faith; but the inner world is invisible and unknowable, while observance is real. Vladimir and his successors – for baptism, clearly, was only the beginning – brought in Christianity as a 'package deal'. From the public square to the bedroom, from the cloister to the battlefield, from the kitchen to the cemetery: the Church spread reminders of itself throughout the familiar environment, permeating ordinary life. Part of its function in the state was to be an instrument of cultural integration and social cohesion, a force for and an essential component of (along with the secular authorities whose power it helped to legitimize) national identity.

Christianity in Rus spread from the top down. It was a public identity before it could become widely assimilated as a private identity, the national before the personal. The national dimension of Rus Christianity, implicit in the 'official' Conversion, was well understood by early ideologists. It is, indeed, the main subject of some of the earliest native writings. Conversion might well involve political calculation or personal conviction or aesthetic inclination or commercial consideration, but above all it provided national justification. Through Conversion the Land of the Rus found its place in the universal scheme, in Divine Providence. Through Conversion – through entering the fold, or joining the club – the Land of the Rus found its true and intended identity. To be was to belong. 'We were blind', declares Metropolitan Ilarion of Kiev in the mid-eleventh century, reflecting on the Conversion; 'we were lame'; 'we were as the beasts and as the cattle'; until 'the Grace of faith spread over all the earth and reached our nation of Rus'.[3] Or, as the compiler of the conversion story in the *Primary Chronicle* explains, baptism showed how Christ loved 'the new people, the Land of Rus'.[4]

Despite such claims, Christianisation was a process, not an event. It was a process which had plenty of time to mature, since for about seven hundred years after Vladimir the Church enjoyed a virtual monopoly of prestigious public cultural space. The articulate ideological statements could reassure the religious and political elite of the significance of their own achievements, but they probably reached a limited audience. More pervasive statements about the new identity were implicit in the transformations of the familiar environment, first in the towns, then seeping more slowly through the countryside. We cannot follow in any detail the process of the spread of Christianity across the vast territories of the lands of the Rus; but it is perhaps indicative that by the early fifteenth century a Christian identity was embedded in the language of self-definition. Newcomers to the modern Russian language note the curious similarity between the word for 'peasant' (*krest'ianin*) and the word for 'Christian' (*khristianin*). The similarity is no coincidence, since in origin the two words are the same: not two different words but variant forms of the same word. From the fifteenth century we begin to find documents commencing 'A petition to lord X from the *krest'iane/khristiane* of village Y . . .', with the variant forms used interchangeably.[5] 'Christian', in this context, simply meant 'peasant', in documents issued by or for peasants themselves.

Often the general label 'Christian' was enough. It defined the community as far as most people could see, whether looking outwards geographically or upwards or downwards socially. It affirmed a common *essential* identity, regardless of the variety of actual popular beliefs and local rituals. And it affirmed a common *contrastive* identity: whether in a theological context, against Jews of the Biblical past ('we, too, with all Christians, glorify the Holy Trinity, while Judea is silent');[6] or against neighbouring pagans of the steppes ('the Polovtsians observe the law of their fathers: to shed blood . . . to eat carrion and all sorts of unclean food . . . But we Christians, of whatever land . . . have one law.').[7] These are assertions of an inclusive Christianity: 'with all Christians'; 'of whatever land'. Inclusive Christianity is by definition non-national, or multinational, where part of national identity is a broad affinity with others. Among themselves, however, 'Christians, of whatever land' were far from unified. Inclusive Christianity coexisted with – and was sometimes overshadowed by – exclusive versions. At the time of the official conversion of the Rus there was in principle still one universal Church. But in local tradition and culture, and in language, and in details of observance, the Roman (western; Latin) and Constantinopolitan (eastern; Byzantine; Greek) branches were already estranged. Already for Vladimir the choice of faith was not just a choice between Christianity and others but between the Christianity of the 'Latins' and the Christianity of the 'Greeks'. He chose the 'Greeks'. In 1054 the patriarch of Rome (the Pope) and the patriarch of Constantinople excommunicated each other, and the schism has remained unresolved for nearly a millennium. Within the Christian world, therefore, the defining contrastive identity was 'Greek', or 'Orthodox', as opposed to 'Latin'. In sacred history, the Greek empire of 'New Rome' (Constantinople) had succeeded the Latin empire of Old Rome, just as after the fall of Constantinople to the Turks in 1453 it was itself succeeded by Moscow (the 'Third Rome'). The 'Greek' heritage provided the justification for the elevation of the national.

The 'Greekness' of Rus Christianity was quite literally built in: the first major showpiece buildings were designed and constructed with Constantinopolitan help, in conscious emulation of the 'Greek' capital; their mosaics and frescoes even displayed bits of Greek writing. Constantinople was the model, the prototype, the source of authority on style as well as on substance. The visible Christian environment – the churches, the liturgical silver, the relic-holders and crosses, the textiles and book-bindings, and perhaps above all the devotional images (the icons) – developed from the 'Greek' tradition. In verbal culture: for seven centuries over ninety per cent of all local writings consisted of works translated from Greek or adaptations and imitations thereof. The exclusive version of Christian identity is therefore implicit, but it is also articulated explicitly in ideological texts almost from the beginning: in chronicle accounts of the Conversion, ('do not accept the teaching of the Latins.'),[8] or in polemical anti-'Latin' tracts by leading churchmen.[9] Its narrative reflection can be found in, for example, the *Life* of the mid-thirteenth-century prince Aleksandr Iaroslavich, also known as Aleksandr Nevskii. As prince of Novgorod he was later to become Grand Prince of Vladimir – Aleksandr successfully defended his land against attacks by Swedes and by Teutonic knights. The Pope, hearing of Aleksandr's prowess, sent a brace of cardinals to instruct him in the true faith. Aleksandr will hear none of it: 'From Adam to the flood . . . to the first Ecumenical Council and to the Seventh – all this we know well, and we will not accept teaching from you'.[10] Thus the glorious Aleksandr – eventually venerated as Saint Aleksandr – repels the 'Latins' both on the battlefield and in the rivalry of Christian identities.

From universal Christianity to Greek Christianity to the narrowest of the available options: Slavonic Christianity. 'Greeks', after all, spoke, wrote and worshipped in Greek, but the Christian Rus (drawing on the tradition already established in Bulgaria) spoke, wrote, and worshipped in Slavonic. The ecclesiastical form of Slavonic, 'Church Slavonic', had been devised specially for the purpose of translating Christian texts from Greek. Rus had no classical antiquity to provide alternative models of cultural identity: no ancient ruins littering the landscape; no classical education bringing direct access to ancient Greek and Latin literature or philosophy. The Church was both source and bearer of Rus learning. Christian identity, Byzantine authority, *and* local distinctiveness were embedded in the very language.[11]

And so it remained almost until the end of the seventeenth century. More or less. Perhaps more, rather than less. Of course culture changes, but here what matters is the perception. Early Russian culture was not *meant* to change; changelessness was its virtue, its pride, and in crucial areas even a theological imperative. Cultural forms were not assessed as products of aesthetic whim, and certainly not vehicles for artistic self-expression, still less innovation. Orthodox 'art' was not really 'art' at all in a modern sense. The physical church and the images within it were devices to make the divine manifest in the material. Likenesses – Greek *eikones*, hence 'icons' – were justified only if true; otherwise their veneration was idolatry. Most of the main icon types were in theory derived from eye-witness descriptions or from authentic visions. The job of the artist, the image-maker, was to recreate, not to invent. One implication of this strong sense of the iconic is that cultural identity becomes very strongly associated with a specific cultural form. The preservation of form can be perceived as a central issue of religious, and hence in this context national identity. The conserved form is not only a likeness of its prototype but also an emblem – a kind of self-affirmation – of the cultural community in which it is venerated.

To sum up so far: in early Rus – roughly from the end of the tenth century right through to the seventeenth – the issue of 'religion and national identity' in Russian culture, though it can be addressed in elaborate abstract theological terms, is at core very simple. It is not an issue at all. Christianity was introduced partly as a device to facilitate the very process of nation-formation and state-formation, to devise and articulate and provide a spiritual focus for national identity. The Church meant to be and became, in effect, the cultural agency of the State. It held an absolute monopoly of public cultural forms and expression in all spaces which defined what we now call the national. And form and expression were of the essence. The Christian – Orthodox – element was simply a given, a fact of the cultural environment, implicit and explicit in the forms themselves; not a question, not a choice; not an issue.

The collapse of this edifice of assumptions, when it eventually occurred, was rapid, at least among the elite. The chasm between two worlds can be appreciated if we consider two types of reform: one in the mid-seventeenth century and one fifty years later at the start of the eighteenth century.

In the mid-seventeenth century Patriarch Nikon, with the backing of Tsar Aleksei Mikhailovich (1645–76) introduced a range of practical reforms aimed at cleansing the faith of accretions, to restore it to pristine purity. The reforms may well strike the modern observer as trivial: points of wording and spelling, the way one holds one's fingers when making the sign of the Cross, and other such details. The result was a bitter schism in the Church, between the official Orthodox and the 'Old Believers'.[12] Although the methods and tools of the reformers were to a degree new, critical, scholarly, the rift was still virulently medieval: neither side advocated innovation, and each presented itself as more traditional than the other. Where was true tradition? In preserving the familiar practices handed down from one's fathers, or in attempting to restore and reinstate unfamiliar practices lost since the days of one's great-great-great grandparents? The schism produced rival articulate versions of Christian Russianness, each claiming to out-archaize the other. It offered no challenge to the identification of national culture with ecclesiastical culture.

The more radical change came with the cultural reforms associated with Peter the Great. Peter put an end to the ecclesiastical domination of the forms and contents of high culture. Writers, painters, printers, and builders were now encouraged – ordered, indeed – to apply their talents to worldly projects. The models were no longer Byzantine but West European. An active interest in West European cultural models can already be observed in the latter part of the previous century: in the beginnings of Latin and Greek learning and of experimentation in literary forms, in paintings modelled on western engravings, or in a variant of Baroque architecture for civic buildings. Peter's new capital, St Petersburg, took innovation to a different level. St Petersburg represents not merely a strategic break from Moscow, a 'window on the West' with direct access to the sea. It was also a dramatic cultural statement, a purpose-built, western-style stage for Peter's new Imperial drama: grand western-style buildings, grand western-style parks and gardens, actors in western-style dress and – most insistently – shorn of their traditional Russian-style beards. Even the city's main church – the Peter and Paul church in the fortress of the same name – was a blatant reminder of western style, with its spire instead of an onion dome. St Petersburg was not the whole of Russia, but it was an immensely powerful declaration of intent, and the eventual consequences of Peter's 'top-down' cultural impositions were perhaps as profound as those of his remote predecessor Vladimir of Kiev.[13]

For many, the comparison amounts to a straightforward contrast: Vladimir Christianized, Peter secularized. But to represent Peter's reforms as secularization can be misleading. Peter was an Orthodox Christian (or conceived himself to be so), and he had no doubt that Orthodox Christianity was a necessary component of Russian national identity. Foreigners could live and work in his empire and practice their own faiths; or they could convert to Orthodoxy and thereby become the tsar's subjects. The conversion of the Empire's non-Orthodox peoples (in a sense, the continuation of Vladimir's initiative) was part of his domestic policy: freedom of conscience or freedom of (or from) worship was not on his agenda; nor was it on the agenda of any of his successors, all of whom regarded their own and their subjects' Orthodoxy as a given; or at least regarded Orthodoxy as an essential component of Russianness, and conversion as part of a process of russification. Anyone who suggested that the former German princess Sophia of Anhalt-Zerbst was anything other than Russian and Orthodox and a defender of Orthodoxy would have met an icy reception, after Sophia's transformation into Ekaterina Alekseevna, otherwise known as the Empress Catherine II, or Catherine the Great (1762–96). Under Catherine's grandson Nicholas I (1825–55), the 'official' version of identity was proclaimed to consist of 'Autocracy, Orthodoxy, Nationality'.[14]

Peter and his successors were not, then, intent on secularising Russian national identity: not Peter with his passion for western technology, not Catherine with her zeal for the culture of the Enlightenment. But it easy to get the *impression* that this is precisely what happened. The impression arises because the Church was firmly displaced from its position of dominance over public and prestigious cultural form and production. The space for ecclesiastical culture was the church. Peter did not secularize Russia, but outside the church he legitimized, created space for, and assiduously promoted secular culture. High cultural form was no longer automatically associated with religious content or identity. The old forms of high culture had been imported and developed in the service of Christianity. The forms themselves had been emblems of that Christianity, true likenesses – icons – of authoritative prototypical Orthodox forms. The new – also imported – forms of high culture had no such associations. They were emblematic of West European secular culture, true likenesses of authoritative models which had nothing whatever to do either with Orthodoxy or with any received model of Russianness. The contagion spread even to religious culture itself, where traditional iconicity was similarly undermined. The spire-topped church in the Peter and Paul fortress did not spark off a new tradition, but neo-classically domed churches became fairly common, and an utterly Westernised art of religious painting even claimed a fairly prominent niche alongside traditional devotional iconography.

The automatic link between cultural form and the expression of religious identity was severed. In post-Petrine high culture, religious or Orthodox identity was no longer immanent in form or dominant in function. Religion was no longer *the* point, or even *a* point; it became merely an optional theme. For some, of course, it was an immensely important theme; not just for tsars and their spokesmen, and not just for a hard core of committed 'Slavophile' intellectuals who tended to hold up pre-Petrine Russia as the 'true' Russia.[15] We need not, for present purposes, doubt that very significant numbers of Russians would have identified themselves as Orthodox. The problem now was not belief about identity, but cultural expression. To adapt a late twentieth-century formula: the medium was no longer the message. In post-Petrine culture a gap was opened between, on one side, explicit ideological or philosophical pronouncements concerning the place of religion in Russian national identity, and, on the other side, implicit representations of the theme in the 'creative' branches of culture.

At a very general level we can see this even in a cursory glance across, for example, nineteenth-century literature. Some writers, perhaps not surprisingly, were either indifferent or hostile to the notion of a religious component in national identity; others simply had literary interests in other areas. More curious, however, are the tensions – sometimes destructive, sometimes wondrously creative – faced by writers who *were* deeply concerned with the significance of religion in personal and national life. The core of the problem was: how to reconcile or harmonize two potentially different types of integrity: integrity to the artistic medium, and integrity to personal convictions.

Nikolai Gogol (1809–52) not only believed firmly in Russia's redemption through Orthodoxy but aimed to exemplify that belief in his planned three-volume novel *Dead Souls*. Only one volume was published, on the basis of which many readers drew precisely the opposite conclusion: that Gogol's implicit message was politically and socially radical. Gogol then produced a set of polemical essays (*Selected Passages from Correspondence with Friends*) to correct the misunderstanding, but laboured unsuccessfully for a decade to realize his true aim in literary form. Gogol's 'Rus' (in *Dead Souls* he tends to use the pre-modern designation) is of course Orthodox at the level of assertion and assumption, but not to even the author's satisfaction at the level of depiction. Lev Tolstoi (1828–1910) did present images of an ideal religiosity in his peasant characters, a pure religiosity thus deeply rooted in Russia, but in Tolstoi's work the ramifications were as much social as national (peasants and children have an uncorrupted spiritual understanding, others by and large do not). Moreover, Tolstoi's religiosity was idiosyncratic: he was excommunicated by the Orthodox Church, and neither Orthodoxy nor nationality were relevant to the 'Tolstoian' communities which sprang up in response to his teachings.

Gogol and Tolstoi were writers of utterly different character and style, yet both were frustrated by the inhospitality of their 'secular' prose forms to their desired type of religious image. Gogol died in tormented frustration; Tolstoi abandoned the form and in effect returned to pre-modern genres (his later stories resemble expanded parables) untainted by the multiple ambiguities of a 'realist' mode of writing. In complete contrast, Fedor Dostoevskii (1821–81) positively embraced such ambiguities. In a way, he shares Gogol's sense of frustration, of yearning for some kind of inner and outer harmony rooted in faith. But his is not a frustration with form. On the contrary, few writers have been so relentless in developing the novel's capacity for openness, for non-resolution, for expressing a multiplicity of contradictory perspectives, for – in the common term derived from the influential critic Mikhail Bakhtin – 'polyphony'. His Orthodox or Slavophile characters have no privileged access to the expression of truth, and there is no question of reducing his complex novels to a simple equation of the Orthodox with the Russian and non-Orthodox with the non-Russian.

These brutal summaries are of course utterly inadequate to the works of diverse and subtle writers, and we will return to literature in more measured fashion later. It is worth reiterating, however, that the theme of this survey is *not* 'the religious views of Russian writers', nor 'the influence of religion on Russian literature (and art etc.)', but, much more narrowly, the treatment of religion in relation to national identity.

Some would regard the Soviet period (1917–91) as a logical extension of the Petrine revolution. The tension between cultural form and 'official' identity was resolved, for official identity itself was, at last, secularized. Far from being identified through its religion, the historical destiny and obligation of the Russian people was to cast off the vestiges of religion and progress to higher truth. This was the age when 'scientific atheism' became an obligatory part of the curriculum. Churches, when not destroyed, might find themselves converted into museums of atheism. Where they were preserved – and the golden cupolas in the Kremlin churches continued to gleam alongside the red stars on its towers – their status was as 'architectural monuments' rather than places of worship, heritage sites sealed off from the present. However, although such generalisations may be broadly valid, Soviet culture, too, was capable of ambiguity, of harnessing – in appropriate circumstances – the old religious or quasi-religious associations of forms and images if to do so served present purposes: in particular (and revealingly) if the aim was to stir patriotic fervour. The Soviet national anthem itself (adopted in 1944)[16] proclaims the role of 'Great Rus', not 'Russia': very much the pre-Petrine notion, redolent of princes in fur caps, onion domes, walled monasteries, and solemn Church Slavonic, not the modern march of ideological and technological progress. The Second World War in particular (or the 'Great Fatherland War', to give it its normal Russian designation) was the definitive experience in this respect. All weapons were legitimate, including evocations of past heroic struggles against the invading infidel, be he Napoleon's Frenchmen, Batyi's Mongol hordes, or those ancient 'Latin' foes, the Teutonic knights repulsed by Aleksandr Nevskii. Poetry, film, and painting had in such circumstances license to draw on the accumulated store of imagery, to imply a depth of historical identity, and even a kind of affinity with a religious identity, which normal Soviet rhetoric and culture would tend to oppose.

The post-Soviet age has seen an extraordinarily rapid and assertive re-entry of the Church into public space – as Church, not as museum. The process perhaps began in the mid-1980s, as the *glasnost'* and *perestroika* reform movements coincided with preparations for marking the thousandth anniversary of the baptism of Rus, set for 1988. For the first time, one of the large Moscow walled monasteries (the Danilov monastery) was restored and returned to the Church, as the headquarters of the Patriarch. Within a very few years this significant but limited gesture of tolerance had become dwarfed by the phenomenal scale of church restorations, repairs, and rebuilding projects across the land (from Red Square to remote villages), by 'de-museumisations' and reconstructions, by the re-opening of monasteries, by the virtually obligatory presence of senior churchmen at major state and public ceremonies, by the reintroduction of religious rhetoric into public discourse, by advocacy of a 'return' to religious values, by legislation which by implication favours the Orthodox Church over other faiths in the Russian Federation: in short, by a flood of phenomena which, whatever the constitutional position, have had the effect of reinstating a perception of Orthodoxy as an 'official' religion, as the 'established' Church, of implying visibly, tangibly, and audibly that Orthodoxy is the natural, traditional, and (for some) necessary component of the identity of the nation and the state.

Such phenomena are easy to observe, and easy to react to, but hard to interpret reliably. Specific instances of the post-Soviet use of religious emblems are considered in more detail elsewhere in the present book.[17] Some would, of course, wish to see in this phenomenon simply the Russians grasping the freedom to be themselves once more. Others find the phenomenon aesthetically vulgar, a trivialisation of the past, a theme-park, a currently fashionable Disneyland-type reconstruction of an imagined identity. Others take the phenomenon more seriously and regard it as politically sinister, not just a celebration of the national but an assertion of the threateningly nationalist: prescription masquerades as description, irrespective of the millions who regard themselves as culturally or ethnically Russian but not Orthodox, or who are politically Russian (i.e. citizens of the Russian Federation) but identify with different faiths or with none. Others adopt a more pluralist view: after all, the two new monuments which now dominate the central Moscow skyline are the rebuilt (formerly nineteenth-century) Church of Christ the Saviour, and an almost equally vast and equally controversial monument to Peter the Great. The high rhetoric of Orthodox nationality is the preserve of a cluster of newspapers and journals, just one part of a spectrum. Orthodoxy is one strand in a complex process of heritage revival.

We come back, in a way, to a problem which arose with regard to the Conversion of the Rus a thousand years earlier: the relation of the outer to the inner, of the sign to the faith, of identity to belief. After the Second World War, huge resources were poured into the restoration of the opulent tsarist palaces outside what was then Leningrad (now St Petersburg). This was an official project sponsored by a fundamentally anti-tsarist regime. The restoration could likewise be perceived on many levels: as a healing of the wounds of war; as an act of defiance to show that the Germans had failed; as an indication of care for the cultural heritage or for aesthetic values; as an assertion of local pride; as an expression of covert nostalgia, or perhaps, for some, of a hope for the future. The one thing we can not reasonably claim is that the restoration of tsarist palaces and symbols is a plain index of support for or belief in tsarism. So with the post-Soviet transformations of the built environment: clearly the restorations reflect a very widespread feeling that the physical reminders of Orthodoxy were and should again be, so to speak, part of the furniture (components of a highly eclectic suite), and to this extent they reflect a sense of identity. Belief, as ever, is another matter.

This is not the place to adjudicate or assess. In the context of the present brief overview, the relevant point is plain: that – whatever our personal views and preferences regarding the 'reality', the 'true' essence of Russianness – the relation of religion to national identity has re-emerged powerfully in the post-Soviet years as a cultural issue, as a matter of representation, of debate over cultural form, of the material, visual, and verbal environment of Russia.

2. CASE STUDIES: IDENTITY AND THE PROBLEM OF FORM

Our first 'case study' is taken from nineteenth-century literature. We have remarked that the theme of Orthodoxy and national identity is far more prominent in ideology than in representation, and that even writers who were in principle interested in the theme could find it difficult to project it persuasively in literary form. Here we can look at an exception: at the successful artistic strategies of a writer who is not so well known in the English-speaking world as the 'front-line' classics, but whose reputation in Russia has been and remains high. The writer is Nikolai Semenovich Leskov (1831–95), and the work in question is his short novel *The Enchanted Wanderer* (*Ocharovannyi strannik*; 1873).

In 1860 Leskov came to St Petersburg with the intention of becoming a professional writer. The signs were not promising. The grandson of a village priest and son of a provincial civil servant, Leskov was nearly thirty, had no literary 'track record', had lived all his life in the provinces, had worked as a clerk at the Orel criminal court, at an army recruitment office in Kiev, and as agent for the estate manager to one of Russia's wealthy aristocratic families. Yet Leskov chose a good time. In 1860 the provinces were in vogue. Great reforms were in the air, and in anticipation of the emancipation of the serfs (1861), every intellectual and salon-raconteur in the capital was an expert on the state of the peasantry. Nikolai Leskov had actually been there. He was just the kind of man everybody wanted to patronise.

Fashion helped launch Leskov's career, but talent maintained it. He turned out not to have the views that his initial reformist friends thought he ought to have. But he could write stories: real 'page-turners', lively, dramatic, amusing, shocking, pathetic, macabre. A characteristic skill, known as *skaz* technique, was for getting inside the voice of a fictional narrator, often in idiosyncratic non-standard Russian. In other writers the effect of such stylization was often caricature, or perhaps sentimentality. In Leskov the effect was a sense of affectionate authenticity: not a way of distancing the fictional narrator from the educated reader, but a way of letting the semi-educated speak with their own dignity.

Leskov was a versatile writer, but his most consistent project, reflected in many of his works, was the creation of a particular type of character: in Russian the *pravednik*, whose somewhat over-solemn English equivalent (Leskov is not a solemn writer) is the 'just' or 'righteous' man. Leskov's *pravedniki* are not necessarily people who always do righteous things (a recipe for the insipid or the didactic), but they are in some way motivated towards what is right. Leskov makes no attempt to erase or disguise the ordinary messiness and failures and petty comedies and tragedies of a human life – the 'facts' are those which others might treat as depressing – but the human and spiritual integrity of the *pravednik* lends an affectionate, life-affirming aura to the whole.

In Leskov's short but action-packed novel *The Enchanted Wanderer*, the hero, Ivan Severianovich Fliagin, tells the story of his life, much to the wonderment of a group of travellers he meets on a boat on Lake Ladoga in the north of Russia. Ivan is an extraordinary man. His adventures – sometimes funny, sometimes horrific, mostly bizarre, and always entertaining – show him to be capable of extreme fortitude and self-sacrifice, a willing scapegoat; but he is equally capable of brutality, obstinacy, and impulsiveness. He has endured pain and inflicted it, he has casually saved lives and casually taken lives, he has loved intensely, and has abandoned numerous wives and children. He has, of course, been a monumental drunkard. His wanderings have taken him the length and breadth of Russia and beyond. Brought up a serf, he has lived for ten years in the steppes among the Tatars, who used his skills as a horse-doctor and prevented him from fleeing by sewing horse-hair under the skin on the soles of his feet. He has served in the army, has played the devil in religious plays, has been saved from drink by a drunken 'magnetizer' (hypnotist). Whatever happens he accepts, without introspection or regret.

The Enchanted Wanderer can be enjoyed simply as a *tour de force* of narrative verve and vigour; but it is also a remarkable and quite radical attempt to solve the problem of the novelistic representation of a national, Orthodox identity. In his very name Ivan Severianovich (Ivan, Son of the North) Fliagin (the Boozer), is represented as a kind of Russian Everyman. He is larger than life: physically a big man, with big qualities and big adventures, like a hero of Russian folk epic, a *bogatyr*; deeply national by implication, therefore. And his charmed existence (he is the 'enchanted' wanderer) is rooted in his Orthodoxy. As a boy he had accidentally killed a monk, who later appeared to him in a dream, told him he had been promised to God by his mother, and prophesied: 'many times you will be dying, yet not once will you die until your real death, and then you will remember your mother's promise and you will become a monk'.[18] Hence his many tribulations, which would have killed ordinary men. And he has, indeed, become a monk. His outrageous stories are sanctified by the narrative frame of the prophecy and its fulfilment.

For Fliagin, Orthodoxy is not experienced as a body of theological or ethical teachings, but purely – sometimes in shockingly raw form – as identity itself. The Tatars provide him with wives ('Natashas') for his comfort, and he fathers many children ('Kolkas'). Does he miss them or regret leaving them?

'I didn't consider them my own children.'
'What do you mean you didn't consider them your own? Why on earth . . . ?'
'How could I, when they weren't baptized or anointed with the holy oil?'
'But your own parental feelings?'
'What's that?'[19]

We might almost be back in the world of the eleventh-century chronicler, such is the definitive significance of baptism for identity. Similarly the sense of affinity with visibly Orthodox, familiar Russian space. As Fliagin contemplates the flat and endless steppes, his mind drifts:

'You stare and stare, at nothing in particular; and suddenly, from nowhere, it's as if you can make out the shape of a monastery or a church; and you remember your baptized land, and you weep.'[20]

As themes, therefore, Orthodoxy and Russian national identity are woven tightly together in the fabric of Leskov's narrative. But thematisation is not enough. Anybody can choose a theme. What distinguishes Leskov's novel is the way in which thematisation is amplified into mythologisation. *The Enchanted Wanderer* resonates on many levels. It can be read as a Picaresque novel, an episodic adventure-story in the tradition of *Don Quixote*. For a Russian reader it is reminiscent of Gogol's *Dead Souls*, with Russia reflected in the encounters of its travelling hero. Alternatively, Fliagin is Ivan the Fool, the charmed simpleton of Russian folktale. Or, more grandly, the novel can, as we said, be perceived as a modern recasting of Russian folk epic, of the deeds of a *bogatyr*. Or we can listen for the echoes of a quite different type of prototypical hero, from within Christian tradition. The wanderer is a pilgrim (the Russian word *strannik* has both meanings) and the novel is a sort of 'pilgrim's progress', a spiritual journey. Or it is a 'journey through torments', a 'Descent into Hell' (in Russian *Khozhdenie po mukam*). Or it has generic features of hagiography, the *Life* of a saint, of a man marked out for sanctity in childhood and following his arduous but divinely protected path to the monastery.

Such a multiplicity of generic associations might in some writers have had the effect of undermining any clear interpretation. It could produce a kind of destabilizing 'polyphony'. Not so in Leskov. Here it serves to amplify the resonances, to enhance Fliagin's mythical aura, but without distancing him through subordinating him to any single generic prototype. Fliagin is too secure in his own identity to be threatened by literary or moral subversion. Leskov's truly radical quality – especially in the context of mid-nineteenth-century Russian literature – is his absolute refusal to admit even the vaguest possibility that contradiction, paradox, or ambivalence might constitute any kind of a problem. And if one does not acknowledge a problem, there is no need to search for solutions. In a way, Leskov turns the expected response on its head. What for others among his contemporaries might have been a cause for doubt and the spur for a painful spiritual or intellectual quest, was in Leskov a matter of simple affirmation. Fliagin, Leskov's quintessential Russian, is both magnificent and appalling: no less appalling because magnificent, no less magnificent because appalling. His fellow-travellers, representing a 'normal' contemporary response, are continually amazed that Fliagin seems unaware of the oddness of his story, of the issues which it ought to raise: the a-morality, the cruelty and imperviousness, the outlandish scale. The fellow-travellers inhabit a contemporary novel, where moral ambiguity exists to be explored and dissected; but Fliagin combines the moral insouciance of epic with the moral certitude of hagiography. There are no 'issues' in *The Enchanted Wanderer*. Fliagin is who Fliagin is, and introspection is irrelevant. 'Issues' are dissolved in the celebration of an all-engulfing, gloriously affirmative identity.

In this highly individual amalgam of the novelistic and the mythological, of the contemporary and the folkloric and the ecclesiastical, Leskov came closer than most to transcending the post-Petrine formal dilemma in the literature of religion and national identity.

Our second 'text' is the film *Aleksandr Nevskii* (or *Alexander Nevsky*), made in 1938 by Sergei Eisenshtein (1898–1948), with music by Sergei Prokofev (1891–1953). We have already noted one aspect of an early expression of religious identity in the medieval *Life* of Aleksandr Nevskii, and it is instructive to see how the story migrates across media and across centuries, from thirteenth-century hagiography to Stalinist cinema.

Rus is under threat from the Germans. Teutonic knights, with the Livonian Order of the Brothers of the Sword, have taken the northwestern city of Pskov and are subjecting the defeated population to unspeakable cruelties. Novgorod will be next. Novgorodian merchants and monks wish to negotiate, but the people resolve to fight. They need a leader, so they send for the renowned prince Aleksandr Iaroslavich, known as 'Nevskii' after his victory over the Swedes on the Neva river in 1240. Aleksandr has turned his back on war, and on Novgorod, and he is to be found casting fishing-nets on Lake Pleshcheevo a long way to the east. Yet on hearing of the imminent danger he agrees to return to Novgorod and defend Rus from the invader. On 5 April 1242, Aleksandr and his Novgorodians destroy the mighty Germans in battle on the frozen Lake Chudskoe. Aleksandr liberates Pskov, a romantic sub-plot is resolved, and the captive soldiers (but not their masters) are magnanimously released, and sent off with a message to the world: 'He who comes with a sword shall die by the sword. On this Rus stands and will forever stand.'

The film was temporarily withdrawn in 1939 when the Soviet Union and Germany signed a non-aggression pact, but after the German invasion of June 1941 it came fully into its own as a stirring and prophetic parable of heroism and patriotism. It was a classic – perhaps *the* classic – mid-Soviet appeal to and representation of Russian national identity.

Aleksandr Nevskii is not a religious film. Indeed, it can in several respects be seen as an anti-religious film. Aleksandr fights for his people and his land, not for the Lord. He is a secular warrior, not a saint. By comparison with the medieval narratives, for example, there are no prayers before battle or thanks to God after it, no miracles, no divine intercession. Aleksandr's troops rally to heraldic banners, not to icons. No bishops or priests bless

6.1 The occupation of Pskov: from *Aleksandr Nevskii*, dir. Sergei Eisenshtein, 1938

his undertaking or share his counsel, and the monk – Ananii – is aligned with the merchants as an advocate of appeasement instead of patriotic war. The evil Germans, by contrast, simply ooze religiosity. The focus of their encampment is the bishop's tent. They celebrate the Latin rite and sing psalms. Crosses are everywhere: on their clothes, on their banners. 'There is but one God in heaven', says their bishop, as the fires are stoked to burn the children of Pskov (fig. 6.1), 'he has one representative on earth. One sun warms the universe and communicates its light to other orbs. One Rome shall rule the earth.' Like the medieval *Life of Aleksandr Nevskii*, therefore, the film is virulently anti-'Latin'; but unlike the medieval *Life* the film ostensibly contrasts militant Catholicism with secular heroism alone rather than with heroism tinged with and inspired by Orthodox sanctity.

In view of this general contrast between pious Germans dedicated to God and brave Russians dedicated to Russia, it is particularly curious that, if we look more closely, religious-based signs of Russian national identity are nevertheless deeply embedded in Eisenshtein's film on every level.

They surely resonate to some extent in the very choice of subject, regardless of its realization: barely twenty years after the Bolshevik revolution

6.2 News of the German knights' advance reaches Novgorod: from *Aleksandr Nevskii*

of 1917, not everyone will have forgotten that Aleksandr was a national saint, with a very public prominence (Nevskii Prospekt, St Petersburg's most famous thoroughfare, leading to the Aleksandr Nevskii monastery, Petersburg's most prestigious cluster of ecclesiastical buildings). They are present in the visual imagery, where grand set-piece patriotic speeches take place with the lone speaker silhouetted against the gleaming white background of the cities' main churches in front of which the people congregate when grave issues are at stake (fig. 6.2). They are present, albeit discreetly, in ritual: after his grand speech on the open square in liberated Pskov, Aleksandr does go into the cathedral, preceded by icon-bearing clergy. They are present in the sounds, when church bells ring out to proclaim the liberation. In Eisenshtein's scenario – though not in the eventual film – they were present even in gesture: twice the traitor Tverdilo, in the German camp, is described as switching in confusion between Orthodox and Latin modes of making the sign of the Cross (an astonishing detail, clearly designed to imply a confusion of identities).[21] And the religious associations appear momentarily but very prominently in the language itself: in the very final scene, pronouncing solemn judgement on all that has happened, Aleksandr warns his people never to forget, 'for if you do forget, you will be a second Judas – Judas to the Russian land'. A 'Judas to the Russian land'? Is this a slip of the pen, merely a turn of phrase? Or is a betrayal of Russia equivalent to a betrayal of Christ?

In image, in ritual, in sound, in gesture, in phrase, these emblems of religious identity occur at critical moments. In a film of heroic patriotism, where religion is, for the most part, a conspicuous and utterly negative attribute of Russia's bitterest enemies, such varied – even though restrained – indicators of Russian religious identity are especially significant. This is not, of course, to claim that Eisenshtein's film was an attempt to promote or disseminate Orthodox belief. The emblems represent identity, not belief; or perhaps they represent belief in identity. This is not a statement of Russia's essential Orthodoxy, nor yet a call for Russia to become Orthodox. It is, however a demonstration of how deeply the visible, tangible, audible signs of Orthodoxy could be embedded in the representation of an essential Russia.

Eisenshtein's *Aleksandr Nevskii* and Leskov's *The Enchanted Wanderer* are both attempts at national myth-making, attempts in different media to create an ideal and identifiably national hero. Our final text also aims to generate an aura of authority, but on this occasion not by evoking epic or hagiographical archetypes but by basing itself in the solid, reassuring genre of reference-book. The text is modern, post-Soviet. It does not in any sense stand for all post-Soviet cultural evocations of religion and national identity,[22] but it provides an instructive and in some ways complementary contrast to the other texts considered here.

Holy Rus: An Encyclopedic Dictionary of Russian Civilization, edited by O. A. Platonov, was published in Moscow in 2000.[23] The title is already a slightly confusing hybrid. The notion of an 'encyclopedic dictionary' suggests scholarship, rationality, science, objectivity, dryness, whereas 'Holy Rus' tends to suggest a more lyrical and partisan type of writing. Still, titles are, in part, marketing devices and should not predetermine one's view of the substance. The book's format reinforces the first of the two impressions, the idea of an encyclopedic dictionary as a repository of solid, authoritative, fact-based information: sober maroon binding; large format; over a thousand pages in double columns of smallish print; some five thousand articles (at a rough estimate), most of them signed; plenty of black-and-white maps, plans, and inset illustrations; an eighteen-page bibliography of 'basic sources'. Many of the articles do treat religious topics, as might be expected in a reference-work on 'Russian civilisation', but the genre-signals point towards a standard academic model, a mainstream factographic neutrality, which suggests that the other part of the title ('Holy Rus') is to be apprehended as if in quotation marks.

We begin to browse at random. The page falls open in the early part of the entries under the letter 'S'. Our initial impression is comfortingly confirmed by the sequence of brief and dry notices: Semenov (a small town in the Nizhnii Novgorod region); Semenov, Nikolai Nikolaevich (a physicist); Semenov-Tian-Shanskii, Petr Petrovich (a nineteenth-century geographer); *semik* (in the Orthodox calendar, the seventh Thurdsay after Easter); Semipalatinsk (a town in Siberia); the Semirechenskoe Cossack army; Sengilei (a town in the Middle Volga region); Senin, Aleksei Alekseevich (journalist, b. 1945). This last entry perhaps causes one to pause: why include a living journalist? What is his peculiar distinction? 'Since 1991 editor-in-chief of the patriotic newspaper *The Russian Messenger*, which defends the national interests of the Russian people, opposed to the Judaeo–Masonic ideology of the West'.[24]

The uninitiated reader might well need to reread the entry two or three times, just to check that it really does say what it appears to say. Whatever one's response to the ideology, the most striking feature of the final phrase is its sheer incongruity in its ostensible generic surroundings. The first impression of the book crumbles. Apparently the 'Holy Rus' part of the title does not, after all, come with implied quotation marks. Or perhaps the 'Senin' entry is an isolated anomaly that eluded the editor's vigilance? No. Any doubt is dispelled by the book's substantial entry on the expression 'Holy Rus' itself (*Sviataia Rus'*; following on from the entry on the *svoz*, a medieval procedure for tracing runaway peasants). Holy Rus is defined as 'the particular, divinely endowed quality of the Russian people that makes it the bastion of the Christian faith throughout the world.'[25] Or, on 'Orthodoxy' (*Pravoslavie*; just over the page from 'Poiarkov, Vasilii Danilovich', a seventeenth-century Russian in Siberia): 'the Christian teaching which preserves the instructions of Christ and the Apostles in their pristine purity'; Catholicism has turned Christianity into a mere 'decorative screen to conceal vice and sin', so that 'the main guardian of Orthodoxy is Russia.'[26]

Thus the 'encyclopedic dictionary' turns out to be a cover (in all senses) for the recognisable utterances of those who, in the post-Soviet years, have quite successfully appropriated for themselves the use of the word 'patriotism'. The issue here is not whether such sentiments are typical of a post-Soviet sense of Russian religious identity (for some they are, for others they are not). The present survey, we recall, is not primarily about 'true' identity but about cultural expression. In this context the noteworthy feature is the formal ruse, the resort to genre hybrid (by contrast with, say, the direct ecclesiastical rhetoric of the churchman cited in the epigraph to this chapter). Here, despite the many obvious differences, this specimen of post-Soviet 'patriotic' cultural production can be compared to our previous texts, Leskov's *Enchanted Wanderer* and Eisenshtein's *Aleksandr Nevskii*.

All three texts, in various ways, reflect the paradoxes and dilemmas of the cultural expression of a religious national identity in the post-Petrine era, when devotional culture ceased to be the sole, the dominant, or the most authoritative vehicle for prestigious expression. All three texts are, to a degree, hybrids. All three reflect ways of embodying or embedding signs of religious identity in secular cultural modes; or at least in modes which (unlike most medieval genres) do not automatically convey any religious connotations. Leskov's knockabout novel combines secular and religious archetypes into a highly distinctive form of non-idealised myth-making. Eisenshtein's heroic film reinforces an ostensibly anti-religious message with the discreet (and at the linguistic level perhaps even accidental) aid of habitual religious markers. The 'encyclopedic dictionary' wraps its highly partisan message in multiple layers of thick borrowed packaging which suggests an impartial, academic, institutional, one might almost say 'secular' respectability. Whatever we may choose to believe about the 'real' place of religion in Russian national identity, its modern cultural expression remains an intriguing problem, a source of tension, whose resolutions span the full range from, at one extreme, innovative and potent art to, at the other extreme, incongruous absurdity.

CHAPTER 7

Music of the soul?

Marina Frolova-Walker

Towards the end of 2000, a great controversy developed over the new Russian national anthem – not over the words, which were not yet settled, but over the music. Not only was Russia stirred up, but the news media all over the world picked up on the story and a rash of new websites appeared in many different host countries, all devoted to the Russian national anthem issue. What was the cause of this storm over a mere tune? There were many accounts in Russia. According to one popular narrative, it all began with the unexpectedly poor showing of the Russian football team in the 1998 World Cup. Many remarked on the sight of the sullen-faced players as they stood in line while their anthem was played before the match. The players later complained that the post-Soviet anthem introduced under President Eltsin, an unfamiliar melody with no words attached, could never inspire them to the great patriotic effort needed for success in such an enterprise. Beside all the other competing nations, they were unduly handicapped.

Their complaint did not pass unheard in the Kremlin, and President Putin realized that bold and decisive action was called for: the Eltsin national anthem must be ditched, and the old familiar melody of the Soviet anthem restored. Nothing less would suffice. Exactly how much, if any, of the old Soviet lyric was to be retained could be settled later, but the main thing was to bring back the old tune, a tune that would recall the proud and mighty Russia that existed before the chaos and humiliations of the 1990s destroyed the nation's confidence. Seven years earlier, Eltsin had scrapped the Soviet anthem, which had been pressed into service as the anthem of the Russian Federation without any alteration – just as Soviet passports were still issued to Russian citizens well into the decade. For many, the old Soviet melody was the abiding symbol of a relatively comfortable and stable past: this was the melody which had been broadcast on the radio at 6.00 am every working day, awaking them for the resumption of decently paid work which was always there for them. By 1993 that was gone, and to mark the new, grimmer, reality there was a new anthem. For the rest of the nation, which still thought it could see light at the end of the tunnel, the old tune could never rise above its associations with Stalinist oppression and Brezhnevite apathy. By the time Vladimir Putin was installed as president, however, hopes had been dashed of a prosperous liberal-democratic future, but the dismantling of the Soviet state had also advanced much further, removing any possibility of a full-scale restoration. Some welcomed the return of the anthem, many acquiesced, while others imagined it to be a sinister omen.

Such is the symbolic power of music, a power which often takes us by surprise. In this chapter, we shall examine the musical construction of Russia's national identity from the late eighteenth century, when music first became entangled in nationalist discourse, through again to President Putin and the start of the twenty-first century. We shall resume our discussion of the national anthems and other ceremonial music of the state. Then we shall look at how folk, popular, and church music was used by composers of opera and concert pieces for nationalistic purposes. Thirdly, we shall examine how the myth of the Russian tragic soul was founded on a very partial view of Russian folk music, and how the later development of Russian nationalist music ran counter to this myth.

I. CEREMONIAL MUSIC: NATIONAL ANTHEMS

The power of music to excite strong emotions was well known in ancient times, and Plato asserted that some kinds of music should be banned, lest they stir up dangerous mobs. The unifying and exhilarating power of collective songs was well tested in labour, battle, and revolution over the centuries. It is therefore no surprise that by the early nineteenth century collective songs were enlisted to unite the masses behind the nation state, to induce 'involuntary fervour' among them, as one commentator put it at the time. England had led the way with 'God Save the King', which became the universal song of resistance to Charles Stuart's forces in 1745, although the melody may have been over a century older; neither composer nor lyricist were remembered – like the nation itself, it is always most convenient if the origins of these things are shrouded in mist. As it happens, official sanction was only accorded as late as 1821, when the song was used during the coronation of George IV. By this time, the *Marseillaise* had come and gone as the French national anthem, and, ironically, 'God Save the King' had already been adopted by a number of European states, with translations of the lyrics altered where necessary.[1]

The struggle against Napoleon was the principal motivation for these counter-*Marseillaise* anthems, but the 1812 Russian campaign failed to produce any Russian anthem. During the Congress of Vienna, however, the Tsar and his diplomats began to sense the lack of any ceremonial song to mark their own presence at the negotiations, so in 1816 Alexander I followed the pattern in adopting the English tune and translated lyric: *God Save the King* became *Bozhe, Tsaria khrani*. By the early 1830s, however, under Alexander's successor Nicholas I, the core nationalist idea that every country possesses its own, unique national spirit, had percolated through to the Court, having become common intellectual currency among essayists and artists; thus in 1833, the Court inaugurated official state nationalism with the slogan 'Orthodoxy, Autocracy, Nationality'. The reactionary import of 'Orthodoxy' and 'Autocracy' were clear, while the third term 'Nationality' or *narodnost'* was left undefined.[2] In this context, it was hardly surprising that Nicholas I skirted around the issue of nationalism when he declared the need for a new, home-grown anthem: he said he was simply 'bored of the English music which had been used for so long'. The existing lyric was largely to be preserved, although it was thought appropriate to introduce some reference to Orthodoxy. The new melody was commissioned from Aleksei Lvov (1798–1870), who conceived his task in consciously nationalist terms: he said that he 'sensed the need to write an anthem that would be majestic, strong, and full of feeling, accessible to everyone, bearing an imprint of nationality, and suitable for the Church, for the army and for the people from the learned to the ignorant'.[3] In effect, he supplied the nationalist rhetoric lacking in the words. The Tsar characteristically reacted in French – *C'est superbe*! – and the critics were entirely in sympathy with Lvov's nationalism:

The honour of this great Empire demands that on its expanses, a seventh part of the world, the millions must express lofty feeling not through borrowed sounds, but through sounds of their own, sounds pouring from the Russian breast, sounds penetrated by the Russian spirit![4]

Thus *Bozhe, tsaria khrani* became the first Russian national anthem. Owing to its suppression during the Soviet period, when even Chaikovskii's 1812 overture was censored, it is enjoying some kind of cult status today; in one web page, the Western author claims that the melody is in fact a hymn tune from the Orthodox liturgy. This is completely untrue, but the author passionately wants to believe it, since it allows her to say that this melody uniquely 'embodies the heart and soul of Russian people', and so it is Russia's true national anthem, whatever the official choice may be. Let us remember, this is an anthem whose words are almost entirely taken from its English counterpart, and whose freshly composed melody bears no relation to the musical style of Mikhail Glinka (1804–57) and 'the Five' (see below) which was later to become established as characteristically Russian.

The ensuing changes to the national anthem faithfully reflected the state's changing attitude to Russian nationalism. The Soviet Republic replaced the Lvov anthem with the *Internationale*, the very negation of national anthems. The expected revolutions in Europe failed to develop, or were defeated, and Stalin instituted the policy of 'Socialism in One Country', but the *Internationale* retained its status until the 1944 Soviet anthem brought about a partial restoration, with elements of Russian nationalism placed in the context of the Soviet Union. The phrase 'Great Rus' appeared in the anthem in harmony with the new tendency in Stalin's war-time speeches. The conflict with Germany was officially known as the Great Fatherland War, in which the 'great Russian people' were destined to be the *most* heroic, the *most* courageous nation in the fight against fascism. The new anthem was accordingly designed to sound Russian, and the music critics rushed to demonstrate how it was rooted in the music of Russia's nineteenth-century classics; they even pointed to the unhurried Russian expanse that they heard in the melody's long and stately phrases. The anthem stayed in place until the dissolution of the Soviet Union at the end of 1991, when the non-Russian republics naturally celebrated their independence by instituting national anthems of their own. In Russia, however, the old Soviet anthem lingered on for another two years, until finally the new regime had heard enough of it. Whereas in 1944 its Russianness was most striking, now it was heard as a relic of Soviet times. In its place, the Kremlin chose a melody that had lain dormant in Glinka's sketchbooks for nearly a century and a half, but in the years which followed, only the music was ever heard, for no words were ever attached to it. Boris Eltsin's regime worried that whatever national image was presented in a lyric for the anthem, half the population was bound to reject it. With the arrival of President Putin, the wordless Glinka anthem was scrapped, and as we have already seen, the Soviet anthem of 1944 was reinstated.

Although this brings us back to the present, we should pause to consider the ready alternative which Putin did *not* choose. There was in fact another Glinka melody which is much better known and which functioned as Russia's semi-official second national anthem under the last four tsars and, after Stalin revived it, through the rule of six Soviet leaders and, finally, through the presidency of Boris Eltsin. This was *Slav'sia*, ('Glory!'), the final chorus from Glinka's opera *A Life for the Tsar*. The opera was written in 1836, three years after Tsar Nicholas I had inaugurated official nationalism, which this opera expresses eminently well. Its plot glorifies the establishment of the Romanov dynasty, and the court, duly pleased by the work of its loyal servant, chose this opera to celebrate the opening of a grand new building for the St Petersburg Imperial Theatre. No expense was spared, and a delighted Nicholas I presented Glinka with a golden, bejewelled ring, then a little later granted him a post with the Court Cappella. Beside Glinka's *Slav'sia*, with its rousing march rhythms and chant-like melody, Lvov's national anthem was a bland affair, and far less effective as a means of enlisting the nation's emotions in the cause of Orthodoxy, Autocracy, and Nationality. Even Glinka's harmonies were strongly reminiscent of the Orthodox chant harmonisation practised in countless provincial churches, as opposed to the more Westernised music of the great St Petersburg and Moscow churches. Thus the music brought together Orthodoxy and Nationality, while the words praised Autocracy. The Lvov anthem was not displaced, but *Slav'sia* was given a special importance only one rung lower, and the opera was always performed on the first night of the season in the Imperial Theatres. *Slav'sia* fell silent in the early Soviet period, but it was able to re-emerge when the opera returned to the stage in 1934, now furnished with a new libretto expunged of any reference to the Tsar; the words of *Slav'sia* were also modified accordingly. *A Life for the Tsar* was transformed into *Ivan Susanin* and restored to its position as season-opener. Glinka could now rejoin Pushkin and Tolstoi in the Pantheon of Russian classics which Stalin promoted as the artistic foundation of Socialist Realism, providing continuity between the Russian Empire and the Soviet Union. During the *perestroika* period of reform under President Gorbachev in the late 1980s, the original version of the opera was rehabilitated, and even improved upon, with changes to the somewhat stilted libretto justifiable on purely artistic grounds. *Slav'sia* thus returned with its original text even before the fall of the Soviet Union, but for all its popularity it suited the purposes of neither Eltsin nor Putin. At the end of 1993, Eltsin decided it was time to rid the new Russian Federation of the old Soviet anthem, but having violently overthrown his rivals in Parliament just a few months earlier, his regime faced great hostility. In this context, it would have been unwise to adopt anything with ideological baggage; hence the unfamiliar wordless melody. When Putin, in turn, scrapped the Eltsin anthem, his immediate political need was to co-opt the Communist Party and its masses of disgruntled, poverty-stricken supporters; *Slav'sia* was useless – only the familiar Soviet anthem would do. Even among those who disdained the ineffectual Communist Party, many or most wanted some restoration of order and national pride, so the Soviet anthem was no longer anathema to them.

2. FOLK AND POPULAR MUSIC

Now let us turn to the music of the peasantry and townspeople, first looking at them on their own terms, then examining how they were used by composers, song collectors, and others for nationalistic ends. The very notion of a single entity called Russian folk music was itself a creation of late eighteenth-century Romantic nationalism. Remove the imperative to find a unitary Russian folk tradition and what we have left is a collection of regional traditions, often limited to surprisingly small areas; and any attempt to specify a few near-common denominators would mean the admission of much music from outside Russia proper. In any case, the differences are too great, even if we limit ourselves to the music of Russian Slavs west of the Urals. The idea of a Russian identity to be found in folk music is simply an invention of the literary-minded gentry whose knowledge of peasant musical practices was hazy in the extreme, and always at one or two removes from the village and field. After a century's elaboration on this gentry conception of folk music, the discovery of actual peasant practices, through a series of pioneering phonograph recordings, thoroughly shocked most of those who had long considered themselves folksong enthusiasts. The rough timbres of untutored voices, the whoops, the shouts, the odd intonation – all this shattered the received notions of folk harmony.

From the 1770s, collections of Russian folksong lyrics began to appear, but it was not until two decades later that the first collections with music were published. These were settings for voice and piano; the vocal melody was heavily filtered through the expectations of transcribers versed in Western music theory, while the piano harmonies had nothing at all to do with folk polyphony (of which these transcribers knew nothing) and everything to do with Italian opera or French romances. The transcribers were content to hear a version of each song from a coachman or domestic servant who had learnt the song from their native village; if the original was normally sung in a polyphonic version, then of course only the principal line was ever heard by the transcriber. As a further step away from peasant sources, a genre of so-called Russian songs became fashionable: these generally owed little or nothing to the style of melody found in the folksong collections – a little rustic colouring in the lyric was sufficient, it seems, to turn any French-style chanson into a Russian song. And in the midst of a fashionable soirée, any society girl could imagine herself at one with the mysterious spirit of the Russian people.

This enjoyable pretence continued undisturbed until the late 1850s, when one of the foremost literati of the time, Prince Vladimir Odoevskii (1803/4–69), published a series of essays attacking the Russian song genre and calling for a return to authentic folk melodies, a precious repository quite unlike anything to be found among the nations of the West.[5] French and Italian folk melodies, he argued, had lost all their original innocence because of the encroachments of a strong civilised musical culture over the centuries. Russian folksongs, on the other hand, offer all the strangeness of an ancient tradition still healthy and vital. His criticism of the Russian song genre was certainly correct, although his conception of genuine folksong was based on nationalist mystification rather than any direct experience of peasant practices. But Odoevskii ventured a more concrete claim about genuine Russian folksong: that its melodies were constructed on the basis of the ancient Greek modes. This was misconception piled upon misconception, grossly distorting both Greek modal theory and the actual melodies of Russian peasant music, and positing startling connections between cultures distant in both time and space without offering a shred of historical evidence in support. To understand this strange turn in Odoevskii's argument, it is sufficient to locate his motivation. This requires no great detective work, since he provides the information himself. The link with Ancient Greek culture was supposed to lend Russian music a prestigious lineage, tapping directly into the roots of Western Civilization, where other Western national cultures had obscured their Attic origins through the decadent accretions of many centuries.

At this point, Odoevskii's argument meshes neatly with Slavophile ideas:[6] Odoevskii accepts only those songs which were supposedly traceable to the pre-Petrine era, since everything else was contaminated by Western influence, as the Slavophiles said. After Odoevskii, musical discourse in Russia was long dominated by the quest for the most ancient music, and the stripping away of Western accretions. Each successive generation pictured itself as digging deeper in the search for the final bedrock of true Russianness. Glinka, in the 1840s, was thought to have cleared away the Westernised music of previous Russian composers. Then a couple of decades later, the 'Five', much as they respected Glinka as a pioneer, saw that he had only assimilated urban popular music, whereas now the Five were absorbing, for the first time, the ritual and epic songs of the Russian people. The next generation then claimed that the Five had only acquired a very imperfect knowledge of folksong and, worse, that they had adapted and exploited folk melodies to suit their own musical styles. This generation had the advantage of hearing the first phonograph recordings of peasant song; one of their number, Aleksandr Kastalskii (1856–1926), tried to codify folk harmony from the polyphonic songs he heard, but even if he began sincerely, his abstractions and generalizations became ever more remote from their source; the fantastic end product was supposed to replace Western harmony tuition in Russia's conservatoires.[7] Kastalskii political enthusiasm allowed him to continue this project through the first decade of the Soviet period, long after most composers had abandoned nationalism for more cosmopolitan and modernist styles.

3. CHURCH MUSIC

Let us now look at the development of Russian church music, which for many is the most powerful evocation of Russianness. It seems that few who encounter it can remain unmoved at the entry of the characteristic low basses who translate into sound the dark and mysterious interiors of Orthodox churches. Russia, of course, received its original corpus of Orthodox chants from Byzantium but over the centuries the Russian *znamennyi* chant tradition developed along independent lines. This much is accepted by all parties. Over the seventeenth and eighteenth centuries Russian church music assimilated a variety of Western influences. These imported novelties were generally accepted with equanimity; only the 'Old Believers' (regarded as schismatics from the mid-seventeenth century) preserved liturgical practices in a more or less pre-Westernised form. The changes were profound. First, Western polyphonic singing was transmitted from Catholic Poland to the Ukraine, and then carried by Ukrainian emissaries to Russia. Secondly, the whole corpus of ancient chants fell into disuse. Finally, in the second half of the eighteenth century, the vacuum was filled by the choral concerto, an entirely Western genre of an elaborate and virtuosic type altogether at odds with the character of previous Russian liturgical music. The acknowledged masters of the genre, Dmitrii Bortnianskii (1751–1825) and Maksim Berezovskii (1745–77), both studied their craft in Italy. A reaction to this thoroughgoing Westernisation only developed in the mid-nineteenth century, and as we saw in the case of folksong, this was Slavophile in character, dividing the supposed pure Russianness of pre-Petrine culture from later practices. No matter that these pre-Petrine traditions had largely disappeared, making a genuine revival impossible; in any case, there was no desire to abandon polyphony and return to the single line chants of Russian and Byzantine tradition. Such an impoverishment of sonority would have been acceptable neither to priests nor to the laity. Far better instead to devise a fantasy in conformity with present tastes, shaped as they were by two centuries of Westernisation; so long as the result sounded sufficiently different from the music of recent years, it could be labelled as a revival of ancient traditions, a return to authentic Russian ways. And so whatever chants they could find were dressed up in a new harmonic style, sometimes drawing from Palestrina, the late sixteenth-century Italian master, sometimes drawing from a spurious theory in circulation at the time which supposed that Russian folksong and chant repertoires were based on common principles. Although church and state officials welcomed the revival of the old chant melodies, the methods of harmonisation were often received badly by the deacons who had to implement the changes – in particular, they had begun to associate such sounds with folksongs, since these harmonisations had already become established in that area. In the end, the nationalist reform of liturgical music was a failure, not because of its unscholarly constructions and spurious claims to authenticity, but precisely because it satisfied no one on nationalist grounds, for if there was one kind of music that all social strata identified with, it was Russian church music as it had been shaped by *post*-Petrine Westernisation. Perhaps it did sound more than a little like eighteenth-century Italian opera, but these were the sounds which all Russians, high and low, associated with the most important moments in their lives. This, in short, *was* Russia's national music. Even though many would have taken the claims of the liturgical reformers at face value – that the new harmonies were a retrieval of true Russian practices – they found the result devoid of that quality most valued in Russian church music: *umilenie*, or tenderness. The Italianate music of Bortnianskii held its ground. The new chant harmonisations were initially forced on churches across the land, but they gradually receded to a subordinate position within the repertoire. This was a defeat for nationalist theorizing, even with the support of the most powerful in Church and state.

4. THE INVINCIBLE 'TRAGIC SOUL'

We now move on to another conflict between two musical representations of Russianness, but with two differences: both representations were created by musicians and essayists; and this time the new, rival representation enjoyed its success more through the popular acceptance of its artistic results than through the persuasiveness of its theories. The earlier representation was established during the first half of the nineteenth century: Russian folk music, according to this view, was a melancholy art, reflecting the essential sadness at the core of every Russian. Out of this, after much literary elaboration, grew the myth of the Russian tragic soul. The new counter-representation developed from the later music of Glinka, composed in the 1840s, and from the music of the 'Five', or the 'Mighty Handful' – Milii Balakirev (1837–1910), Modest Musorgskii (1839–81), Aleksandr Borodin (1833–87), Nikolai Rimskii-Korsakov (1844–1908), and César Cui (1835–1918) – composed from the 1860s to the beginning of the twentieth century. This new trend presented the joyful, festive aspect of Russian folk music, an aspect which the partisans of the tragic soul had altogether ignored. To the extent that earlier Russian operas and concert music were of a professional standard, they were thoroughly Western – usually Italian. The tragic soul music was the preserve of amateurs, and generally limited to modest songs with piano accompaniment. Now at last, with the music of the 'Five', there was a body of music which satisfied the highest standards but was at the same time original in style, and purportedly based on a profound understanding of Russian folksong. Yet despite the musical success of the 'Five', the tragic soul myth retained much of its hold over the Russian literary imagination and continued to appeal to many Westerners as the essence of Russianness.

Let us look in more detail at the development of the myth of Russian melancholia. The first writer to make the crucial connection between the songs of a people and national character was Aleksandr Radishchev (1749–1802), in his *Journey from Petersburg to Moscow* (*Puteshestvie iz Peterburga v Moskvu*; 1790):

My horses are rushing me along; the coachman has struck up a song, a gloomy one as usual. Those who know the sound of Russian folksongs will admit that there is something in them which signifies the grief of the soul. Nearly all of these songs are in the minor mode. One ought to learn how to set the style of government according to this disposition of the people's ear. It is here that the soul of our people is to be found.[8]

Over the course of the next hundred years, these sentiments were repeated and elaborated by countless belletrists, scholars, and travellers, both Russian and foreign. During this period, a single folksong genre, the *protiazhnaia* (literally a 'drawn-out song') came to be seen as a paradigm for all Russian folksong, or even as the essence of Russian creativity and the 'Russian soul' itself. The enormous variety of music practised by the Russian peasantry remained largely unknown to the urban literati: even those who spent part of the year on their country estates were unlikely to attend a peasant wedding or any seasonal festivities – this would have been considered improper on both sides. Russian gentlemen did, however, hear individual servants or coachmen singing, and these songs were almost always *protiazhnye*, precisely because this genre was independent of any work-related or ritualistic context. These long, slow songs with elaborate melodies now found many receptive listeners among a gentry which was newly interested in discovering (as they thought) what Russianness was. Such listeners all noticed a general mood of melancholy, although there is little to suggest that they were interested enough in the lyrics to follow the slow unfolding of the entire narrative in each *protiazhnaia* – the mood set by the music was enough to take root in their imaginations, so that they could spin their own fantasies about the meaning and cause of the songs' melancholy. Thus the *protiazhnaia* became urbanised and began to influence Russian art song (then at an early stage of its development). In this manner, the art songs which came under the influence of the *protiazhnaia* formed a link, however tenuous, between the gallant Francophone salon of the Russian gentry and the coarse and pungent hut of the Russian peasant. Listening to the sounds of *protiazhnaia*, the gentlemen pitied the peasant and himself at the same time, the two distinct classes coalescing into one Russian people in their imagination.

Returning to Radishchev, a few pages after the last quotation, we encounter another group of peasants, girls and young women, merrily singing and dancing – the song mentioned in the text is the round dance 'A birch-tree stood in the field' (*Vo pole bereza stoiala*). But Radishchev's narrator cannot enter into the merriment:

I could not reach the round-dance. My ears were clouded by sadness, and the joyful voice of simple merriment did not penetrate my heart.[9]

What does this tell us? Radishchev, through his narrator, is on the brink of admitting that the jovial and the melancholy exist side by side in the music of the Russian peasantry, and that the impression of universal melancholy is determined by the predisposition of the observer from the gentry, not by the thing observed.

Forty years later Pushkin wrote a skit on Radishchev, his *Journey from Moscow to Petersburg* (*Puteshestvie iz Moskvy v Peterburg*), reversing the direction of Radishchev's original journey. Pushkin derides the cult of sentiment which flourished among fashionable people in the decades around 1800. He placed much of the blame on Johann Wolfgang Goethe's maudlin tale, *The Sorrows of Young Werther* (1774), and no doubt its superior artistic quality played a major role in extending the lifespan of this spate of emotional self-indulgence. Pushkin saw Radishchev as a product of this school, and makes the connection in the following sarcastic sketch:

A blind old man sings a verse about Aleksei, a man of God . . . The peasants are weeping; Radishchev weeps along with those assembled . . . The name of Werther had appeared at the beginning of the chapter – it explains a lot.[10]

Pushkin saw that sentimentalism could act as a filter, bringing everything into conformity with its sickly hue. He noticed accordingly that the perceived melancholy of Russian folksong conveniently matched the sentimentality of contemporary salon verses and romances, hence the mocking lines in his poem 'The Little House at Kolomna' (*Domik v Kolomne*; 1830):

> From the coachman to the greatest poet,
> We all sing gloomily.[11]

But even Pushkin's highly developed sense of ironic detachment deserts him on one occasion if Nikolai Gogol is to be believed. Gogol reports that after he had read out the first chapters of his novel *Dead Souls* (*Mertvye dushi*; publ. 1842), Pushkin cried out, 'How sad is our Russia!'[12] Gogol's celebrated work is indeed a turning point: no one managed to embody vague Romantic philosophising about Russia, its people, and its destiny in images so powerfully vivid and so highly poetic. The image of Russia as a flying troika became a cornerstone of emergent Russian self consciousness and to the present day remains one of the nation's favourite images of itself. And it is remarkable that the lingering song of the coachman becomes one of the most important components of Gogol's rich image of Russia, together with the troika and the journey without end. It is the *protiazhnaia* that imparts a poignant sense of longing into these lyrical soliloquies; it becomes a double metaphor: as the song stretches out, so too do the expanses of the Russian soil and the Russian soul:

But what is that inexplicable force that draws me to thee? Why does thy plaintive song, which rises all over the length and breadth of thee from sea to sea, constantly resound in my ear? What is there in it, in that song? What is there in it that calls, and sobs, and grips the heart? What are those strains that poignantly caress and torment me, that stream straight into my soul, that entwine themselves around my heart? Russia! What dost thou want of me?[13]

In a later explanation of these lyrical digressions which Gogol attempted in his *Selected Passages from Correspondence with Friends* (*Vybrannye mesta iz perepiski s druziami*; 1846), his direct experience of the *protiazhnaia* manifests itself even more clearly:

Even today I still cannot bear those plaintive, heart-rending sounds of our song, the song that streams all over the limitless Russian expanses. These sounds hover near my heart, and indeed I am amazed that everyone else does not feel the same. Those who look at this desert, until now an uninhabited and shelterless space, and yet do not feel melancholy, those who do not hear painful reproaches to themselves in the plaintive sounds of our song . . . those are the people who have either fulfilled their duty already or who have nothing of Russia in their souls.[14]

As we see, Gogol's outlook is hardly different from Radishchev's. If the birth of the Russian intelligentsia is associated with the first pangs of conscience the upper classes experienced when contemplating the plight of the lower classes, then we may consider the Russian *protiazhnaia* an important agent of this process.

An even more colourful example of the same equation of the *protiazhnaia* with the Russian soul is found in *The Singers* (*Pevtsy*), a short story by Ivan Turgenev (1818–83) written in 1850. The story gives an account of a rare meeting of the two distinct worlds, when a gentleman at sport seeks refreshment in a rural tavern. He witnesses a competition between two folk singers, where the first sings a dance-song which brings his listeners to their feet, while the second sings a *protiazhnaia*, and makes them weep. Of the latter, he says:

I should confess that I have rarely heard such a voice: it was slightly broken and rang as if cracked; at first it even seemed somewhat sickly, but it also had a genuine deep passion, youth, strength, sweetness, and some enticingly careless, melancholy sorrow. A true, ardent Russian soul sounded and breathed in it, and it gripped your heart, gripped the very Russian heart-strings.[15]

The simple people, after a wave of emotion, resume their drinking, their banter, and their dancing as if nothing had happened, but the cultivated sportsman cannot bear to stay, since he is afraid of 'spoiling the impression'. This moment of melancholy must have matched his image of the soul of the Russian people, and he wanted to preserve it, removed from its context. The dance song of the first competitor and dances that followed the competition are forgotten, and only the *protiazhnaia* stands out as the climax of the story. The *protiazhnaia* is romanticised and thus incorporated into the gentleman's version of Russianness, while the dances are filtered out to satisfy his romantic sensibilities.

Tellingly, when it came to finding a name for the *protiazhnaia* in the story, Turgenev dipped into the folksong collection assembled by the Slavophile Petr Kireevskii (1808–56) and selected a title, at random it would seem. He had assumed that the song under that title was bound to be melancholy – weren't folksongs supposed to be the groanings of Russia's tragic soul? One of Turgenev's friends knew better, and pointed out that the chosen item was in fact a joyous song for dancing. Turgenev decided to play safe on his second attempt, and now used the title of a *protiazhnaia* which was already well known, and which he knew to be suitably melancholy.[16] Equally telling were Turgenev's arrangements for a private staging of the song competition depicted in the story. Evidently he hoped to experience the same series of emotional states which he ascribed to the narrator of the story. Did he invite peasants? No, they might bring in mud on their boots, or steal the silver. Instead, he deemed it more appropriate to bring in two educated connoisseurs of Russian song, the painter Kirill Gorbunov (1822–93) and the writer Lev Zhemchuzhnikov (1828–1912), and no doubt they made very good peasants for the evening.[17]

As we have seen, the *protiazhnaia* was widely perceived throughout the nineteenth century as a paradigm for all Russian folksong and as a Romantic image of all that was essential to the Russian soul. The Bolshevik revolution of 1917 swept this away, and Stalin's bureaucratic retrenchment, for all its restoration of older cultural traditions, did nothing to encourage this image of Russianness: a culture which held up the hyper-productive coalminer Aleksei Stakhanov as the ideal for all workers had no time for languor and self-pity. Socialist Realist art (the official Soviet dogma from the 1930s) called for everyday heroism, and required strong, optimistic endings to every tale, whether in novels or operas. Only in the later Soviet period, from the 1960s and 1970s, as the bureaucracy eased its grip, did the tragic soul come back into fashion, and it has retained its popularity ever since. Moreover, it has proved to be a marketable phenomenon: Western audiences are only too happy to pay for an evening of Russian melancholy.

Finally, we return to the alternative Russian nationalism developed in opera and concert music from the 1840s onwards. We recall that the composers of the 'Five', taking up the lead given by their predecessor Glinka, decisively rejected the tragic-soul view of Russian folk culture and the Russian national character. Together with the influential music critic and essayist Vladimir Stasov (1824–1906), this small band of composers established themselves in the public mind as the 'New Russian School', and managed to cast their shadow over Russian music through the rest of the nineteenth century and well into the second half of the twentieth after a temporary dip in their influence in the two decades either side of the Bolshevik revolution. While they still failed to acquaint themselves directly with the musical traditions of the Russian peasantry, they did provide an important corrective to the melancholy *protiazhnaia*-based view of folksong propagated by their predecessors. They greatly expanded the variety of folk-song types used in opera and concert music, including wedding songs and songs performed at calendar rituals. In their eyes the *protiazhnaia* had become too compromised by its sentimentalisation in the salon songs of previous generations, and for this reason they usually avoided it. The ritual and dance songs they adopted led them to consider folk texts which differed greatly from the melancholy previously favoured; accordingly, their nationalist operas feature epic narratives (*byliny*) and fairy tales, and they were able to return to Pushkin's humorous folk-style tales, largely ignored by the intervening generation. These story lines were full of heroic images and witty pranks, but low on opportunities for expressions of Romantic melancholy. Among the many celebrated works resulting from this new perspective on folk culture are Borodin's *Prince Igor* and his *Bogatyr Symphony*, Musorgkii's *Great Gates of Kiev*, and numerous fairy-tales operas by Rimskii-Korsakov such as *The Snowmaiden*, *Tsar Saltan*, *Kashchei the Immortal*, and *The Golden Cockerel*. All these works of the late nineteenth and early twentieth century present a Russia that was above all colourful, festive, and heroic.

Music was not isolated as a medium for this new image of Russianness. By the time the Five were well established, the painters of the important *Mir iskusstva* (*World of Art*) group developed a parallel interest in ornamentation and wild colours. Sergei Diagilev (1872–1929), an entrepreneurial genius, saw the export potential in the creations of these musicians and artists, and staged a series of concerts and exhibitions in Paris; eventually, and with resounding success, he united the two arts in his opera productions, and most famously in the Ballets Russes. He finely tuned his repertoire on the basis of the earlier concerts: Chaikovskii for example, had to be abandoned since the Parisians found him too Western beside the exotic novelties of the Five which they were already learning to associate with true Russianness. The Parisians love for the most exotic strains ensured the warmest reception for Borodin's *Polovtsian Dances*, Stravinsky's *Firebird*, and new ballets based on the music of Rimskii-Korsakov's *Shekherezade* and *Golden Cockerel*, and Balakirev's *Tamara*. The stage sets and costumes were designed by some of the most prominent painters of the *Mir iskusstva* group, and enhanced the impression of wild, colourful exoticism; the result was so popular that even the haute-couture houses of Paris had to adjust their fashions accordingly. But in all the excitement of dressing up in Oriental garb and chattering about those famous Russians, Parisians had no time to draw careful distinctions between Russia proper and the genuine Asiatic cultures at the edges of the Russian Empire; all were mixed together so that

Russia was transferred from Europe to Asia in the popular imagination. For the French, and later for the English and American audiences of Diagilev's *Saisons*, Russian music was associated with its colourful packaging, and so perceived as bright, decorative, exotic, and fantastic. There was scarcely a Russian tragic soul in view.[18]

The purpose of this survey is not simply to debunk essentialism, to show how the 'tragic soul' version of Russianness was an early nineteenth-century construction. Even if we treat the 'tragic soul' myth with the greatest scepticism, there is still the danger that we can lose sight of major traditions within Russian culture simply because we assume that nothing of importance lay wholly outside the tragic soul's field of influence. A survey of the dominant nationalist tradition within Russian musical life demonstrates that much creative and discursive energy was directed towards an entirely different picture of Russianness, a picture which was based on a less partial, though still far from perfect, understanding of peasant culture. This does not mean that we replace one version of the Russian national character with another. National characters are constructed within cultures, they are not the given foundation of a culture, nor can even the most accurate research into peasant cultural practices somehow produce evidence of the 'true' national character. As is apparent from several of the chapters in the present book, in the ideological vacuum left by the collapse of the Soviet Union many Russians have been engaged in myth making: some return to nineteenth-century nationalist myths, others idealise Soviet life, others turn to Orthodox Christianity or to various imported religious cults. All such versions are real enough to those who identify with them, and it is not our business to pick and choose between competing Russian myths so as to favour that which appeals to us either as the most picturesque or as the most politically congenial.

CHAPTER 8

Identity in language?

Boris Gasparov

I. APPROACHES TO IDENTITY IN LANGUAGE

Since the emergence of a Romantic philosophy of language at the beginning of the nineteenth century, the idea of a link between a nation's language and its self-consciousness and identity has been prominent in studies of cultural history. In Russian culture, the conflict between the two main approaches to the problem of 'language and identity' – they can loosely be called 'nominalist' and 'realist' – has played a significant role over the past two centuries. In the 'nominalist' view, language is a tool whose shape and development are contingent on the changing intellectual and cultural needs which it is supposed to serve. In the 'realist' view (approximating to an approach which elsewhere in this book is termed 'essentialist'), the native language itself is the embodiment of its speakers' collective mentality and cultural tradition. Thus, according to the 'nominalist' view, the Russian literary language emerges and develops as a series of responses to specific cultural challenges and influences: from the adoption of Church Slavonic after the baptism of Rus in the late tenth century and its gradual assimilation by indigenous (East Slav) linguistic practices, through the adaptation of West European discourses and narrative techniques in the early and mid-nineteenth century, to the post-Soviet influx of Americanisms. According to the 'realist' (or 'essentialist', or perhaps 'organicist') view, language through-out its history, despite apparent changes, retains fundamental features that bear the imprint of national character.

These two paradigms clashed with each other most directly in the first quarter of the nineteenth century, in the polemic between followers of the writer Nikolai Karamzin (1766–1826) and the essayist – and eventually Minister of Education – Aleksandr Shishkov (1754–1841). Karamzin and his party, which included such literary luminaries as Vasilii Zhukovskii (1783–1852) and Pushkin, believed that the Russian language should be open to all the various modes of expression necessary to render it capable of meeting the ideological, intellectual, and aesthetic needs of the European culture of its day. Shishkov argued that the language must arrive at this state in an organic way, by developing the potential within its own Slavonic tradition. The presumption here is that only through nurturing of the Slavonic tradition could Russia preserve and enhance its own linguistic (and hence cultural, and hence national) identity. Although the Karamzinian school prevailed in making the decisive impact on the language itself, their opponents' view had a strong influence on the way in which the Russian language was perceived – in relation to its West European counterparts – by later generations of linguists and cultural theorists. Thus the Slavophiles took the 'realist' or 'essentialist' view, interpreting fundamental structural differences between Russian and West European languages (such as the presence in Russian of verbal aspect, along with a reduced system of tenses; or the proliferation in Russian of impersonal constructions without a grammatical subject) as signs of the uniqueness of the Russian national character. For example, in the loose usage of tenses in typical Russian discourse they saw the linguistic symbol of Russia's rejection of an over-rationalist way of ordering all events as either past, present, or future; and in the frequent absence of a grammatical subject they perceived a way of expressing the collective and existential tendency of Russian spirituality. Recent Russian scholarship of the late Soviet and post-Soviet period reflects a surge of renewed interest in this 'realist' or 'essentialist' approach, and there have been numerous fresh attempts to read a Russian national 'mentality' directly into certain features of the semantics and grammar of the Russian language.[1]

Both sides – the 'nominalists' and the 'realists' – have a point, which they then both proceed to over-stretch. On the one hand, obviously language changes, sometimes radically, in response to challenges posed by intellectual and ideological needs. Equally obviously, on the other hand, different languages do have different ways of expressing thoughts, which necessarily have an impact on the shape and texture of those thoughts, if not on their logical content. The present chapter is not an attempt to adjudicate between the two approaches but to show instead some aspects of their dynamic interrelationship, for in fact the process works in both directions. Different languages do have their own peculiar ways of shaping meaning, and therefore leave their mark on the character of that meaning. This does not justify the Romantic notion of language as a bearer of national character and identity encoded and implicit in the lexicon and grammar themselves. However, by examining the concrete historical circumstances in which certain morphosyntactic, idiomatic, and rhetorical features of a language have developed, we can discern the ideological values and cultural goals that motivated such development; and, in their turn, those motivations for shaping language in a particular way give the resultant shape certain semantic implications. We can follow the sequence: first the choice of linguistic tools of expression in specific historical, cultural, or ideological circumstances; then, after these tools become established facts of language, their residual perception as bearers of certain ideological values.

A prime example of this twofold process is the way the Russian language adapted to and assimilated Church Slavonic. Church Slavonic was the sacral language developed on the basis of South Slavic (Old Macedonian, Old Bulgarian) dialects, and imported into early Rus from the Balkans along with Christianity. For a millennium, it has been one of the principal driving forces in the development of the Russian literary language. The close linguistic proximity between Church Slavonic and the native vernaculars spoken by various Slavic peoples made the medieval cultural situation in the Slavic Orthodox lands quite different from that of nations whose sacral or high-status cultural language was only distantly related to, or altogether different from, their native tongues. It was not, therefore, directly comparable to the situation in, for example, Northern European Catholic lands whose population spoke Germanic, Celtic, or Slavic languages while using Latin as their principal cultural vehicle, or to the situation in non-Arabic Muslim nations. In Rus, however, the linguistic situation in the eleventh to thirteenth centuries, with regard to the relationship between the local East Slav vernacular and Church Slavonic, was broadly equivalent to the situation experienced at the same time by speakers of Romance languages vis-à-vis Latin.

The decisive difference between Italians using Latin and Eastern Slavs using Church Slavonic lay in the scope and history, and therefore the character, of the respective languages. Latin was represented by a vast and diverse literary tradition comprising texts of different genres and ideological provenance, secular and sacral, artistic and pragmatic; it had been thoroughly explicated by grammarians, philologists, and rhetoricians, and taught with the help of standard grammars and texts. The use of Church Slavonic, on the other hand, rarely expanded outside a limited range of genres relating to liturgical services and pious reading, from the Gospels and the Psalter to sermons, prayers, and hagiography. The language itself, at least in the first few centuries of its existence, did not receive any explicit codification: no early formal grammatical descriptions of the language survive, nor is there evidence that any was produced. The first grammar of Church Slavonic appeared in the Balkans in the fourteenth century, almost half a millennium after the language was created; in the north, the first Church Slavonic grammar appeared much later, in 1596.[2] In the sixteenth century, Muscovy, if judged by West European standards on the basis of the availability of scholarly texts (original or translated), and on the basis of its institutions of teaching and learning, still looked like intellectual virgin soil.

How, then, could the tradition of Church Slavonic writing survive several centuries that witnessed drastic changes in the political and cultural map? This happened in an implicit way, through mnemonic absorption, more then through explicit learning, explication, or codification. A linguistic and cultural tradition rooted in Church Slavonic books was maintained by generations of its adherents, from the clergy to educated classes to common people, through repeated reading, listening to, copying, and memorizing a limited corpus of texts, from the liturgical core to a somewhat broader variety of pious and didactic reading. This tradition of collective memory served as an implicit body of knowledge about the language, and the principal means of its learning; one learned the language not by studying its structure and norms but through the practice of reading and by copying texts which one already knew, more or less accurately, from previous experience. Alongside this process, and in the same implicit way, one would absorb a body of knowledge contained in the texts, from theological concepts and metaphysical problems, to rhetorical tools and narrative modes of expression.

This situation made the state of the language contingent on the state of the linguistic consciousness of its users. In the absence of any explicit norms (other than available precedents), norms had to be deduced – in effect reinvented – on every occasion that the language was used, be it in the copying of an older manuscript or in the creation of an original (though always clearly derivative) composition. A copyist, writer, or reader had to negotiate between, on the one hand, his or her linguistic intuition (inevitably influenced by spoken practices, due to their proximity to the cultural language) and, on the other hand, the concrete examples offered by earlier manuscripts, which, for all the authority they exuded, might look counter-intuitive at certain points: either unduly archaic or even outright 'foreign'. This sense of 'foreignness' might arise in particular with regard to books of Balkan provenance, or when Russian Church Slavonic books were subjected to correction by invited Greek and Bulgarian scholars. Out of such negotiations between the available precedents and current linguistic sensibilities, new implicit norms would emerge, to be passed, through newly produced copies or original compositions, to subsequent generations, which in their turn would confront these precedents with their intuitive linguistic perceptions.

For centuries linguistic tradition – and the whole cultural tradition that was almost entirely dependent on it – was being passed through the air, so to speak, rather than proceeding on firm ground. The negative side of the process became evident by the sixteenth and seventeenth centuries, by which time the lack of explicit norms had led to a very large accumulation of defects in the practices of book production, while all attempts to correct such defects ran against existing linguistic sensibilities, which were all the stronger because of their implicit, non-codified character. The controversy lingered for a century and a half, culminating in reforms of liturgical books at a Church Council in 1666/7. The reforms led to a schism, which stemmed from the inability of a substantial part of the flock to accept even minor changes. When confronted with a minuscule correction in the Church Slavonic Creed – the phrase 'born, not created,' instead of the traditional and habitual 'born and not created' – people expressed their willingness to die rather than give up that 'and'. One might even say that the less significant the changes may have looked to an outside observer, the more striking was the effect they produced on those who perceived the alterations as intrusions into their world of memory: a corrected expression evoked a sense of discord which made the whole text seem like a form of diabolic subversion. The 'Old Believers,' as they called themselves, repudiated the new liturgical books, along with the churches that used them in the services. They left the official church, establishing their own communities on the periphery of the state, which have survived for several centuries, outliving Muscovy, the Russian Empire, and even the Soviet Union.

This uncompromising resistance to any alteration in the holy books did not mean, however, rejection of any innovation. On the contrary, the precarious fluidity of mnemonic tradition inspired, in fact necessitated, creativity. What was not acceptable to the opponents of the reforms of 1667 was an abrupt implementation of codified changes. Yet at the same time it was common practice to reinvent language, sometimes quite radically, in the guise of paraphrasing remembered precedent. Because of its intuitive character the process of the selection of grammatical forms, syntactic patterns, or specific turns of phrase was susceptible to symbolic interpretation. New usage of known grammatical forms and derivative patterns, (emerging out of the process of negotiation between the older examples and current linguistic sensibilities) acquired secondary symbolic values, which could turn the forms into principal bearers of ideas, ideological trends, and aesthetic values. In such circumstances the language itself could come to be treated not simply as the *means* for expressing the foundations of faith or philosophical ideas and ethical principles, but as the very embodiment of those ideas and principles.

Thus the 'realist' (or 'essentialist') view of the word as the embodiment of the concept it designates – the view that form is a bearer of meaning – which in the Western scholastic tradition established itself as a major philosophical trend, found on Russian soil no less powerful (albeit not fully articulated) practical expression in the way language was used. It was typical for the culture of medieval Rus to address intellectual and ideological problems obliquely, through the implied secondary meanings bestowed by tradition on certain patterns and structures of language. To an outside observer seeking explicit, articulate signs of intellectual and spiritual life, early Rus might well have looked quite barren, incapable of development. To an insider attuned to nuances of linguistic behaviour, it presented a rich and ever-changing field of spiritual stimuli, which were all the more exciting for their elusive and volatile character.

This approach to the use of linguistic form can be illustrated with a few examples from the culture of early Rus, taken from several periods in the six centuries of its development before its radical transformation around the time of Peter the Great. We will then look briefly at how the phenomenon may be conceived in more modern times.

2. LINGUISTIC MEMORY AND THE SEMANTICS OF FORM

In his latter years, Prince Vladimir Monomakh (Prince of Kiev 1113–25) wrote an *Instruction*, or *Admonition* (*Pouchenie*), ostensibly for his sons, in which he told of his own experiences and set forth ethical and political advice on how a prince ought to behave. Monomakh begins, after a brief introduction, with a dramatic episode in his life when he repudiated his cousins' offer to join them in an assault against another branch of the ruling dynasty: an excruciatingly difficult decision, since it would destroy the crucial alliance with his kinsmen. After dismissing the envoys, Vladimir continues:

I took the Psalter, opened it at random in my sorrow, and this is what has been drawn for me: 'Why art thou cast down, O my soul? and why art thou disquieted within me?' – and the rest. I gathered then all the beloved words, and arranged them in an order, and wrote this. If you are not pleased with the latter, accept the former.[3]

Remarkable is the degree to which Monomakh relies on his readers' memory. He does not need to quote at length Psalm 43 from which the cited phrase is drawn. Moreover, the quoted fragment constitutes no more than the tip of an iceberg in Monomakh's and his readers' corpus of remembered or partially remembered textual passages – hence the addition of 'and the rest' at the end. What is meant by 'the rest' is not so much the remaining text of the Psalm as a multitude of passages from holy books that could be recalled by memory in association with the text quoted. Indeed, Monomakh himself responds to the appeal to his and his readers' stock of memory. The quoted phrase triggers a lengthy string of quotations from the Psalter, the Gospels, and books of the prophets; one quotation evokes another by association, the process evolving with no end in sight until, some two pages later (in the modern edition), the author stops himself by adding once more: 'and the rest'. After scores of quotations, 'the rest' remains as nebulous and at the same time as evident, as infinite and yet as easy to grasp, as after the initial prompt.

Ultimately, Monomakh claims that own writing is no more than a re-arrangement of the 'beloved words' of Holy Scripture 'collected' by his memory. Monomakh's humble (and conventional) posture of someone whose writing is just a periphrasis of the sacred source in fact allows him to assume the didactic authority he could not have claimed as an 'original' author in the modern sense. His acknowledged imperfection as a writer, whose ineptitude may 'displease' his readers, turns out to be his highest virtue, for he recreates the act of the incarnation of the sacred Word into the world. If the reader does not like 'the latter' words (those which come from Monomakh's own pen) he has to bow to 'the former' words (Scripture, the Divine words, the implied ultimate source of Monomakh's writing).

The shared memory of the 'former' words is also the shared memory of their language, Church Slavonic. A close connection between the language used by a writer and the metaphysical and ethical position he assumes could be maintained due to the special relation between the holy books and the language in which they were received by the Orthodox Slavs. Church Slavonic existed, at least in theory, solely for the purpose of rendering the sacred texts and their ostensible periphrases in pious and didactic writing. By presenting his writing as nothing more – and nothing less – than an exercise in using the sacred 'beloved words', an author, solely by virtue of using Church Slavonic, could assume the mantle of spirituality and piety.

At the same time, however, the norms of Church Slavonic remained so nebulous, its conflation with everyday speech practices so ubiquitous and natural, that such authority could never be full or exclusive. Every instance of creative writing, from a sermon to narrative prose (such as

Monomakh's *Instruction*) to private letters, showed the Church Slavonic and indigenous (East Slav) linguistic material mixed in different proportions, from an almost complete dominance of the Church Slavonic lexicon and grammatical forms, to their sporadic appearances amidst indigenous discourse. The worldly imperfection of every new attempt at writing would be readily acknowledged; even the loftiest discourse could only approach the ideal of the original sacral language, that ideal itself remaining elusive and largely imaginary, since no normative texts of the holy books, let alone their explication in a grammar, ever existed. The closer a certain text came to the perceived ideal of Church Slavonic purity, the stronger would be the aura of piety, spirituality, and didacticism that it exuded. By the same token, the prevalence of indigenous linguistic material would draw the text towards the sphere of the worldly, the practical, and the material. Thus the first written code of law, the *Russkaia pravda* whose first version dates from the mid-eleventh century,[4] was written in a plain, informal language, almost completely devoid of Church Slavonic forms – a type of discourse that looks, from a modern perspective, unexpected in a code of law; yet in the medieval scale of values avoidance of Church Slavonic and closeness to the native vernacular was fully appropriate for a text dedicated to matters of worldly justice.

Church Slavonic, as the principal indicator of the spiritual bent of a text, could alternate with indigenous language in infinite variations, depending on the genre and the theme. Every increase in using Church Slavonic forms would immediately cause the spiritual temperature of the text to rise in the writer's and readers' intuitive perception, while an influx of indigenous forms would draw it down to earth, to the realm of practical matters.

Monomakh shows great skill in using this symbolic potential of the language, by no means limited to direct quotations from the Psalter. Immediately before the passage cited above, Monomakh narrates the following encounter:

I was met on the Volga by my brothers' envoys who told me: 'Hurry to join us, let's chase away Rostislav's sons and take their land; if you do not go along, then we shall mind our business, and you will mind yours.' And I spoke: 'Even if this would anger you, I cannot go with you, nor transgress the cross [of my vow].'

The envoys' speech is informal to a point of outright crudeness. It is saturated with words whose morphemic composition or phonetic features reflect their indigenous East Slavic origin: the forms for 'hurry' (*potsnisia*), 'let's chase away' (*vyzhenem*), 'land'/'possession' (*volost'*), 'if' (*ozhe*) and the reflexive pronoun (*sobe*); the syntax is very simple, and the only compound sentence (with the conditional *ozhe*) is reminiscent of plain conditional formulas in *Russkaia pravda*. In his own reply, Monomakh changes the linguistic tone entirely. He begins with the verb of speech in the simple past tense (aorist): 'I spoke' (*rêkh"*). The aorist was used almost exclusively in carefully styled written texts. In informal discourse, such as private letters, the normal form was the perfect. Moreover, in this instance Monomakh chose not even the plain aorist but an archaic version of it (by Monomakh's time, the form *rêkh"* had largely given way to a regular modernized version: *rekokh*). The very appearance of the aorist raises the moral and intellectual level on which Monomakh is preparing to make his reply, and the effect is still further enhanced by the archaic solemnity of the particular form. And in case the point should be lost, the archaic aorist is immediately followed by a Church Slavonic conditional conjunction (*ashche*) in marked contrast with his opponents' East Slav conditional (*ozhe*). Monomakh's syntax features a single negative – a rarefied device that deviated from the spontaneous Slavic speech pattern of double negatives. Even in the oldest Church Slavonic, which did adopt the single negative in imitation of Greek, it was never used consistently, but lapsed into the double negation on some occasions.

By the standards of the pragmatics of communication, Monomakh's response to his cousins could be deemed a failure. Instead of trying to make his point understandable for his interlocutors by adjusting his speech to theirs, he resorts to archaic and difficult forms drawn from the most rarefied sphere of language, in marked contrast with the simplistic discourse of his interlocutors. However, the pragmatic incoherence of the dialogue is beside the point, since Monomakh's linguistic behaviour was motivated not pragmatically but didactically. By using different discourses, the speaking parties place themselves on different planes on the scale of spiritual versus earthly matters. Monomakh's cousins and their envoys speak about worldly affairs; with his lofty reply, Monomakh shifts the dialogue into the sphere of moral judgement and heavenly justice. The whole situation is instantly recast from that of a political dilemma into a moral test. This shift is conveyed not so much by the content of Monomakh's speech as by the level of discourse used in it; even before he has uttered a word, the introductory verb *rêkh"* already says it all to the reader. The linguistic fabric of the message becomes a crucial component of the message itself, since it creates a mode within which the message is to be perceived. Had Monomakh rejected his cousins' offer in plain language, the subject matter of the situation would remain the same, yet its meaning would have been purely pragmatic, that of a political offer and its repudiation. Drawn into the pious mode by his own speech, he turns to the Psalter for words to render his state of mind.

More then five centuries later, in the mid 1670s, Archpriest Avvakum, the leader of the Old Believers, wrote his striking *Life of Archpriest Avvakum by Himself* (*Zhitie protopopa Avvakuma, im samim napisannoe*). This piece of auto-hagiography was produced in anticipation of the imminent end of the world, in a situation when no future hagiographer could be expected to record the last chapter of sacred history, the story of Avvakum's own martyrdom. Describing one of his numerous confrontations with the authorities during his exile, Avvakum uses virtually the same stylistic tool as Monomakh half a millennium before. The brief exchange is described as follows: 'He was barking at me, but I said (*rekl"*) to him: "Grace be in thy mouth, Ivan Rodionovich!"'[5] Avvakum introduces his speech with the same verb of speech as Monomakh: a past tense of *rekou*, 'I say', although here he chooses the perfect form, since by now the aorist had become a markedly bookish form, hardly appropriate even in a stylized dialogue. However, he chooses the archaic version of the perfect: *rekl"*, instead of the simplified *rek"*. Again, therefore, even before he begins speaking, the very form of the introductory verb indicates the shift from crude worldliness to piety. And again the writer's own speech is replete with Church Slavonic expressions: 'grace' (*blagodat'*); an ornate archaic form *ustnêx"* instead of the plainer *ustakh"* for 'mouth'; a solemn syntactic formula of exhortation (*da budet*).

In narrative texts, the alternative use of aorist and perfect worked for centuries as a device for locating the discourse along the axis between the worldly and the spiritual. In the second half of his *Instruction*, Vladimir Monomakh tells of the numerous adventures he has experienced in his life. He describes the many dangers he confronted as a hunter, using for this worldly subject, quite appropriately, the perfect rather than the aorist – until a crucial point at which he caps his story with its didactic conclusion, whereupon aorist appears again:

Two bisons tossed [*metala* – perfect] me and my horse on their horns, a stag gored [*bol"* – perfect] me, one elk stamped [*toptal"* – perfect] upon me while another gored [*bol"* – perfect] me, a boar once tore [*ottial"* – perfect] my sword from my thigh, a bear on one occasion bit [*ukusil"* – perfect] my kneecap, a wild beast jumped [*skochil"* – perfect] on my flank and threw [*poverzhe* – aorist] my horse with me. But God preserved [*s"bliude* – aorist] me unharmed.[6]

As the translation suggests, the choice of aorist or perfect has little to do with temporality of the actions. Instead, it serves as an indicator of the discourse's spiritual mode. The shifts to the aorist in the last sentence, in which God's providence is cited, is understandable. However, that shift had in fact already occurred in the previous sentence, which in theme and in temporal logic belongs to the preceding list of events which, until that point, had been rendered in a chain of perfects. Why, then, this premature change to the aorist? It seems that the narrator already at this point anticipates the coming shift of the story to the pious mode, and it was this anticipation that triggered the use of the aorist in the last 'worldly' segment, as a kind of foreshadowing of the imminent pious conclusion. The switch of form was quite possibly inadvertent, prompted by a surge of pious didacticism. Remarkable in this example is the spontaneity with which the shift of the authorial position could be translated into the choice of linguistic form.

Avvakum's treatment of the aorist is quite similar to that of Monomakh, in spite of the fact that by the late seventeenth century the aorist had receded further from spontaneous speech practices than in Monomakh's time. Yet it continued to be consistently used and remembered in liturgical texts, and its symbolic significance as the token of sacred discourse remained keenly felt: to such an extent, indeed, that Avvakum's usage of the aorist turns out to be even more consistently atmospheric than Monomakh's. This is how he begins the story of his life:

My father was a priest, Petr by name, my mother was called Maria, Marfa by her monastic name. My father was given to strong drink; but my mother was given to fasting and prayer, and did most constantly instruct me in the fear of God . . . And in that village there was a maiden, she too was an orphan, who was wont to go continually to church, and her name was Anastasia. Her father was a blacksmith Marko, exceedingly rich, but when he died all his substance was wasted.[7]

Introducing his father, Avvakum uses an aorist of the verb 'to be': 'was a priest' – *byst' sviashchennik*. However, when a few sentences later his future bride's father is mentioned, Avvakum uses the perfect for the same verb, in a syntactically identical sentence: 'was a blacksmith' – *byl kuznets*. The shift from one form to the other was, in all probability, purely intuitive: mention of a priest, even the one 'given to strong drink', attracts the aorist, a form associated with Church Slavonic discourse, while a blacksmith triggers the choice of the perfect, a form typical for indigenous spoken speech. Even the fact that the priest was a drunkard is conveyed in a lofty Slavonicized expression – 'was diligent in the drinking of alcohol' (*prilezhashe pitiia xmelnova*) – which uses another rarefied form of the simple past (here the imperfect) alongside an abstract noun in its Church Slavonic version (the vernacular form would have been *pit'ia*).

3. RHETORIC AS A KEY TO KNOWLEDGE

The hero of the *Life of Stefan of Perm* (*Zhitie Stefana Permskogo*) by Epifanii the Wise (c. 1400) dedicated his life to missionary work among the Permiaks, a remote heathen Finno-Ugric tribe in the Northern Ural region. He translated the Gospel into the Permian language, created characters for writing it down, baptised the people and preached Christianity in their native tongue. The *Life* by Epifanii, the saint's disciple, is one of the foremost examples of the ornamental style known as 'word-weaving'; its discourse is replete with long convoluted periods, multi-layered parallelisms, ornate periphrases, and dense sound repetitions. Originating in the Balkans in the previous century, the style of 'word-weaving' eventually came into vogue in Muscovy.

The subject of Epifanii's *Life* must have been particularly inspiring to him and his readers, since Stefan's saintly feat recreated the achievement of the 'Apostles of the Slavs', Constantine (Cyril) and Methodios, who had in the ninth century translated the Gospel into the Slavic tongue and had written it down in newly created characters, the event that marked the beginning of Church Slavonic and of Slavic Christianity. By the time of Epifanii, the original Church Slavonic had receded into a remote and rather vague past. This did not change, however, its role as the primary source of spiritual authority. To assume the mantle of such authority, a writer had to present his words as being directly derived from this sacred linguistic source, the repository and guarantor of all holiness and wisdom. Such an appeal was largely symbolic, since in fact the implicit norms as perceived by a fifteenth- or sixteenth-century writer were already fairly remote from ninth- or tenth-century Church Slavonic in phonetics, morphology, and even in the lexicon. To pursue the ideal of archaic purity, one had to reinvent this presumed ideal in such a way as to make one's writing appear awe-inspiringly authentic with respect to the original, yet not outright 'foreign' to modern perception.

Epifanii achieves an apparent paradox: he conveys the impression of archaic solemnity by being strikingly innovative. He creates numerous neologisms, some of them extremely daring. For instance, the Permian people complain, in their lament after the saint's death, that they are now doomed to be 'mountain-confined and wolves-preyed' (*goroplennym*

i volkokhishchnym byti).[8] These fancy composites are reminiscent more of
Homeric compound epithets than of anything one might encounter in
genuine Church Slavonic texts. Epifanii's syntax, while following rhetorical patterns of the Church Slavonic oratorical style (which in turn had
emulated patterns in Greek originals), stretches them to such a degree that
the text sometimes seems almost to collapse under the weight of constant
ornamental elaboration.

This futuristic reinvention of the archaic gave a strong impetus to the
symbolic use of language. Here, too, the choice of a certain expression
or grammatical form appears to be motivated not so much by linguistic
norms (vague as they were) as by the perception that a given choice carried
symbolic overtones. By manipulating skilfully these secondary, symbolic
meanings, the author could express complex metaphysical and theological
ideas without ever addressing them directly, simply by using language in
a certain way. By reading a pious text, one could gain access to complex
metaphysical, theological, ethical, and even scientific concepts embodied
in the use of certain rhetorical patterns. Instead of being merely a means
to convey conceptual knowledge, language turned into the body of that
knowledge itself.

To clarify these general assertions, we can consider a passage in the *Life of
Stefan of Perm* in which Epifanii praises the saint's achievement in creating
Permian writing:

For so many years many Hellenic philosophers had been assembling and constructing the Greek alphabet, and barely succeeded after much time and labour.
Yet Perm writing was composed by one monk, built by one, created by one, there
was one elder, one hermit, one monk – I mean Stefan, bishop of eternal memory –
one at one time and not, as them, over many years; it was one hermit, the sole one
in his solitude, the unique one in his uniqueness, one invoking One God's help,
one praying to One God.[9]

At first glance, this passage contains little more than a fairly standard
device used by the ideologues of an upstart nation to boost its pride in its
identity: 'others' may have achieved this earlier than we did, and therefore
received all the credit, but 'we' in fact did the same thing much better
albeit later. However, the thesis that Stefan 'alone' fully achieved what
'many Hellenic philosophers' had barely succeeded in doing is repeated
in so many ways, and its various periphrastic expressions are so densely
packed (playing on the repetition of 'one' – *edin"* – and derivatives), that the
reader's attention is inevitably drawn to the opposition 'one versus many'.

Following this opposition as it evolves through a multitude of variations, we notice that its meaning gradually drifts away from a straightforward assertion of Stefan's uniqueness (by contrast with the plurality of Hellenic philosophers) to the solitude in which he invokes God's help in prayer, and finally to the key theological idea of One God. Following this continuum of symbolic overtones, we begin to perceive in the multitude of 'philosophers' a deficiency deeper than just their inferior productivity by comparison with the achievement of the lone Russian hermit. Somehow, according to the implicit logic emerging from the fabric of the text, the idea of 'many' philosophers who spent 'many years' and 'many labours' on their task runs against the ideal of One God; it takes 'one hermit', in his solitude, to attain an intimate proximity to that ideal. To put it plainly (as Epifanii does not, of course), the ancient philosophers' multitude smacks of paganism, the holiness of their task notwithstanding, while the genuine holiness of Stefan's deeds can be attested by the fact that he emulated God's uniqueness; or, even more specifically, he emulated the solitude of God at the moment of the creation of the world.

However, the assertion of Stefan's uniqueness as a sign of his intimate proximity to the One God is only part of the implied message. The complexity of the theological concept of God consisted in the fact that the absolute assertion of God's oneness was balanced by the ascription to him of a multitude of attributes, hypostases, and names. The complex, even paradoxical nature of the idea of God's unity, most obviously manifested in the Holy Trinity, was the central point around which all medieval theology and metaphysics rotated. Epifanii never mentions this scholarly tradition, yet he addresses it obliquely, in the way in which he uses certain rhetorical patterns for portraying his protagonist. The most pertinent feature of Stefan of Perm, as Epifanii depicts him, is that he unites in one person a multitude of roles and functions that are normally dispersed among many different persons: those of a writer, translator, calligrapher, baptiser, preacher, moral guide, and so on. Unlike the multiplicity of 'Hellenic philosophers', his is an integrated multiplicity, similar to that of God. The variety of Stefan's functions, like that of God's attributes, springs from the inexpressible absolute which is whole and unique; the broader the variety, therefore, the stronger the idea of ultimate unity that emerges from it.

The symbolic subtext of saying how Stefan performed all his deeds 'alone' becomes even more clear in an extensive postscript, in which the author addresses his readers directly, in the first person. The apparent subject of this address is the author's perceived inability to find adequate words to describe the greatness of his subject – a typical device in epic or oratorical discourse. Epifanii uses this common rhetorical ploy in a way that makes it reverberate with his message of godly unity in multiplicity. He claims to be at a loss in trying to find a fitting name for Stefan in the light of his many deeds. However many names Epifanii proposes, none is adequate:

And I, a great and unlearned sinner, following the words that eulogize you, do knit words and create words, attempting to glorify you with words. Gathering the words of praise, and adding and weaving words, I ask: How else shall I name you? Shall I call you the pastor of those who have gone astray, redeemer of those who have perished, teacher of those who were tempted, leader of those whose sight has been darkened, cleanser of those who have been defiled, guardian of soldiers, consoler of those who are afflicted, nourisher of those who hunger, provider for those in need, punisher of those who are simpleminded, sustainer of the offended, the one who prays fervently, the faithful intercessor, saviour of the heathens, curser of demons, breaker of idols, destroyer of graven images, servant of God, upholder of wisdom, lover of philosophy, protector of chastity, defender of the truth, writer of books, creator of Permian letters? Many names have you received, O Bishop, many titles have you won, many gifts have you deserved, many blessings have enriched you![10]

This extraordinary list of 'names' bestowed on the saint evokes the multitude of God's names in the Bible; the author's claimed inability to find a single formula for his subject, resorting to the list of 'names' instead, puts him in a metaphysical position of acknowledging the human limitation of creative ability, and of language when dealing with the transcendental and the absolute.

Such theological and philosophical concepts as unity in plurality, the relations between the empirical and transcendental, or the limitations of language as a worldly incarnation of the absolute, are never mentioned explicitly in Epifanii's work. Yet these problems are being addressed, with great intensity and ingenuity, indirectly, through various configurations of the language itself. This strategy of addressing the cardinal problems of being and faith in a 'silent' way, through periphrases and the symbolic use of language, may be perceived as one of the channels through which to express the 'apophatic' belief in the inaccessibility of the infinite. Thus, once again, the very choice of linguistic means – rather than any direct assertion – implicitly affirms crucial aspects of the writer's values and identity.

The consequences of the status of Church Slavonic as the linguistic foundation of Russian cultural history have been ambiguous. On the one hand, the East Slavs received a rich cultural language that could be absorbed into all facets of communication, from the sublime to the pedestrian, by various degrees of osmosis. Church Slavonic was simultaneously close to and different from everyday speech: so close that it could not effectively be separated from it, yet also standing distinctly above it, as its sublime extension. This opened an infinite field of possibilities for playing with different degrees of the presence of Church Slavonic, in order to create various symbolic effects. The choice of language could thus be the principal means of expressing ideological values. On the other hand, however, this situation created a culture which was largely 'mute' to the world outside, and which tended, moreover, to perceive this very muteness as a sign of its sacred uniqueness. The absorption of speakers into the world of implicit meanings created by the perpetual co-presence of the sublime in their language was so deep that it gave little stimulus for reaching out to other perspectives, or other languages. The relations between Church Slavonic and the East Slav vernacular conditioned both the scope of linguistic expression and the limitations of a sense of linguistic identity.

A straightforward analogy between the world of medieval Rus or Muscovy and modern times would be imprudent. From the eighteenth century onwards the cultural language has no longer been monopolised by the enclosed relationship between Church Slavonic and the indigenous vernacular, and, as we saw at the start of this chapter, Russian has in practice been open to a far broader range of external stimuli. Yet one can still sense the medieval heritage in the very intensity of polemic surrounding language in Russia and the Soviet Union throughout this period. Such polemics have addressed not only the larger philosophical questions of Russia's linguistic peculiarity and identity, but have often expanded into social issues such as the methods of language teaching, editorial policies in the media, and publicly approved stylistic taste. And despite all changes in the language itself and in the ideological values it has been called upon to express, nevertheless the very fact that such issues of language have remained controversial has helped to sustain certain fundamental features of the medieval tradition. In particular, a continual awareness of controversy over different levels and sources of language sustains the potential for writers to use linguistic form as an implicit emblem of meaning, to enhance the message by purely stylistic and rhetorical devices. Far from receding with time, such opportunities were expanded in the age of Modernism and the subsequent Soviet era. Post-Soviet speech practices have added a new layer to this ever transforming, yet enduring tradition: the opportunity to recycle 'Soviet' turns of phrase as parody, where once more the writer's attitude and values are conveyed in the choice of linguistic form rather than through explicit statement. Thus in actual cultural practice, regardless of whether ideological fashion veers towards 'nominalism' or 'realism', Russian culture retains an enduring tradition of perceiving and manipulating the very forms of language as bearers or markers of ideology and identity.

CHAPTER 9

Byt: *identity and everyday life*

Catriona Kelly

I. THE NAMING OF EVERYDAY LIFE

The Russian word *byt* means something extremely basic, but cannot be translated by a single word, or even a single phrase, in other European languages. Everyday life, daily life, quotidian existence, material culture, private life, domestic life: all of these various shades of meaning are present in the term. Sometimes, but by no means always, *byt* is defined by being opposed to *bytie*, spiritual existence: in this context, the translation of *byt* would come close to 'earthly existence' as well as to 'material life'. Additionally, *byt* is sometimes used as a value-laden term – a circumlocution like 'the dreariness of quotidian life' would capture the flavour. At the same time, *byt* is often used more restrictively, to mean 'way of life' – as in 'the way of life of the Russian peasant' (*krest'ianskii byt*), for example.

It is common for analysts to move from linguistic specificity to psychological distinctiveness, and to argue that the fact that *byt* cannot be translated means that Russians have a different attitude to daily life from Western Europeans. In a recent article, for instance, the literary critic Igor Shaitanov observed, 'The Russian word *byt* has a right to gain entry to dictionaries in foreign languages alongside "samovar", "intelligentsia", "borzoi", and "sputnik". The point is that other nations do not have *byt*. Nowhere else, it would seem, is there such a tense relationship with the everyday, balanced on an unstable border between hatred and an intense desire to possess and dominate.'[1] Shaitanov's assertion is unusual only in that it allows the possibility of an ambivalent attitude towards *byt* on the part of Russians. More often, it is argued that hostility or indifference to *byt*, especially in the sense of domestic existence, is a persistent distinguishing characteristic of Russian identity. The historical evidence invoked to support this interpretation runs from Orthodoxy's reverence for what is 'not of this world', and its suspicion of secular life, through the asceticism of Russian intellectuals in the nineteenth century, and on to the political activists and avant-garde artists of the Soviet period. In the words of Svetlana Boym: 'Nineteenth-century Westernizers and Slavophiles, Romantics and modernists, aesthetic and political utopians, and Bolsheviks and monarchists all engaged in battles with *byt*. For many of them what mattered was not physical survival but sacrifice, not preservation of life but its complete transcendence, not the fragile human existence in this world but collective happiness in the other world . . . In a culture in which the eschatological and the apocalyptic are closely linked to the conception of national identity, there can be very little patience for the ordinary, transient, and everyday.'[2]

Commentators on Russia, no doubt because the place is so large, diverse, and bewildering, have been particularly prone to attempt to make sense of it through generalisations. For instance, it is often argued that Russians have a profound and emotional commitment to authoritarian rule, that they have a deeper-rooted sense of the spiritual than Westerners, or that they are particularly and passionately attached to literature. The idea that Russians have a special relationship with *byt* belongs to this order of simplification (indeed, it is the flip side of the notion that Russians are particularly attached to the spiritual – this would of course require them to feel indifference to material things). This view is quite popular among foreigners, both because it is straightforward ('Russia in a nutshell'), and because it emphasises Russia's difference. The country's long period of semi-isolation under Soviet rule, and the fact that bureaucratic regulations and the unfamiliarity of the language make travel in Russia relatively difficult, have produced a conviction that everyday life there must be different from everyday life elsewhere. Pubs may well be reckoned typically British, but few, on reflection, would argue seriously that a visit to a pub gives access to the essence of British identity, or indeed that putting on lederhosen and going for a walk in the Bavarian Alps will make you understand the rise of the Third Reich. But books and articles suggesting that a few hours at a Russian kitchen table or inside a Russian bath-house will let you comprehend the innermost recesses of the Russian mind seem far more respectable.[3] However, the idea that attitudes to daily life are quite specific in Russia is not purely Western. Russian commentators have been just as inclined as Westerners to subscribe to it (Boym and Shaitanov being two cases in point). Indeed, the idea that Russian intellectual culture has a peculiarly intense relationship with *byt* (usually, one of detestation) became, in the second half of the twentieth century, one of that culture's defining myths.

The myth is no less powerful for standing on shaky historical foundations. Like all Christian cultures, Russian Orthodoxy had, over the centuries, an ambiguous attitude to worldliness. On the one hand, Orthodoxy monitored sexual activity particularly strictly; on the other, Russian monasteries and nunneries – where inmates of high social status were allowed to keep their own furnishings in their cells – were in some respects more, rather than less, worldly than the Benedictine monastery, with its priestly monks entirely removed from the day-to-day business of domestic life. Moving into the area of secular life, it is doubtful that Russian academics would have tolerated the regulations imposed by Oxford and Cambridge colleges, where an official prohibition against marriage and family persisted until the late nineteenth century. And Russian political radicals and modernist artists were typical, rather than exceptional, in their desire to escape from quotidian cares. All over Europe and in America, avant-garde advocates of 'healthy living' aimed to reduce domestic existence to a state of ascetic minimalism, with waste products and domestic clutter removed from view, and open planning used to stress the hygienic and innocuous character of the human activities which went on within a given dwelling. Streamlining was temporal as well as spatial – the importance of regimen, from defecation according to timetable ('regular habits') to the punctual consumption of meals, a practice to be learned from the earliest years. The Sentimentalist and Romantic cult of 'natural' behaviour had given way to an ethos of taming and regulating nature.

Mistrust for the domestic was not uniquely Russian, then; equally, Russian culture embraced more than one attitude towards the domestic. The belief in a special, Russian, self-denying, ascetic, and stoical attitude to *byt* in general, and to adversity in particular, became dominant during peculiar historical circumstances. It started to take hold during the early twentieth century, when the Russian Symbolists expressed their discontent with the ordinary material world in favour of another, higher reality, of existence on a spiritual plane of radiance and beauty. The elevation of *bytie* (a more abstract concept of being) to a favoured position and the denigration of *byt* went together. In his memoir, *On the Border of Two Centuries* (*Na rubezhe dvukh stoletii*; 1930), the poet and novelist Andrei Belyi (1880–1934) was to describe his father pityingly as 'a prisoner of *byt*', unlike his son, who had been transformed into a precocious Symbolist by a bout of scarlet fever at the age of two.

Despite the Soviet regime's commitment to state atheism, a negative attitude to *byt* survived the Bolshevik revolution of 1917: willed asceticism now became a way of lending lustre to the perpetual shortages and discomforts that Russians had to endure under Soviet power. This was particularly true among intellectuals, such as writers, who were opposed to Soviet power: to repudiate *byt* came to seem a form of covert political resistance once Stalin proclaimed in 1934 that every Soviet citizen had a right to a 'prosperous existence'. The more the Soviet government assured its subjects that prosperity was legitimate, the more those opposed to Soviet power came to despise any involvement with *byt*. Contempt for *byt* became particularly widespread among dissidents in the post-Stalin era, when the Soviet government still more vigorously asserted every citizen's right to material comfort (ensuring which became official Communist Party policy at the Twenty-Second Congress in 1961), but failed to ensure the manufacture and distribution of the consumer goods, and at times even of the basic foodstuffs, that would have been required to sustain the myth. As Soviet journals launched consumer pages, and complaints about non-provision came to be regarded as legitimate, an ability to rise above material need began to seem the token of true intellectual superiority.

At other periods of Russian history, though, attitudes to domestic existence among intellectuals were different, and less ascetic. Certainly, it is possible to trace the idea of a national identity rooted in the survival of adversity back to the nineteenth century, and in particular to the Romantic notion of Russia as a 'northern country', where sincerity and directness compensated for lack of polish, and endurance for guile. But identity, even at the most patriotic periods of Russian history, was always defined in far more ways than in the sense 'Russian as opposed to foreign (western), northern as opposed to southern'. Russians defined their identities in terms of their relationship to other Russians, as well as to the outside world: and the use of different definitions of *byt* was an important weapon in these struggles. So far from being stable in terms of its meanings and associations, then, the term *byt* was subject to constant modulation. It was also a socially divisive term, used to claim authority on the part of the socially and intellectually advantaged, and to allow them to shape the space where the disadvantaged might realise their identities.

This survey addresses both these aspects of the history of *byt*, beginning with a brief outline of important shifts in the meaning of the word over the course of the nineteenth and early twentieth centuries. This preliminary discussion is then used as background for the second part of the chapter, a case study of the campaign to transform the daily life of children (*detskii byt*) during the 1920s, which was an especially instructive instance of how a Russian political and social elite attempted to mute the expression of Russian identities (in the plural) in order to forge an effective myth of national identity (in the singular), but also of the obstacles that were experienced in the course of this procedure.

2. THE USES OF 'BYT': THE HISTORY OF A TERM

In the late eighteenth and early nineteenth centuries, the term *byt* was in most common use among conservative nationalists, who used it to evoke the precious tradition of Russian household practices: the way of life preserved in patriarchal extended families, but not in the atomised households to be found in the modern city. The word was used in this sense in a poem by the late eighteenth-century poet Gavrila Derzhavin (1743–1816), 'In Praise of Country Life' (*Pokhvala sel'skoi zhizni*; 1798), which spoke of the wife's part in ensuring 'the household *byt* / According to the custom of honest Russian wives'.[4] It was also so used by the nationalist Slavophile thinker Ivan Kireevskii (1806–56) in his 1852 essay 'On the Character of Enlightenment in Europe and its Relation to Enlightenment in Russia' (*O kharaktere prosveshcheniia v Evrope i ego otnoshenii k prosveshcheniiu v Rossii*). When *byt* was used in ethnographical work produced by members of nationalist conservative circles, it also had this resonance. As Nathaniel Knight writes in a pioneering study of the Russian Geographical Society:

The concept of *byt* – the totality of material and cultural elements comprising a particular way of life – was unique to Russian ethnography. Unlike the notions of civilization, enlightenment, or culture that dominated the thinking of imperialist ethnographers both in Russia and the West, *byt* was nonhierarchical and non-comparative: there are no levels or stages of *byt*. The very etymology of the word, derived from the verb 'to be', betrays its essence: *byt* simply is.[5]

There are numerous texts that bear out Knight's contentions. Among them are not only the various writings of his main subject, the ethnographer Nikolai Nadezhdin, but an 1842 study of *Old and New Russian Byt* (*Zapiski o starom i novom russkom byte*) by Ekaterina Avdeeva (1789–1865), also the author of household manuals meant to help country-dwelling Russians put the ideal of *byt* into practice.

Yet Knight is not correct to argue that for commentators of this kind, 'there [were] no levels or stages of *byt*'. To be sure, there existed an unchanging nationalist *ideal* of *byt*, in the sense of a level of Russian civilization as yet uncorrupted by Western and urban influence. But *byt* could change, if only for the worse: there was such a thing as 'new *byt*' as well as 'old *byt*. And the term was sometimes used with neutral relativism: even the conservative lexicographer Vladimir Dal (1801–72), compiler of the famous *Defining Dictionary of the Living Great Russian Language* (first published in 1861–67) gave his imprimatur to relativistic usages such as 'gentry *byt*', 'peasant *byt*', and indeed 'English/German *byt*'. In a sense, then, the use of *byt* by groups of this kind was analogous to the uneasy employment of the term *kul'tura* in the late Soviet period, or of 'culture' in contemporary Britain or America: it meant at one and the same time any way of life, however lived, and the ideal of how life should be lived.

Equally controversial was the question of how *byt* should be organised in a practical sense, as addressed in humbler sources such as the many treatises on housekeeping, hygiene, and other aspects of day-to-day behaviour that poured from Russian presses in the mid to late nineteenth, and early twentieth centuries. By the early twentieth century, a full-scale rift had opened up between one type of manual, advocating streamlined and ascetic forms of 'rational living', and a second type, which with equal vehemency propounded high spending and elaborate decoration. It was at this period when the association between plain living and high thinking moved out of the radical fringes of intellectual culture into the mainstream. One of the few kinds of advice literature not to be parodied by intellectuals in the early twentieth century was the manual of health and fitness; at the same time, the desire of the early-twentieth-century new rich to acquire expensive decorative items was satirised relentlessly in liberal periodicals such as *Satirikon*, whose contributors, not coincidentally, tended to come from established intelligentsia families. This distaste for frills and self-indulgence carried over directly into the Soviet era, in part because of the tastes of the most powerful intellectual in Russian history, Vladimir Ilich Lenin. Lenin was a health and fitness fanatic, whose capacity for work and serious conversation, and intolerance of smoking, daunted even his close associates. Returning by rail to Russia from Switzerland in 1917, Lenin 'stipulated that all smoking should be confined to the lavatory', and 'introduced a priority system whereby those wishing to smoke were issued with a "second-category" pass and had to give way to those with "first category" passes.'[6] The health and hygiene-obsessed atmosphere of the first Soviet years, not to speak of the obsession with passes (*spravki*) that haunted the system till long after its demise, was already, quite literally, in train.

Yet even in the early Soviet period, more than one interpretation of *byt* was in circulation. The ethnographical, relativist usage made itself felt, for example, in the creation of 'museums of *byt*', historical exhibitions which set out the daily life of specific social strata – for example, the merchants of St Petersburg. This usage was also evident in the numerous early Soviet studies of worker *byt*, such as an important book on the daily life of Moscow workers by E. Kabo, published in 1928. Among modernist writers, on the other hand, the term *byt* was used as an absolutist term of abuse, referring to the banal and ordinary existence that they neo-romantically spurned. A third usage, characteristic of (but not limited to) official propaganda, was structured round the binary opposition *novyi byt/staryi byt*, and might be best translated 'the new order/the old order'. The slogan *Za novyi byt!* (Toward a New *Byt!*) expressed in a single phrase the understanding that traditional Russian life was 'backward' and needed to be 'modernised'. While this idea, in itself, had been been a cliché since the days of Peter the Great, one innovation of the early Soviet period was a partial disaggregation of two processes which had previously tended to be identified, 'modernisation' and 'Westernisation'. The creation of 'new *byt*' would be based on an appropriation of Western practices (for example, 'scientific management' in industry), but these would be revalidated once they were relocated in Soviet society, which was collectivist, egalitarian and just, where Western societies were individualistic, exploitative, and inhumane. The principles of the 'new *byt*' were supposed to include not only industriousness, self-restraint, sobriety, intellectual self improvement, and admiration for scientific progress, all of which could be matched in Western capitalism, but communal living and staunch atheism, which could not.

Byt, then, could be used positively ('new *byt*'). It could be used negatively ('old *byt*'). But it could equally well be used neutrally (as with ethnographical studies of 'worker *byt*'). In point of fact, though, the neutral usage was always marginal, even before the closing of the 'museums of *byt*', and the replacement of ethnographic study by photo-profiles of hero workers, in the late 1930s. And indeed *byt*, particularly in the sense of private, domestic existence, was consistently seen as a subsidiary domain of human endeavour. In terms of official Soviet ideology, *pogruzhenie v byt* or 'absorption in private life' was inimical to full participation in the collective: the Soviet ideal was someone who 'placed the interests of the Party and the working class above his personal interests', to quote from a eulogy of the Pioneer hero Pavlik Morozov (1918–32, most notorious for having allegedly betrayed his father to the Soviet authorities).[7] During the late 1920s, there was a high degree of congruence between official Soviet discourse and members of avant-garde groups of writers and artists. Excessive concern with *byt* was regarded as a trait debarring entry to intellectual life, an indication of backwardness, and a marker of affiliation to the despised *meshchanstvo*, or petty bourgeoisie.

3. *BYT* AND SOCIAL IDENTITY: THE DIVISIVENESS
OF EGALITARIANISM

Russian intellectuals themselves understood their ascetic intolerance of *byt* as egalitarian, as a gesture of solidarity between the intelligentsia and the working class. Obviously, there was some foundation in this view: an ideology based on self-restraint was indeed more accessible to the disadvantaged than one based on relentless acquisition. And there was an egalitarian note, too, in the words in common use for cultivated behaviour in the late nineteenth and early twentieth centuries. Unlike earlier terms (for instance, *porodistost'*, or 'breeding'), the terms *kul'turnost'* ('culturedness') and *intelligentnost'* ('behaving in the manner befitting a member of the intelligentsia') made cultivation a question of behaviour, and not of birth. As a result, before and after the Revolution, some of the most eloquent expressers of intelligentsia anti-*byt* were self-made intellectuals from humble backgrounds such as the writers Anton Chekhov (1860–1904), Maksim Gorkii (1868–1936), and Kornei Chukovskii (1882–1969). In a famous letter to his brother, Chekhov set out a credo of intelligentsia behaviour in which a fastidious attitude to domestic existence was seen as an essential prerequisite of intellectual life. Well-bred people must not sleep in their clothes, regard bed-bugs with indifference, breathe dirty air, step on to a spit-covered floor, or over-indulge themselves sexually with women. They must regard women as 'mothers, not tarts', and their motto should be *mens sana in corpore sano*.[8]

As Chekhov's reference to different ways of regarding women also reveals, though, the egalitarianism of *intelligentnost'* was far from all-embracing. The boundaries of the ethos were porous in class terms, but less so in gender terms. To live in a cultivated manner required that squalor be kept under control, yet becoming mired in domesticity was an obstacle to cultivation. This double-bind was easy enough to escape for men, who were able to abandon housework to wives or servants,[9] but less so for women, most particularly after the Revolution, when domestic service was no longer anything like so widespread as it had been before 1917. Modernist women writers, like their male counterparts, understood *byt* as a living hell: the theology of the narrative poem 'The Staircase' (*Lestnitsa*), by Marina Tsvetaeva (1892–1941), in which *byt* disappears in a purifying conflagration, has much in common with a poem by Arsenii Tarkovskii (1907–89) portraying the nineteenth-century culinary writer Elena Molokhovets (1831–?), whom he sees as permanently enslaved, even in the after-life, by the obscenely physical processes of food preparation.[10] The difference was that women writers saw hell as a place that they, as well as other people, might have to inhabit.

What one might call the 'discriminatory egalitarianism' inherent in Russian attitudes to *byt* and identity was also evident in Soviet propaganda for 'new *byt*'. The most important targets for this propaganda were the socially subordinate and the socially marginal: members of the working classes and the peasantry, and above all women, who were seen as the most backward section of the proletariat and the peasantry. There was direct continuity between the missionary endeavours of Soviet campaigners for 'new *byt*' and the attempts of the pre-revolutionary radical intelligentsia to take education and culture to the Russian people. The kind of intellectual populism expressed in the 'going to the people' movement of the 1870s, or in Tolstoianism, which attempted to find common ground between peasant custom and 'modern', 'hygienic' ways, had no currency in early Soviet propaganda and agitation. Rather, popular practices were cited exclusively in the context of exhortations that they be changed – culinary literature, for example, attempted to persuade peasant women of the virtues of the hay box and the primus rather than the traditional stove.

4. REFORMING CHILDREN'S DAILY LIFE: THE TRANSFORMATION OF PLAY

A hierarchy of age was as central to the 'differential egalitarianism' of campaigns for *byt* as a hierarchy of gender. The ideal body of hygiene propaganda was one that was not only muscular and male, but youthful, supple, and energetic, *zakalennoe*, or 'tempered like steel' by a programme of *zariadka* (gymnastic exercises, weight-lifting, or 'working out', to use the modern term). So far as 1920s hygiene propaganda was concerned, old age was a disaster to be averted as long as humanly possible, by rejuvenation therapy should all else fail. But as well as being too old to be an ideal subject of Soviet power, one could also be too young. If senile degeneration definitely lay beyond the margins of the permissible, infancy was at best a borderline case. As Evgenii Zamiatin (1884–1937) made clear in his dystopian novel *We* (*My*; 1920), the shining cities evoked by futurists had no room for maternity hospitals; in the real-life clinics, creches, and nurseries of the Soviet Union, infants were meant to be the objects of 'emotional hygiene' as well as sanitary control. 'Picking a child up is quite useless and simply wears out whoever is caring for it,' commented the most prominent child-care guru of the 1920s, Georgii Speranskii. The child was to be in a separate room from the outset, and 'upbringing should start from the first day of its life'.[11] 'Upbringing' was to be achieved not only by means of education, but through the transformation of children's day-to-day existence, their *byt*. Propaganda campaigns were launched (using advice literature aimed at adults, and also the columns of journals and newspapers for children, such as *Pionerskaia pravda*, the junior version of the Communist Party daily) to inculcate hygienic principles: every child was supposed to have its own bed, towel, and eating equipment. Children were exhorted to take schoolwork seriously: in 1932, for example, a 'shock school pupil' drive was launched to accompany the 'shock worker' campaign being carried on in Soviet factories and workplaces.

Once again, all of this was 'Soviet' more in terms of the rhetoric used than of underlying principles: in contemporary Western societies as well, children were seen as the 'future of society', and education was at the centre of political debates. Health and hygiene campaigns were carried out all over the West, and 1920s visitors to Russia thoroughly approved of Soviet efforts in this direction, praising the showpiece baby clinics and kindergartens that they visited. More controversial, and more distinctive in an international context, however, was the official Soviet view of children as nascent citizens in the sense of participants in the political struggle. Children were not only encouraged to participate actively in political discussions, but also to contribute to the transformation of Soviet society. Members of the Pioneer movement, the junior wing of the Komsomol (Committee of Soviet Youth), helped distribute election leaflets, disseminated materials about modern agricultural practices to villagers, acted as couriers taking new books house to house, and took the political struggle into the home, lecturing sceptical and sometimes contemptuous parents and relations about the benefits of Soviet power.

This view of the ideal child as a serious, committed political activist did not, on the other hand, mean that children were placed in full control. Children were always subordinated to adults: the Pioneer movement was, throughout its existence, a department of the Komsomol rather than an autonomous organisation; Pioneer leaders were supposed to be members of the Komsomol rather than senior Pioneers; likewise, teachers were constantly advised that they were not supposed to allow the children too much self-direction. In the words of Beatrice King, a British educationalist who knew early Soviet Russia well, 'the children under twelve can be, and in fact are, only nominally responsible for much of the school life that is supposed to come within their jurisdiction.'[12] Equally, the reform of daily life was adult-directed, with children enacting policy and disseminating propaganda shaped by their elders. A good example of how this happened is the campaign to transform play, or to put it a different way, to inculcate appropriate ways of spending leisure time among children.

For many dominant figures in the Soviet political establishment, such as Lenin's wife Nadezhda Krupskaia (1869–1939), play was an instrumental activity, a branch of 'education for labour', through which children acquired skills that would be of use to them in later life. This attitude to play had a long pedigree: it was expressed in the work of Western educationalists such as Locke and Fröbel. Indeed Rousseau, for all his advocacy of an education based upon non-interference with children's 'natural' state, had also seen play as a tool in moral education: games in the dark, for instance, were useful because they allowed children to combat their fear of the dark: 'Let him laugh when he goes into a dark place, let him laugh when he comes out, so that the thought of the game he is leaving and the games that he will play next may protect him from the fantastic imagination which might lay hold on him.'[13] But by the late nineteenth century, a different attitude to play was starting to evolve: it was now seen as an expression of the child's distinctive psychology, of children's difference from adults. In the words of the Italian psychologist Giovanni Colozza, whose study of children's games was translated into Russian in 1909, play was 'the free and essential expression of those interior things which need to be outwardly expressed'.[14]

It would be an over-simplification to suggest that attitudes to play during the 1920s were uniformly rationalistic. Particularly in the first half of the decade, play was often understood as a free imaginative space, along the lines set out by Colozza (and also by British and American 'paidologists' of the 1890s and 1900s). Several outstanding psychological and ethnographical studies emphasised the significance of games, particularly linguistic games, as expressions of the specific traits of the juvenile mentality. The First Experimental Station of Narkompros (the People's Commisariat of Enlightenment), in existence from 1919 until 1932, did invaluable research on play as part of its pioneering work on the nursery and primary school syllabus. In the nursery and primary schools attached to the Station, self-expression by children was encouraged.

From 1925, though, there was increasing emphasis upon the fact that play should be primarily an educational experience. Ideal Soviet children were supposed to pass their free time in suitably harmonious, decorous groups, with educational toys such as balls, cubes, pyramids, and *natsmen* dolls (dolls in the costumes of Soviet national minorities (*natsional'nye men'shinstva*) – designed to inculcate internationalist attitudes), if they were young enough. Older children were expected to take part in purposive role-playing games.[15] All of this, of course, ignored the possibility of children who

would rather have worn frills and ringlets than linen smocks, would rather
have played with baby dolls than miniature trucks and tractors, or would
have preferred rolling in the dirt and making mud pies to building miniature
Constructivist buildings with wooden cubes. But the question of what
children wanted was of less consequence than the question of what they,
as budding members of the harmonious Soviet collective, ought to have
wanted. As a result, many of the games that children actually played were
represented by normative sources in a thoroughly hostile way, as part of
'old *byt*'. For instance, the 'Letters on Method' published by Narkompros
in the late 1920s, and which were intended to provide guidance for nursery
teachers about what to do with the children in their care, distinguished
carefully between acceptable and unacceptable forms of play. It was vital
that such manifestations of backwardness as 'fights, drinking, superstition,
rudeness, slovenliness, mendacity, laziness, cowardice, deceit, and social
isolationism' should not be reflected in children's leisure activities, the
brochure proclaimed.[16] The supervisor's duty was to remain on hand as the
children played, occasionally stepping in to right the situation if things took
a dangerous direction, and nudging her charges towards games expressing
a positive attitude to Soviet reality. If the children were playing trains and a
squabble broke out, the supervisor should ask, 'But where's the guard?' or
'Where's the driver?'. Children left out of the main train game should be
organised to pretend that they were mending another train back in the
depot, so that the entire group was involved in the same activity. And
as children grew older, they should be diverted from games as such into
activities more closely related to work. Younger children might play 'Uncle
Iakov's Vegetable Garden', a game evidently based on Beatrix Potter's story
Peter Rabbit, in which a group of 'bunnies' attempted to steal Uncle Iakov's
lettuces, but older ones should be encouraged to make and to tend their
own vegetable garden. While some 'space for the child's creative drive' must
be left, it was very important that games should reflect more than just a
fantasy world.[17]

　　Play, then, was supposed to facilitate rapid and unproblematic progression to entry into the rational adult collective: it was supposed to take
place under the supervision of responsible adults (not necessarily parents).
The reverse side of this ideal was a fear of unsupervised play, of children's
capacities for subversion and hooliganism if left to themselves. A story by
Aleksei Tolstoi (1883–1945), written in the mid 1920s, contrasted Vaska, 'a
revolting young man with a snub nose, lips gone yellow with smoking,
and pop eyes, and a forelock hanging down over his low brow', who 'never
did anything, filched money from his mother, and thought about what

mischief to get up to, or how to get hold of fifty copecks for beer and expensive *Samorodok* brand cigarettes', with Mitia Strelnikov, an upright boy who spent his leisure time indoors, reading improving stories about Polar explorers. The Vaska/Mitia conflict was paralleled in a deadly fight between Boor (Kham), a courtyard-lurking feline hooligan, and Snowball (Snezhok), a clean and cultured pet tom-cat from Mitia's own communal flat.[18]

During the 1920s and early 1930s, unsupervised play was usually seen as a manifestation of lack of supervision in a wider sense, of *besprizornost'*, or 'lack of care'. *Besprizornost'* was not only a social problem of vast dimensions (in 1922, Soviet orphanages harboured at least 600,000 inmates, who represented only a portion of the children actually abandoned). It was also – especially in the sense of 'parental neglect' rather than of 'child abandonment' – a central symbolic issue. As the children's journal *Vorobei* put it in 1925:

In every apartment block there live children who are left to their own devices. And nobody shows them how to use their free time. They gather in the courtyard, which is covered in litter and junk and refuse. There on the dumps is where the courtyard children spend their time.

Every morning they gather. 'What'll we do today?' the children ask. There's no answer – there's no-one to give an answer. Yesterday they sang songs, but they went through all the ones they know. They feel like playing a game, but there aren't any to play. They want to go somewhere, but the market's the only place to go to. And so it goes on, day after day . . .

But then they run out of money. Should they swipe some from dad, or go to the market and 'buy' something for nothing from a trader who's looking in the other direction? They get away with it once, but the second time they get caught: and now you've another 'waif' [*besprizornyi*] on your hands.[19]

The courtyard (*dvor*) appeared again and again as a locus of delinquent behaviour of this kind: stories published in *Pionerskaia pravda* during 1927 evoked boys gearing up for fights, scribbling graffiti, making mud-pies, and tormenting birds.[20] But it was not the only place where delinquency was held to flourish. Streets and housing blocks were other places of danger. Zlata Lilina's tract *Parents, Learn How to Bring Your Children Up*, for instance, ringingly denounced the situation in a hostel housing workers at the Staro-Glukhovskaia factory on the Kliazma River, not far from Moscow. While adults drank, 'strummed on the accordion', swore at each other, and fought, the corridor was left stinking, and the children abandoned to their own devices. They spent their time lying on the concrete floor while playing cards for money pilfered from the adults in the hostel, sneaking off to Harry Piel films, getting drunk and vandalising that temple of culture the 'red corner' (*krasnyi ugolok*), roaming the streets till late, or infecting themselves with venereal disease.[21]

As these citations illustrate, campaigners for 'new *byt*' drew no distinction between activities that really were harmful to health (such as drinking), or cruel (such as torturing birds), or illegal (such as theft), and those which simply ran contrary to the aesthetic appreciations of hygienically inclined Soviet adults (for example, playing card games, scribbling graffiti, or watching Western silent films). Equally, leisure spaces that, to children themselves, had very different symbolic resonances – courtyards, the public areas of communal flats or barracks, and streets in cities, fields and streets in villages – were rolled together into a single crucible of deviancy, the haunt of what a troop of Young Pioneers, writing to Stalin in October 1924, disdainfully classified as 'the ordinary childish life, one with no purpose'.[22]

The Pioneer movement, in its 1920s manifestation, was intended to be both the embodiment of such 'purpose', and the means of inculcating this in the child population at large. A central duty of the Pioneers was to carry propaganda for the Communist collective to non-members, or 'unorganised children', to use the jargon of the time. This was managed not only by means of political education as such, but also through the provision of rational leisure. In the words of a 1924 article in *Pioner* magazine, 'A person who can play in a friendly spirit can also live in a friendly spirit.'[23] Both Pioneer propaganda, and Pioneer agitational initiatives, carried out relentless assaults on the traditional pursuits that children went in for when 'hanging round streets' and courtyards. One rural Pioneer group in Moscow province, for example, was supposed to spend July 1925 running singing and sunbathing sessions and games for 'unorganised children', taking them out bathing and mushroom- and berry-picking, and holding readings and discussions of children's literature. All this was supposed to act as 'a counterweight to games of chance'.[24] The plan incorporated most types of rational leisure for children – hygienic activities, intellectual pastimes, and organised sports – but one surprising absence from it is the politically-coloured 'mass games' which were usually a standard feature of rational leisure programmes. In 1924, for example, Pioneers from the working-class district of Khamovniki, in Moscow, took part, wearing white hoods and robes, in 'The Fascists' Funeral', a sort of Communist *auto-da-fé* which used Ku Klux Klan costume (Klan members were known as 'American fascists' in the Soviet press) in order to satirise Fascist rites.[25]

The attempt to transform play into an orderly and purposive activity was, then, a central part of the early Soviet campaign for 'new *byt*'. This campaign was driven by a desire to free children from the burden of tradition, and to liberate them from 'the ordinary childish life, one with no purpose'. It remains to be asked how successful the reformers were in reshaping children's *byt*, and by extension their identity. The well-intentioned attempts to improve the living conditions of working-class children often foundered on practical difficulties. The minutes of parent–teacher meetings held at the First Experimental Station's Central Nursery School reveal a rather tragic confrontation between the idealistic expectations of the teachers, and the intractable circumstances in which families lived. One mother observed that she would gladly give her children separate beds, but she simply had not the space and the money to do this. Another protested that to divide the children up during the winter would have meant that one of them would have had to sleep without a blanket.[26] Even Soviet orphanages, the supposed crucibles of hygienic collective upbringing, were frequently quite unable to enact ideals in practice: reports, both secret and published, abounded of institutions which were filthy, underequipped, and served the inmates an inadequate diet.[27] Educational reform was often bedevilled by physical difficulties of this kind; the recalcitrance of many teachers, who either failed to understand new methodologies, or who were determined not to introduce them, also stymied changes imposed 'from above'.

Of the two types of obstacle – physical and psychological – it was more the latter that counted in the campaign to revolutionise play. Some types of rational leisure required equipment: it was impossible to organise games of football or catch without balls, and yet these remained deficit items until at least the early 1930s. But many other activities – for example, role-playing 'mass games' – could be carried on with no special equipment at all. More problematic was the nature of the human material. The Pioneer movement was supposed to be the hub of activism: yet throughout the 1920s and early 1930s, it remained atomised. Large numbers of its members had only the dimmest idea of what the movement's purpose was. In the words of one exasperated Komsomol activist from the Moscow area, speaking in 1924, 'Often our Pioneers don't know what the very word "Pioneer" means'.[28] Other children were not so much ignorant, as mischievous: the number of cartoons and satirical articles carried by *Pionerskaia pravda* that lambasted bad behaviour at meetings can be taken as an indication of its prevalence. But if some Pioneers were not really qualified to act as the organisers of rational leisure, the active and politically aware did not necessarily respond with enthusiasm to being funnelled off into playing games, however ideologically sound these were. Asked by a foreign visitor why she was not wearing her Pioneer tie, one girl responded in 1932, 'We're not doing anything worth being in the organisation for.' She was irritated at being kept busy with such trifling activities as collecting cuttings and writing to the group of German Pioneers for which her troop was responsible.[29] Given that some Pioneers did not know how to engage in serious political activity, and others were frustrated by being asked to do 'childish' things, it is no surprise that the presence of Pioneers in a particular inner-city area did not necessarily contribute to a diminution in undesirable forms of play.[30]

There were other problems too. The Soviet authorities' motives in attempting to transform the nature of play were not just connected with their desire to shape the new generations into amenable citizens. They also expressed a conviction that every child deserved prolonged exposure to education, freedom from the need to enter paid employment, and access to an upbringing driven by concern about moral education. Prior to the Revolution, this kind of 'extended childhood' had been the exclusive experience of children from the economic and educational elite, and these children had generally played in private gardens, or else in open spaces that were shared with other children from the same class. But the attempt to 'civilise' childhood foundered on the nature of the urban environment, and particularly on the lack of spaces appropriate to 'rational leisure'. While playgrounds existed, these were scarce, and aimed at children of pre-school age; the prestigious 'houses of culture' (and from the late 1930s, Pioneer palaces) and culture parks were places for occasional visits, rather than daily use. Even in the post-Stalin era, the place where most urban children played in Soviet cities was still the courtyard or the street in dry weather, or the corridor of the communal flat or barracks when it was too wet or cold to go outside.

What is more, the jumbling up of different social strata that was a result of the 'compression of living space' (*uplotnenie*), i.e. the resettling of working-class residents in what had once been bourgeois one-family apartments, also led to the 'democratisation' of play spaces. On the whole, it was proletarian children who set the rules in corridors and in flats. In the courtyard of Vadim Shefner's house, the most admired raconteur was a thirteen-year-old boy called Ogurets (Gherkin), who boasted of being friends with Motia Bespalyi (Motia 'Nofinger'), one of Leningrad's most notorious hoodlums.[31] Similarly, one Leningrad resident at school in the 1920s remembered her school playground as dominated by gangs with 'their own etiquette and laws: they valued bravery, agility in games and sports, despised weakness, laziness, greed, and tell-tales'.[32] Rather than the 'cultured' children offering leadership to the 'uncultured' ones (as was imagined in Pioneer propaganda), both in the yards of apartment blocks and in school playgrounds, it was often the 'cultured' children who did their best to blend in. The result was often to foster exactly the kind of 'hooliganish' behaviour that 'organised games' had been meant to stamp out.

To be sure, children themselves usually had a clear appreciation of the distinction between play, however 'unbridled', and criminal behaviour. As Vadim Shefner recalled from his experience in the mid to late 1920s, admiration for characters such as Gherkin did not mean that children belonged to a lawless community. Rather, the courtyard acted as 'a buffer zone between home and the street', and had 'its own rules, which weren't those of the family, the school, or even the street: oddly enough they were closest to the ones we had in the children's home . . . Strength was admired, but so was fair play, and as a rule the bigger children left the younger ones in peace.'[33] And, rather than being subversive, the games played by children often drew directly upon the political orthodoxies of the day. One such game was 'Search and Requisition', played in a suburban Moscow courtyard during the first years after the Revolution. The boys would act as 'Red Army Soldiers' and the girls (well padded-out with cushions) as 'The Swindler' and 'The Fat Bourgeois'. Paper twists of salt and other provisions stolen from the kitchen stood in for the shop goods. The Red Army Soldiers burst their way into the premises of the shop, shouting and yelling abuse, and punching and kicking their victims (this was where the padding came in useful). Having duly requisitioned the 'goods', they departed triumphantly with the words, 'Now we're off to Sukharevka' (the largest and most famous flea-market in Moscow).[34]

In sum, though, children's play remained resistant to reform; indeed, adult attempts to control it often ended up by reinforcing the practices that were the primary target of the attempted control.

Children's *byt* was not only elusive in a practical sense: it was also problematic in a conceptual sense. Most educated Soviet citizens were prepared to endorse intervention in daily life on the level of campaigns against hooliganism, which had been a significant cause of alarm since the late nineteenth century. However, the politicisation of childhood was often seen by opponents of Soviet power as a distortion of 'natural' experience rather than as a measure against deviance. Evgenii Zamiatin, in an essay written not long after his emigration to France in 1930, evoked the typical Soviet child as 'an eight-year-old grown man', turned to a automaton by the political indoctrination imposed on him in schools. For Zamiatin, the fact that 'the influence of the family loses the battle with the influence of the school' was both obvious and tragic.[35] But one did not have to be a political dissident to find child activism problematic. In Soviet official circles, too, there was a good deal of heart-searching about the extent to which children should be involved in serious politics. Politicised through and through, childhood was at the same time beyond the reach of politics. And in turn, childhood began to be a place where daily life could be represented more positively than it ordinarily was in Soviet official discourse. Though the children of Soviet myth, such as Pavlik Morozov, might give lessons to adults as well as other children by the perfection of their commitment to the Soviet cause and their disdain for *byt*, at the same time the depiction of childhood was one of the few areas of autobiography where quotidian details (*bytovye detali*) were considered permissible. A primary target in the campaign to transform traditional life, the everyday experience of children not only eluded complete transformation, but became, when remembered, the space for the imagination of an alternative *physical* reality, evoked through memory, which undermined the conventional hierarchical distinction, fervently asserted by both Soviet reformers and literary modernists, between the 'material' and 'spiritual' worlds.

The Soviet management of children's daily life, then, illustrates both the potency and the limitations of the Soviet ideology of *byt* in a broader sense. The supremely irrational behaviour of infants was to be controlled and policed; older children were to be encouraged to develop their rational impulses, so that play became another branch of 'education for work and citizenship', the driving force of child socialisation. By extension, this transformation of an especially backward sector of society would stand for the Soviet Union's transformation of itself into a dynamic new nation. So far from being forced by the political elite upon a reluctant population, this ideology was widely shared. Kornei Chukovskii, whose ideas about children's play were far closer to Colozza's than to Krupskaia's, none the less saw the transformation of children's lives as a major achievement of the regime:

Nothing does more to indicate the extent of cultural growth in Russia than the unprecedented level of concern for the child that has become apparent in recent years. Suddenly, all at once, one after the other, a whole series of books of a totally new kind has appeared [. . .] And the toy museum! And the museum of children's art. And the Experimental Stations of Narkompros. And the Institute of Children's Reading. And the Verkhoturskii Children's Town. And the Kazan Pedological Laboratory for the Study of Chuvash Children [. . .] And the special 'Theatres of the Young Viewer' in Moscow, Leningrad and the provinces! And the children's books – especially for little children! Never, in the course of two whole centuries, has there been such a rich flowering of the children's book in Russia. Truly, the Epoch of the Child has arrived in our country.[36]

Yet even in the context of these widely approved notions about the importance of transforming children's existence, *byt* remained a slippery and contradictory concept. Ideals were difficult to implement in practical terms, which in turn led to a questioning of ideals. Moreover, concepts of desirable daily life were in any case (even before tested out in practice) unstable and contradictory. Thus, even in the era when there was apparently greatest consensus about the meaning of *byt* (as an area requiring transformation by means of energetic intervention), there existed an alternative view of *byt* as resistant to politics and cherishable on precisely those grounds.

This chapter began by questioning the view that Russians have an extraordinary and unique relationship with everyday life. Certainly, it is fair to say that at some periods of Russian history, the issue of everyday life, named as *byt*, has been controversial. The question, 'How should we live?' has been raised insistently and often, and the use of the term *byt* has carried the suggestion that daily life occupies a discrete domain, whose boundaries may be changed at will, or which may even be effaced from the earth altogether. 'Life without daily life' would sound absurd in English; *zhizn' bez byta* makes perfect sense. At the same time, Russian identity cannot be said to have been defined, even over the last hundred and fifty years, and let alone in the longer term, by a single, straightforward and unchanging, relationship to daily life. Nineteenth- and twentieth-century Russians were neither more nor less preoccupied with daily life than their counterparts elsewhere in Europe; it was the expressions of their preoccupation which had idiosyncratic, though varied and mutable, forms.

SECTION IV

Symbols of identity

Until now, we have considered questions which, at least in principle, relate to substantive 'facts' about communal circumstances, attributes, or activities: questions of history and geography, of ideology and religion, of language, music, and the conditions of life. However, in several cases we have also seen how, in cultural practice, discourse on national identity often functions as much through symbols as through articulated discussion of the 'real' question. Identity may be affirmed or contested through a shared language of signs (flags, pictures, verbal slogans, songs, names, labels, and so on) as much as through 'real' shared practices or qualities. In the final section of the book we turn to such signs themselves, no longer as adjuncts to a thematic discussion. Indeed, one of the strongest points to have emerged is the polyvalence of the signs, the ways in which they have been invested with multiple meanings by those who have used them: as if a shared identity can be maintained through the constant use of agreed signifiers, almost regardless of what is supposed to be signified by them.

Chapter 10 deals with public monuments which have come to acquire this kind of emblematic status. The first section of the chapter is partly a historical survey of such monuments, but partly also an account of the very idea of a public monument in Russia, drawing on the evidence of relatively under-used sources such as guide-books. The 'case studies' in the second section of the chapter illustrate the cultural uses made of two of Moscow's most prominent monuments – the strikingly ornate sixteenth-century church on Red Square popularly known as St Basil's cathedral, and Vera Mukhina's 1937 statue 'Worker and Collective Farm Woman' – from their origins through to the mass reproduction of their images in modern constructs of 'consumable Russianness'.

Finally, Pushkin; or rather, 'Pushkin': not the life or works of the poet Aleksandr Sergeevich Pushkin, but an account of the 'myth of a national poet' that has flourished ever since the death of the man himself in 1837.

No Russian comes to Pushkin for the first time as a student or adult out of an interest in poetry, as a foreigner might. Pushkin is an integral part of the familiar linguistic and cultural environment from earliest childhood. With works for all ages, from fairy tales to love lyrics to historical drama, Pushkin accompanies Russians on the path through life. Even Shakespeare (in an anglophone context) cannot aspire to such a universally acknowledged sense of intimacy. Chapter 11 outlines the general features of the Pushkin myth before concentrating on his anniversary celebrations – in particular the 1999 bicentenary of his birth – when 'Pushkin' is venerated and contemplated with a special intensity, and when the multi-dimensionality and adaptability of the myth are brought most clearly into focus.

CHAPTER 10

Monuments and identity

Lindsey Hughes

In this chapter we consider how Russians and in some cases foreigners have talked about, written about, and represented certain key works of Russian painting, architecture, and sculpture as signifiers of national identity. The 'monuments' to be discussed are not confined to what the Shorter Oxford English Dictionary defines as 'a structure, edifice, or erection intended to commemorate a notable person, action or event'. They are better characterised by the Russian word *pamiatnik,* which has both the narrow meaning of a monument *to* someone or something and the wider sense of a notable or key example of visual, built, or literary culture, as in such combinations as *pamiatnik kul'tury* (monument of culture) or *pamiatnik zhivopisi* (monument of painting) These cultural landmarks may have lasted for many centuries and be widely venerated, like the twelfth-century icon of the Vladimir Mother of God, or they may be of more recent vintage and less generally admired, but still enjoy iconic status, like Vera Mukhina's 'Worker and Collective Farm Woman' sculpture (1937). Some are official memorial-monuments to empire-building, such as the instantly recognisable St Basil's Cathedral on Red Square (1555–61); others are small intimate pictures like Aleksei Savrasov's 'The Rooks Have Arrived' (1871), which, to quote a Soviet art historian writing in the 1980s, is 'linked in our consciousness with the discovery and affirmation of images of our native land . . . as a sort of symbol of Russian realistic landscape. Everyone knows it from childhood.'[1] For our purposes, a statue to a tsar or a memorial to the Second World War in a provincial town, although undoubtedly 'monuments' in the narrower sense, do not qualify. They may serve the collective memory by linking places on the margins with events of national significance, but the objects themselves are famous only locally. Local identities are interesting, but are beyond the scope of this survey, which seeks to explore how Russian national identity has been projected onto prominent visual emblems among a wide public.

These landmark buildings, statues, paintings, most of them in Moscow and St Petersburg, are immediately recognisable to most Russians and in a few cases also to foreigners. They seem to have a peculiar significance and resonance, sometimes transcending their original location or material to appear in other media so that they imprint themselves even more deeply upon the collective consciousness. In some cases they have come to represent a kind of 'consumable Russianness', providing evocative emblems of Mother Russia or other manifestations of the national persona for the marketing of chocolate and cigarettes, vodka and package tours. The first part of this chapter presents an overview of the emergence of such monuments, and indeed of the very notion of a public monument in Russia. In the second part we look in more detail at a few key examples and at some of their cultural uses.

One of the first buildings in Moscow to achieve 'monument' status, and which maintains it to the present day, was the Cathedral of the Dormition (Assumption) of the Mother of God in the Kremlin (fig. 10.1). If the original church (1326) arguably had only local significance – the princes of Moscow were then one of several clans competing for political leadership of Rus – the surviving building, rebuilt in 1475–79 for Tsar Ivan III (reigned 1462–1505) by the Italian architect Aristotele Fioravanti, laid claim to be the mother church of All Rus. In the Muscovite period, of course, when religious identity was far stronger than national identity, such a 'monument' must be viewed in the context of Orthodox Christianity. The cathedral was one of the signifiers of Russia's place in universal history, in that 'grander vision of time' into which Russians fitted 'tales of self-location and self-justification' centred on the notion, after the fall of Constantinople in 1453, that their country was the only independent Christian tsardom left to guard the true faith.[2] The cathedral's family tree can be traced back via the town of Vladimir – where Tsar Ivan III sent Fioravanti to inspect another Dormition cathedral built in the twelfth century – to the eleventh-century Dormition church in the Monastery of the Caves in Kiev, which legend has it was designed by the Mother of God herself, whose Dormition feast on 15 August was associated with Constantinople.

The cathedral was also a key element in one of the founding myths of the Muscovite realm, according to which in 1326 Prince Ivan I of Moscow and the Orthodox Metropolitan Petr achieved the perfect symphony between state and church that was supposed to form the basis of Muscovy's greatness. An icon painted by the Moscow artist Simon Ushakov in 1668 shows the prince and the prelate planting and watering the family tree of the

Москва   Успенскій Соборъ.
Moscou   Cathédrale d'Assomption.

10.1 Cathedral of the Dormition (Assumption), Moscow Kremlin: early 20th-century postcard

Muscovite ruling dynasty and Muscovite saints against the background of the cathedral. Above them is one of the cathedral's most sacred treasures, the 'Vladimir' icon of the Mother of God of Tenderness, which was painted in Constantinople in the early twelfth century and brought from there to Kiev in about 1130. From Kiev the icon was transferred north to Vladimir and in 1395 to Moscow, where it remained (fig. 10.2). Theories about the icon's Byzantine origins were elaborated by art historians only in the last hundred years or so. Well into the nineteenth century it enjoyed a much older and more dramatic provenance, as a portrait of Mary painted from life by St Luke. She promised that the image would confer the grace of herself and her son upon those who possessed it, a prophesy which subsequently applied to the 'chosen' Russian people. Stories about the icon's miraculous intervention on Moscow's behalf in struggles with the Tatars in the fourteenth to sixteenth centuries underlined the specific historical circumstances of Moscow's emergence as the centre of world (i.e. Christian) history. The miracles attributed to the icon were not modest, small-scale ones such as restoration of sight or hearing, but miracles of national salvation. That tradition survived to recent times. In August 1991 when the White House (the parliament bulding) in Moscow was under siege following the attempt to unseat Mikhail Gorbachev, the Patriarch of Moscow is said to have brought out the icon in an attempt to intercede and end the conflict.

Just as Prince Vladimir forced Rus to accept Christianity from Byzantium in the tenth century, Peter the Great (1682–1725) forced Russia to improve its position in the world by accepting and mastering rules worked out by others. For our purposes, this meant following the lead of Western European artists, architects, and writers in adopting the models of Classical antiquity. On the face of it, the eighteenth century, with its belief in the universal virtues of these models, was a lean period for national consciousness in general and for Russian national identity in particular. Russia's indigenous ancient monuments were condemned to oblivion when Peter replaced Moscow with his new, purpose-built capital of St Petersburg, founded in 1703. Dynastic pride was redirected to a new set of St Petersburg monuments, such as the imperial family's new mausoleum, the Western-looking cathedral of Saints Peter and Paul (1712–34), built to the design of the Swiss Italian architect Domenico Trezzini. The building's thrusting spire was said to be redolent of Peter's new 'Fatherland', in contrast to the more 'feminine' rounded domes of the old churches of Mother Russia. Likewise the foreign-designed royal palace at Peterhof (begun 1714), Peter's own version of Versailles, with its formal gardens, fountains and sculpture, presented a completely different ideal of public space and 'monumentality' from Muscovite palaces.

10.2 Vladimir Mother of God; 12th-century icon: modern postcard (from the original in the Tretiakov Gallery, Moscow)

Despite the provision of such new national monuments, joining the 'mainstream' of Western culture comparatively late posed problems for Russian national pride. In the eighteenth century educated (i.e. Western-ised) Russians were alienated from their own cultural monuments, their atti-tudes shaped by the peculiar development of elite culture, which required the prioritisation of Western genres and models and the marginalisation of Russo-Byzantine religious art. By the standards of the Grand Tour of Europe, as undertaken by fashionable gentlemen in order to hone their appreciation of Classical and Renaissance civilisation in warm southern climes, Russia was a blank sheet. It had no Old Masters of its own (although the emperors and empresses from Peter onwards imported them in bulk), neither ancient Classical sites nor grand Renaissance buildings. The transfer of the capital and court to St Petersburg and the abolition of the patriarchate (1721) left Moscow much diminished. In 'Petition of the City of Moscow on Being Relegated to Oblivion' (*Proshenie Moskvy o zabvenii eia*), written by the conservative Prince Mikhail Shcherbatov in the 1780s, a personified Moscow rebukes the monarch for deserting it: 'My ancient ruins can still please and are still useful – they please because they represent my very antiquity and that of your Empire, and they are useful in that they are a reminder of many a service performed for the country.'[3]

In the eighteenth century this plea for Moscow's monuments to be regarded as a focus of patriotic pride was heeded only to a limited extent. The earliest published Russian guide to Moscow (V. G. Ruban's *Opisanie imperatorskogo stolichnogo goroda Moskvy*, 1782), was no more than a laconic gazetteer, lacking any personal response to historic and artistic sights. The only site deemed worthy of the attention of men of the Enlightenment was the newest: St Petersburg. In a preface addressed to Empress Elizabeth (1741–61), the author of the first St Petersburg guide (1779, based on a work written in 1749–51) wrote:

By the energetic efforts of Your Imperial Majesty this City is now so extensive and so adorned with splendid new buildings and so much admired, that it has the advantage over many famous European cities, which are famous for their antiquity, to the great glory of its Founder, and especially to the glory of Your Imperial Majesty . . . Thanks to Your Majesty's efforts this City has risen to the height of fame for its beauty and continues to surpass itself more and more, so that anyone without any prompting can see, as though in a theatre, the glory and beauty of its grandeur; and it is not only those people who live in it who enjoy the glory of its beauty but also those who live in distant countries and marvel just on hearing about it.[4]

The author underpinned his appreciation of St Petersburg and its monu-ments by setting it in the context of ancient history, as well as declaring its equality with Western centres deemed most civilised.

10.3 Monument to Peter I (the 'Bronze Horseman') by Etienne Falconet, 1782: modern view

In this context, one St Petersburg monument in particular marks a turning point in appreciation of native sites. The equestrian statue to Peter the Great, designed by the French sculptor Etienne Falconet for Catherine II (also 'the Great'; 1762–96) and unveiled in 1782, has acquired a life and an identity beyond the technical bravura of a horse standing on its back legs (fig. 10.3). The real Peter the Great, the statue, and Aleksandr Pushkin's poem 'The Bronze Horseman' (*Mednyi vsadnik*; 1833) later became inextricably linked in the Russian consciousness with the 'spirit' of St Petersburg. Even before Pushkin, however, the monument worked on several levels. Chiefly, it expressed the eighteenth-century ideal of great men as exemplars. In the words of the Russian scientist and writer Mikhail Lomonosov (1711–65), who himself had planned a monument to Peter: 'By animating metal and stone, sculptors will represent views of Russian Heroes and Heroines in gratitude to their fatherland and as an example and encouragement to their descendants towards courageous virtue.'[5] Remarkably, Falconet's statue was the first public monument in this sense to be erected in Russia. Until Peter the Great's time the Orthodox Church's hostility to graven images meant there was no sculpture at all.

It was no less a celebration of Russia's inclusion (or desired inclusion) in the ranks of 'civilised nations' as a result of Peter's reforms and the efforts of his successors: the horse tramples the serpent of ignorance and barbarism. It seemed to underline that by 1782, with a string of military victories under its belt, Russia no longer saw itself as a junior partner in world politics. The history of the statue's creation is characteristic of a number of Russian monuments in its association with feats of strength and courage, in this case the hauling into position, inch by inch over many months, of the mighty natural 'Thunder Stone' (*Grom kamen'*) that forms the monument's base.

> Colossus of Rhodes, subdue your proud look!
> And buildings of the lofty Pyramids on the Nile
> No longer consider yourself wonders!
> You were made by the perishable hands of mortals.
> Here is a Russian mountain not made by hands.
> Heeding the voice of God out of the lips of Catherine
> It came to Peter's town across the deeps of the Neva
> And fell beneath the feet of Great Peter.[6]

This poem by Vasilii Ruban, published in 1770 when the stone was moved, vigorously expressed the belief that a Russian monument could outdo those created by earlier civilisations.

Napoleon's occupation of Moscow in 1812 and the subsequent burning of the city, then the entry of Russian troops into Paris in 1814, aroused national feelings in a number of ways, not least by inspiring a sense of protectiveness towards national culture. Some members of the elite took to speaking Russian instead of French, wearing Russian-style dress, and taking a new pride in Russia's past. Long neglected monuments got a new lease of life, boosted by an infusion of patriotic feelings, and new monuments were generated, such as the column to Alexander I on Palace Square in St Petersburg (1834), 'one of the greatest contemporary monuments, worthy of the amazement of the whole civilised World'.[7]

A key work in this process was a guide to St Petersburg published in 1816–26 by Pavel Svinin (1788–1839). Svinin was one of several of his generation who promoted the idea of St Petersburg as Paris's equal, and as a symbol of Russia's full membership, even leadership, of Europe. Foreigners complained, he wrote, that there was no guide to the sights (*dostopamiatnosti* literally, things worthy of remembrance). The capital city of the 'great and strong Russian people', which had attracted the attention and respect of the whole world, languished in oblivion, whereas in other countries even the smallest town was described in detail.[8] Svinin invited his Russian readers not only to appreciate national achievements and heroes, but also to respond to monuments in an *emotional* way. His intended reader was a Russian man of sense and sensibility, ennobled by Russia's victories over Napoleon, who approached his surroundings with the eyes and mind and, ultimately, the heart of a patriot. Svinin refers to him as *strannik* – wanderer or pilgrim – but equally the 'pilgrim' could be described as a sightseer or 'tourist' (the Shorter Oxford English Dictionary dates the first use of the word in English to 1800), either an outsider or an inhabitant of St Petersburg indulging in the civilised occupation of strolling. Interesting passages are devoted to Peter the Great's first cabin, which by its very simplicity aroused a sense of reverence, which in earlier times had been reserved for churches and holy relics. Svinin also directs the traveller's gaze to the landscape beyond the cabin: 'The virtues of the object itself and the unparalleled views will give rise to new, happy outpourings of feelings and imagination.'[9] The humble hut and its surroundings were appreciated through the prism of Romanticism, which prioritised the individual response to the picturesque.

Svinin's was essentially a personal project, influenced by current artistic and philosophical trends. From the 1830s, *official* publications shamelessly strove to manipulate the emotions of Russian 'sightseers' through the doctrine of 'Official Nationality' (Orthodoxy, Autocracy, National Feeling), as promoted by Nicholas I (1825–55).[10] Nicholas's son, the future Alexander II, on the eve of travels abroad, set an example by making a patriotic guided tour of the Kremlin 'in order to fill his soul with its holy antiquity and with such impressions to leave his native capital city.'[11] Various monuments played their part in Russia's version of the 'invention of tradition', by which the state and its elites selected and adapted elements of the past to bind people together and to promote current programmes. It is in this period, not in medieval times, that the term Holy Rus (*Sviataia Rus'*) gains currency, reaching its height in the reigns of Alexander III (1881–94) and Nicholas II (1894–1917) and sparking a sort of re-run of old Muscovite stories about Russia's place in the world.

If in the mid-nineteenth century many Russians were still unfamiliar with national monuments, in the next few decades buildings, statues, and other works of art in the capitals in particular were imprinted upon the consciousness of a wider public as a result of increased travel opportunities (the railways) and wider dissemination of images through reproductions in guidebooks, magazines, prints, postcards, and so on. A woodcut of 1879 shows Pantiushka and Sidorka – peasant 'hicks' up to see the capital – goggling in amazement at the sights of Moscow. Late tsarist guidebooks aimed to transform aimless gawping into well-informed, edifying, *patriotic* observation. According to an 1898 guide, *Moscow, its Shrines and Monuments* (*Moskva, eia sviatyni i pamiatniki*), for example, Moscow was the 'cradle' of Russian national feeling (*narodnost'*). No other town had so many sacred objects and places, of which the Dormition cathedral was said to arouse an especially heartfelt emotion in the true Russian. A 1904 guide to the cathedral for factory workers declared:

An indissoluble spiritual link unites the Russian people with its Sovereign Father and in the heart of every Orthodox person there resides also a feeling of reverence towards the holy Kremlin; here worshippers flock from all corners of Holy Rus. What Orthodox believer, visiting Moscow, will not bow before the Kremlin's holy places? What Russian person can remain indifferent to its historical grandeur? The interior decoration of this imposing building of the [Dormition] cathedral bears witness to the solicitude of Orthodox sovereigns and of the Russian people for the beauty and preservation of the chief holy place of the capital . . . Shielded by the protecting veil of the holy things within it, filled with the fragrance of unceasing prayer, a witness to all Russia's many-centuries-long heroic struggle to create a unified, powerful Rus, the cathedral of the Dormition expresses in itself all that history, being at the same time a symbol of the unwavering Orthodox belief and invincibility of the Russian state, sacredly preserving its behests.[12]

There were alternative discourses, however. A 1914 guide to St Petersburg instructs rural teachers in preparing their classes for a trip to the capital. To help the children to appreciate the difference between the 'good order' of the town and the lack of culture (*nekul'turnost'*) of the village, teachers were encouraged to arrange a visit to a modern apartment block where their charges would see plumbing, doorbells, lifts, stairs, and (if they managed to sneak a look inside) cleanliness, elegance, comfort, telephones, and lights, 'in sharp contrast to their own dirty, small, empty huts (*izby*)'.[13] Teachers were advised to show their pupils a postcard of Peter I's cabin, drawing attention to its 'modest dimensions', then later to compare it with a picture of the grandiose Winter Palace. This little book is infused with a modern spirit: there are almost no appeals to patriotic emotion, no exhortations to 'fall in reverence' before semi-sacred relics of the tsars.

Late Tsarist guidebooks also directed visitors to art galleries. Until the latter part of the nineteenth century, Russian secular painting, perhaps with the exception of portraits of rulers, made virtually no impact on a wider public. Galleries such as the Hermitage displayed predominantly foreign works. One exception, Karl Briullov's (1799–1852) vast 'Last Day of Pompeii' (1833), which created a stir both in Russia and abroad when it went on show, was not an image of Russianness – painted in Italy, it depicts people fleeing the eruption of Vesuvius in AD 79 – but a monument to Russian achievement in the wider world of art. Knowledge of Russian art grew from the 1870s when a group of realist artists known as the 'Wanderers' or 'Itinerants' (*peredvizhniki*) explored contemporary national scenes and themes and the Moscow merchant Pavel Tretiakov began to collect and exhibit their works. In particular, landscapes by such artists as Ivan Shishkin (1832–98), Aleksei Savrasov (1830–97), and Isaak Levitan (1860–1900) achieved iconic status, featuring such set-piece Russian components as birch trees, onion domes, forests, and endless horizons. None of the *peredvizhniki*, even the most famous painter of the era Ilia Repin (1844–1939), achieved anything approaching Briullov's fame in the outside world, however. Their Russianness appealed mainly to consumers at home, transferring easily into the Soviet era when their most famous works adorned both classroom walls and chocolate box lids.

In the nineteenth century, artists also began to explore Old Russian history and legends and to study medieval architecture and icons. In this respect, 'Epic Warriors' (*Bogatyri*, 1898) by Viktor Vasnetsov (1848–1926) was a major landmark, which was actually envisaged by its creator as a patriotic 'monument' (fig. 10.4). The artist claimed that he got the idea from three mighty oaks at Abramtsevo to the north of Moscow: 'This is our mother Russia. Like those oaks you won't catch her with your bare hands. She is not afraid of snow storms or hurricanes nor the passing centuries.'[14] The sturdy warriors of legend were inextricably linked with what Vasnetsov understood as inexhaustible and powerful national forces. The critic Vladimir Stasov (1824–1906) compared and contrasted 'Epic Warriors' with Repin's 'Bargehaulers' (1873): 'In both paintings one sees all the strength and might of the Russian people. Only in Repin's work this strength is oppressed and still downtrodden . . . but here [in Vasnetsov's

10.4 'Epic Warriors' (*bogatyri*); cigarette packet from the 1980s, after the 1898 painting by Viktor Vasnetsov

picture] their strength is triumphant, calm, imposing, fearing no one and carrying out by its own will what it pleases and what it deems necessary for everyone, for the people'.[15]

At the turn of the nineteenth and twentieth centuries, icons – cleaned and restored – were reinterpreted as works of 'national heritage', above and beyond their function as cult objects. The most striking 'discovery' was Andrei Rublev's 'Old Testament Trinity', painted in the early fifteenth century (fig. 10.5). Unlike the icon of the Vladimir Mother of God, which was a processional image whose fame spread through tales and legends in medieval times, the Trinity icon's modern elevation to monument status centred not so much on Russia's place in the scheme of universal history as on its place in the pecking order of world culture. For centuries Rublev's icon was hidden away under a metal cover and known chiefly through

10.5 Old Testament Trinity; 15th-century icon by Andrei Rublev: modern postcard
(from the original in the Tretiakov Gallery, Moscow)

copies, falling into deeper obscurity in the eighteenth century along with
other Early Russian icons. Then in 1904–5 the casing was removed and its
contours were revealed. The critic Nikolai Punin described Rublev's Trinity
as 'an icon of divinely inspired beauty', which has remained hidden from
the world: 'The path of our art is stony and the crown of our artistic genius
a crown of thorns. If we have not been mindful of our treasures, if we

have lost and forgotten them, even so we remember the valleys where once, divinely great, we were in possession of them. We must look for our lost greatness, for no art can live without traditions. Where are our traditions?'[16] The process of recovering these traditions, of assessing icons as works of art, was furthered by public exhibitions of other cleaned icons in St Petersburg in 1911 (where they were seen by Henri Matisse, among others) and in Moscow in 1913 for the tercentenary of the Romanov dynasty.

In 1917, emerging notions of what constituted 'national heritage' were thrown into disarray. As a result of the Bolshevik revolution some monuments to people and events were destroyed, while new ones were erected to the New Soviet Men and Women. Some monuments to 'bourgeois' taste were condemned. But 'revolutionary iconoclasm' was coupled with attempts at re-education about those parts of the past which were to be retained. There were some unexpected beneficiaries. Andrei Rublev, for example, was included in a list of monument-worthy notables in Lenin's 1918 edict 'On Monumental Propaganda' (*O monumental'noi propagande*). That year, his Trinity icon was cleaned again, to reveal more or less the colours we see today. At an exhibition of restored icons held in Moscow in 1920 the Trinity and the Vladimir Mother of God were united for the first time in what one writer later described as 'a world of ancient beauty' liberated by Soviet power.[17] Thereafter, Rublev's career, of which almost nothing was known, and his artistic heritage were reconstructed virtually from scratch.

In general, city guides now started from sites with revolutionary associations such as Lenin's apartments or modern housing and industrial complexes. An evocative example was *A Peasant's Guide to Moscow* (*Putevoditel' krest'ianina po Moskve*), published in 1928 to cater for peasant visitors. The advice was primarily practical – how to get on and off a tram safely, where to buy seeds and tools, how to pay a visit to President Kalinin and other officials – but there was a sight-seeing section that focused on such new landmarks as Lenin's mausoleum, the Lenin institute, and the Museum of the Revolution. The main point of visiting the Kremlin was now to see the places where Lenin worked. The one general reference to churches and 'other historic places' was the assurance that they were fully preserved and maintained by the state.

Such guides hint at a new ideological framework for sights and museums. Soviet citizens were to enjoy better opportunities for seeing and appreciating approved monuments, based on the idea of the fusion of science and accessibility. Artistic and architectural monuments were now the 'property of the people' In 1918 the Tretiakov gallery was nationalised. In the view of Nikolai Mudrogel, a veteran worker in the gallery, Soviet citizens visited their monuments differently from foreigners, who were only interested in icons and rushed through. 'Our Soviet people don't view an exhibition like that. They go round and look seriously, in detail, always with guides.'[18] Increasingly, icons on show were accompanied by 'health warnings'. In 1933 the gallery issued a guide to anti-religious excursions. The 'idealistic-mystic' world view, it stated, was inimical to the proletariat and its struggle with the capitalist world. Icons 'impelled the oppressed masses to reject the class struggle'.[19] At the same time, the radical ideas of the 1920s about creating new futuristic cities gave way to a vision of extending 'bourgeois' refinements to the lives of workers. The architecture of the 1930s made free use of 'aristocratic' Classical idiom for public buildings. The Moscow Metro (itself undoubtedly deserving of monument status) provided workers travelling to their jobs with a palatial (if increasingly overcrowded) environment embellished with columns and friezes, chandeliers and statues. Inhabitants of far-flung regions were encouraged to talk about 'our' Metro, which thus entered the general consciousness.

The Great Fatherland War of 1941–45 brought some adjustments to perceptions of monuments. The 'Bronze Horseman', for example, seemed to share in the dangers, emerging unscathed from the siege of Leningrad. In the words of a 1944 guidebook: 'This most precious artistic treasure of Russia symbolises the immeasurable creative forces which lurk within her, the greatness of a state created by the Russian people and transformed by Peter.'[20] Monuments that perished, such as Peterhof palace, after the war were restored as symbols of resistance and rebirth. Even paintings played their part. Repin's 'Zaporozhians' (1880–91), a historical study of Cossacks, for example, which had the distinction of being one of Stalin's favourite pictures, was declared to be 'truly national' (*narodnaia*) and close and comprehensible to ordinary people. A 1943 pamphlet explored the image of seventeenth-century Cossacks, allegedly defenders of Muscovy's borders, at a time 'when our people with unheard of heroism are resisting the invasion of these New Age barbarians-Fascists'.[21]

In the immediate post-war period the official line reflected, on the one hand, the Soviet Union's confidence in itself as a world power ruling the roost in its own Eastern bloc, on the other, fears about the security risks created by the new configuration of borders and the threat of nuclear war. Comments on Vasnetsov's 'Epic Warriors' reflect both these attitudes. As one writer declared, despite the fact that the work was created in a 'period of reaction', when the people of autocratic Russia were without rights and subjected to intolerable oppression, Vasnetsov 'saw the slumbering gigantic strength of the Russian people and believed that in the not too distant future it would awaken and display itself in all its *bogatyr*-like power'.[22] The Soviet armed forces, 'fighting for peace in all the world and vigilantly guarding the borders of our Motherland especially cherish these images of the defenders of the Russian land, just keepers of the people's peace.'[23]

Optimism became more marked with the onset of the Soviet space programme – the launch of Sputnik in 1957, in 1961 the first man in space (Iurii Gagarin) – which itself generated new landmarks such as 'Conquest of the Cosmos' near the Exhibition of Economic Achievements in Moscow. It is no coincidence that the supposed 600th anniversary of Andrei Rublev's birth in 1960 was marked in particularly upbeat fashion. Dozens of writers produced anniversary tributes, infused with the belief that Rublev's icons, particularly the Trinity, were 'deeply national' and 'true to deep national artistic traditions', proof that Russian medieval painters did not lag behind their European contemporaries.

We can consider subsequent recent changes in the concept of monuments in the context of a more detailed exploration of some emblematic monuments. Perhaps nothing is so widely perceived as epitomizing 'Russianness' as the church generally known as St Basil's cathedral on Red Square in Moscow (fig. 10.6). Built in 1555–61 and officially dedicated to the Protective Veil (*Pokrov*) of the Mother of God, it commemorates Tsar Ivan IV's conquest of the Tatar stronghold of Kazan in 1552. Its popular name marks the fact that in 1588 a separate chapel was added to house the tomb of St Basil (Vasilii) the Blessed, a holy 'fool in Christ'. Basil roamed around Moscow half-naked, dressed in rags and heavy chains, and was famous for his prophecies. The chapel dedicated to him may have been an architectural afterthought, but the name took over in popular parlance and partly obscured the original purpose of the church, creating a tension between official and popular ideas of national piety. The original nine-chapel cathedral (each chapel with its own altar and capped with its own cupola) was a text to be read as a guide to Russia's place in universal history after the fall of Constantinople. The central chapel is dedicated to the feast of the Protective Veil, 1 October being the date of the final assault by Ivan's armies on Kazan. Other chapels commemorate saints' days associated with key stages in the siege, while the western entrance chapel of the Entry of Christ into Jerusalem commemorates Ivan IV's triumphant return to Moscow from Kazan. The parallels between Ivan's progress and Christ's were strengthened by the Palm Sunday ritual on Red Square first described by Anthony Jenkinson in 1558, in which tsar and patriarch re-enacted the entry into Jerusalem. The cathedral can

10.6 'St Basil's' Cathedral [Church of the Intercession of the Veil], Moscow, Red Square: first-day cover in the 'Monuments of History' series, 1989

also be analysed as part of a sacred landscape in which the whole of Red Square is seen as a church, with the cathedral as its sanctuary.

This medieval symbolic landscape became outmoded after Peter the Great relocated Russia in world time. St Basil's now evoked an image of a Russia that the Westernised elite no longer recognised or understood, and even found offensive. Not only its architecture – a mix of 'Asiatic' and 'Gothic' in the view of some writers – but also its historical associations made it distasteful to Enlightenment thinking. Holy fools were no longer in vogue, while some of the legends associated with the cathedral suggest barbarism. In a famous tale, Ivan IV asks the architect whether he is capable of building anything better; when he replies in the affirmative, the Terrible tsar has him blinded, literally the antithesis of Enlightenment.

In the 1770s–80s Catherine II, who had a taste for the Gothic, funded a programme of renovation, but no other Russian ruler took an interest. When in England in 1814, Alexander I was shown an earlier picture of the cathedral without the mass of outbuildings that had sprung up around it, he apparently did not recognise it and said 'I'd like to have one like that in Moscow.'[24] Despite enhancing its credentials as a national monument by being threatened with destruction by Napoleon (who thought it was a mosque), St Basil's remained out of keeping with Russia's preferred self-image, a very visible reminder that Russia was not quite European, but at the same time suggestive of some hard-to-define creative force. In the 1830s, one writer reflected on the problems of fitting the church into any known architectural style 'It may serve as an example of Russian architecture, which does not have the perfection of Gothic as building art . . . but underlying it there is a certain poetic glimmer of a people emerging from a state of barbarism and beginning to sense their individuality.'[25]

St Basil's was famous from the outside, featuring in many of the postcards that were sold from the 1890s onwards, but probably few people entered its cramped interior. The impression that it was neglected is confirmed by the heartfelt appeal of the architect V. V. Suslov in a pamphlet published in 1912. There were cracks throughout, damp and rot, a basement filled with rubbish, and poorly maintained stoves in the belfry, which constituted a fire risk. 'It was painful to see all this unsightliness and the state of ruin into which this priceless historic building has fallen.' Dismissing ill-informed theories about the church's origins, that it was, for example, Indian, Suslov summed up its significance. It was, he wrote, a profoundly holy object of the Russian people, a historical monument to a great victory; and a fine example of national (*narodnyi*) art. It was 'an original (*svoeobraznyi*) monument of Russian life, combining within itself all the features of religious, everyday and political self-identity of the country.' Suslov concluded with an impassioned outburst against the indifference that seemed at odds with official promotion of historic monuments.

Where is the self-awareness of Russian society which now exhorts us to partake of all that is national? Where is the faith in the firm structure of Russian life when the most vivid traces of that structure are treated with criminal neglect? . . . We cannot be true citizens of our fatherland until we truly value our ancestral heritage.[26]

In the Soviet era St Basil's remained a sort of touchstone for attitudes towards national culture. On the one hand, certain revolutionaries and some avant-garde artists wished to wipe the slate clean. Several radical architects advocated demolishing everything older than ten years, including the entire Kremlin. In the words of the writer Sergei Tretiakov (1892–1939):

> All for combat
> Force is best.
> A bullet in the brain
> of Basil the Blest
> Smash all the icons
> And the signs They have made.
> Explode the Iverskaia
> With a hand grenade.[27]

But party leaders, inspired by Lenin, generally wished to 'preserve the best of bourgeois culture'. After suffering some shell damage during the resistance to the Bolsheviks in Moscow in 1918, the cathedral was saved by being one of the first monuments of 'national and world significance' to be placed under state protection. It opened as a 'culture-historical museum' in May 1923. In Konstantin Iuon's (1875–1958) painting 'Red Army Parade' (1924) the ancient cathedral is integrated with symbols of the new era, including marching troops, revolutionary banners and an airship. St Basil's survival required its reinterpretation as a monument of secular culture and 'Heritage', as well as a monument to Ivan IV, one of Stalin's few heroes from the Russian past. There are various stories about Stalin's attitude towards the cathedral, some that he wished to demolish it to make more room for bigger military parades, others that he saved it. One features a Politburo meeting to discuss the reconstruction of Red Square. On the plan the maquette of St Basil's was deliberately made detachable. At one point in the discussion, one of the Politburo members, Lazar Kaganovich, surreptitiously removed it from the board. 'Leave it where it is!' growled Stalin.[28] Whatever the case, the cathedral survived to become one of the USSR's main attractions when the country began to open up to foreign tourists in the 1970s.

In post-Soviet Russia, like many such monuments, St Basil's is the subject of a battle between the secular and religious authorities, between commercial and spiritual interests. 'For the Orthodox heart a church is not a tourist site but a holy place,' writes the author of an article in the nationalist press. 'It is our spiritual treasure and it was given to us, the Orthodox, by God, as a house of prayer, as a memorial to the dead, as a memorial to glorious days for all the Christian world and our faith.'[29] In contrast, for Russia's new business enterprises it represents the best in 'consumable Russianness', sometimes quite literally, being a favourite motif for sweet boxes and chocolate bars (fig. 10.7). It remains an immediately recognisable logo even to foreigners. As an English guidebook puts it: 'foreigners have always seen it as a cryptic clue to the mysterious Russian soul.'[30] If for foreigners the 'Russian soul' is associated with alterity, 'otherness', then you can't get much more 'other' than St Basil's, with its vivid colours, onion domes, irregular silhouette, and somewhat sinister labyrinthine interior. Most foreign guidebooks to Moscow choose it for their front covers and it can also add instant Russianness to anything from the dust jackets of spy thrillers to film sets. Even guides to St Petersburg tend to illustrate its lookalike, the nineteenth-century Church on the Spilled Blood, rather than St Petersburg's much more characteristic but Western-looking Neo-Classical landmarks. Tourists crave the buzz of differentness, which St Basil's

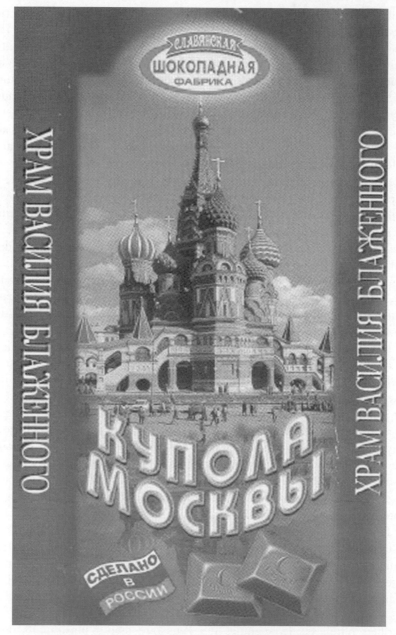

10.7 'St Basil's' Cathedral: 'Cupolas of Moscow' chocolate wrapper, c. 2000

delivers in large doses. It continues to be the photographic backdrop to prove you have been to Russia, as numerous snapshots on web pages attest.

St Basil's, it seems, constantly adapts to the changing times, but our next monument has proved less flexible. Judging by recent visits, virtually no one nowadays goes to have their picture taken in front of the monumental sculpture 'Worker and Collective Farm Woman' (*Rabochii i kolkhoznitsa*) by Vera Mukhina (1889–1953). Probably the best-known piece of Soviet art in the world, it was designed for the Soviet Pavilion at the 1937 Paris Exhibition (fig. 10.8). Rising above the neighbouring exhibits in the heart of the old world, against the background of the Eiffel tower, the pavilion embodied Soviet achievements. Rivalry between the two worlds was of the essence; Mukhina noted that the Statue of Liberty in New York took eleven years to build, as opposed to six months for her sculpture. Its construction – nine tons of steel to create its 24.5 metres, twenty-eight wagons to transport it to Paris – was achieved by high-grade 'shock'-working or, as Mukhina herself wrote, 'Miraculous Soviet pride made people work three or four shifts on end, to work in a blizzard, on ice-covered scaffolding.' She explained that she had tried to give her figures 'that cheerful and powerful impetus that characterises our country'. She did not have to invent the pair: such young people were all around her, bold and confident in their task and of their victory.[31]

Back in Moscow the statue was set up by one of the entrances to the All-Union Agricultural Exhibition, later renamed the Exhibition of Economic Achievements (VDNKh). It was reproduced in more media than any other work of art of the Soviet era, as 'the most vivid achievement of Socialist Realism in our figurative arts'.[32] From 1947 it provided the opening image for movies made by Mosfilm studios. Mukhina, like Andrei Rublev, was elevated into the canon of Great World Artists. The Grand Hall of the Shtiglits Museum in St Petersburg, for example, has a frieze installed in the 1950s, in which Mukhina's relief portrait sits alongside plaques to sculptors of world renown such as Michelangelo and Donatello.

In the late Soviet period the monument began to fall from favour. There was some talk about putting it on a more suitable plinth, but nothing was done. In December 1988, the paper *Sovetskaia kul'tura* printed a letter bewailing its 'catastrophic' condition. By the late 1990s it was isolated next to a car park behind a broken-down fence. Approaching it from inside VDNKh, one had the impression of a new civilisation installing itself in the ruins of another which was dead and gone, except for its inscriptions and emblems. Words from the old Soviet national anthem inscribed the base of the central dome of a pavilion, now home to TV and computer sales. The

10.8 Vera Mukhina, 'Worker and Collective Farm Woman': Soviet Pavilion at 1937
exhibition in Paris (with thanks to Prof. E. B. Mozgovaia)

gold fountains of female national types and heroic workers and peasants on pediments seemed as distant and archaic as the statues of Egyptian gods and Mukhina's sculpture, viewed from the small north gate of the exhibition, like some relic of a dead Pharaoh. And yet, despite the dire predictions, the statue is still standing. As an example of Soviet 'kitsch' it continues to provide material for advertising. Indeed, the appropriation of the image by companies dealing in cars, financial services, vodka, beer, and cigarettes prompted Mukhina's son to launch a law suit. At the time of writing there is talk of the statue finally being moved to a more central location and raised on a higher pedestal, although the context in which it may be presented remains uncertain.

How will our other monuments fare in the future? Perhaps there is no cause for concern, for Heritage and 'Consumable Russianness' are making themselves felt in new guises. The Tretiakov Gallery, for example, offers a catalogue of prints for framing, drawing customers' attention to a 'collection of reproductions of pictures from our own collection of painting and graphics. We share with you a small part of our common property. We hope that our reproductions will adorn your interiors, last for a long time and give you pleasure.'[33] With the proliferation of modern retail outlets in major Russian cities, Western-style notions of exercising choice about interior design and of art predominantly as adornment of private space have taken over from attitudes shaped by shortages and fear of standing out from the crowd. Auction houses such as Christies and Sothebys in London report a strong demand among Russian clients for such artists as Boris Kustodiev (1878–1927), who specialized in colourful urban scenes, crowds milling around stalls groaning with produce, and waiters pouring tea from cheerful crockery adorned with floral motifs. In advertising, Russian Heritage has been utilised to challenge the domination of the market by Western brand names. Thus 'Peter the Great' cigarettes vie with Marlborough and 'Cupolas of Moscow' and 'Streltsy' chocolate with Snickers and Cadburys. You can eat 'Boyar' frozen food from packaging imprinted with cartoon-like magnates in seventeenth-century costume and Russian ham adorned, incongruously, with the domes of the Dormition cathedral, washed down with 'Epic Warriors' tea. Russia patriotic consumerism is apparently intended as much for the home market as for tourists. Other new forces are at work based on Western marketing practices, including making good-quality postcards and souvenirs available at relevant outlets. In the Soviet period such stalls often contained nothing related to the monument in question.

An intriguing example of the new commercialisation of monuments is the Moscow Cathedral of Christ the Saviour. In its first incarnation

10.9 Cathedral of Christ the Saviour, Moscow, 1839–83: early 20th-century postcard

it commemorated the patriotic resistance to Napoleon in 1812. It took forty-four years (1839–83) to build and dominated the Moscow skyline for fifty more (fig. 10.9), but disappeared in just a few minutes when the Communists blew it up in 1931 to make way for a replacement to celebrate the new order, the Palace of Soviets. To quote from a 1937 article: 'This task is indeed great and honourable: to build a monument to last for many hundreds of years to the greatest genius of mankind Vladimir Ilich Lenin, a monument to the Stalin epoch of victorious socialism.'[34] But the Palace was never built and for decades a swimming pool marked the spot. In 1997–2000 the cathedral was restored in replica as a monument to the values of yet another new order (fig. 10.10), President Eltsin's epoch of victorious capitalism and to the revived fortunes of the Russian Orthodox Church.

The cathedral has become a focal point for discussions of Heritage and how best to create new or revive old national symbols to replace the discredited Soviet versions. It remains unpopular with many Muscovites. Curators and consultants working in older, 'genuine' monuments such as St Basil's regard the restored cathedral as a modern 'fake' which soaks up funds that their monuments desperately need. Non-believers regard it as a grotesque attempt to shove religion down people's throats. As the Saviour Above the Garage (a pastiche of a traditional-sounding name for a church), it has been

10.10 Cathedral of Christ the Saviour, Moscow: view of the reconstructed cathedral, 2001

the butt of countless jokes. The gift shop is one of the best in Moscow, offering models in a variety of materials, T-shirts, cardboard construction kits, and 'Christ the Saviour' exercise books. Some observers believe it was more effective when it was invisible, a 'church-martyr' which symbolised the Stalinist disregard for everything.

Meanwhile, not far away in the church of St Nicholas next to the Tretiakov gallery, the icon of the Vladimir Mother of God now resides to the left of the iconostasis in a purpose-built free-standing wooden case with glass on both sides to reveal the previously hidden reverse of the icon. A steady stream of worshippers pray in front of it. The parish priest explained that in the past decade the icon was removed from its regular place in the icon galleries two or three times a year for festivals, but its fragile condition made this inadvisable, so it was brought into the museum church (*khram-muzei*), where proper atmospheric conditions are maintained. It continues to be labelled like an exhibit, with a caption stating that 'the greatest miracle' is the fact that since 1930 the icon has always remained accessible and visible to the public. At the time of writing, Rublev's Trinity remained inside the gallery, where people nevertheless pray in front of it. As one curator admitted, having 'sacrificed' the Vladimir icon, they do not want the Trinity to go to the church, where, they fear, it will quickly deteriorate.

'Pushkin' and identity

Stephanie Sandler

The love for Pushkin, which is incomprehensible to foreigners, is the true sign of a person born of Russian culture. You can like or dislike any other Russian writer, that's a matter of taste. But Pushkin as a phenomenon is obligatory for us. Pushkin is the pivot on which Russian culture turns, he connects the past to the future. Take away the pivot and the connections will disintegrate.[1]

Lidiia Ginzburg

Jubilee Pushkiniana, 1999: vodka bottle, tea cosy, tea cup, plastic shopping bag, wall hanging, book mark, calendar, quill, key ring, pin, playing cards, candy wrapper, advertisements.[2]

1. THE PUSHKIN MYTH

More than two hundred years after his birth, Aleksandr Pushkin (1799–1837) stands as a towering emblem of Russian culture, as more than just a monument: the example of his life and work is perceived as giving meaning to the nation's identity. This myth was articulated well by the conservative critic Stanislav Rassadin: 'we who seem to have lost everything there is to lose – above all, ourselves as a nation and as a people – we possess a hope of remembering our face and suddenly repossessing our soul *when we look at Pushkin*'.[3] When Russians 'look at Pushkin' in this sense, they see all that they hope to be: a symbol of integrity, creativity, and spiritual values, and a dynamic, liberating mind that challenges what seems stultifying or intolerant elsewhere in their culture. Rassadin, a supporter of national ambitions that inform his language of nostalgia and fervent affection, reminds his readers that he speaks from a historical moment of disarray (the early 1990s), but his hopes for Russia are meant to be timeless. Pushkin lives as if outside of time, and contemplating him offers the possibility of reacquiring a soul, itself a timeless notion of identity and spirit.

Pushkin's place in the culture was described differently by a contemporary St Petersburg poet, Elena Shvarts, who speaks from a more marginal cultural position (she was an underground writer in the Soviet period). Writing at about the same time as Rassadin, the early 1990s, she focuses on death, not life, and on myth-making, rather than national self-understanding: 'To a certain extent all poets are mythological figures. There is nothing real about Pushkin or Baratynskii.[4] The real person dies and the myth is all that's left.' She adds, 'the greater the poet, the more inescapable the myth.'[5] Shvarts also puts Pushkin outside any specific temporal frame, because of cultural processes that cross over time's boundaries. She suggests a new question: how a myth comes into being. She sees the poet as trapped by the processes of mythmaking and, unlike Rassadin, she does not celebrate its benefits for ordinary Russians. What matters is how the moment when 'the real person dies' figures in the poet's 'inescapable myth'. The myth is as inescapable as human mortality, and it makes Pushkin a mortal man, rather than the god-like figure imagined by Rassadin. Myth begins where life ends, so, for her, the Pushkin myth draws its energy from the premise of his death.

Pushkin's death has held the attention of every generation since 1837, the year of his fatal duel. Death, 'the most meaningful event in his biography',[6] centres Russia's myth of a national poet. Pushkin lives, but he thrives beyond a death that Russians have loved to contemplate. He *became* Pushkin only when he died in a duel, and those who believe that 'Pushkin Lives!' have never stopped exploring the circumstances and symbolic meanings of his death. He has been imagined as both alive and dead, one state sustaining the other; he is animated into a present that mourns his absence.

Who actually built Pushkin's legacy? This is another way to ask who has imagined Russian identity through the Pushkin story. Shvarts implies that this work occurs inevitably, and as if anonymously. For Rassadin, the viewer, the reader, and the museum visitor make the myth: every Russian who sees into his or her soul by means of contemplating Pushkin renews the myth. The divergence between Shvarts's and Rassadin's points of view here has its own history, suggesting for Pushkin two identities. The first, Pushkin as the founder of a culture, takes him as a praiseworthy public figure, as someone whose achievements can be studied; the second, Pushkin as the cherished object of affection, brings closer contact with him. It is personal, even intimate. It permits identification and self-exploration, whereas tributes to his cultural primacy come not from *individuals* but from *Russia*, undifferentiated and united in the ways symbolic nations always are.

The dispute over 'my' vs. 'our' Pushkin has existed since he was first mourned; at times polemics have grown out of one side's outrage at the attitudes of the other, but the two sides have also often co-existed. Pushkin has maintained his hold on Russia's cultural imagination because he has seemed 'our' Pushkin as well as 'my' Pushkin. For Rassadin, he is largely a shared symbol, yet individuals can contemplate the poet's meanings with private reverence. Shvarts, too, works from the premise of a public figure, one who is made into a myth, yet, like some in the dissident camps of the Russian intelligentsia, she implies that only an individual's view of the poet is legitimate.

Often this idiosyncratic appropriation of the poet has been expressed as a form of love. The poet Fedor Tiutchev (1803–73) wrote 'Like a first love, / The heart of Russia will not forget you'.[7] Pushkin created modern Russian culture not because he gave things their names, like some Slavic Adam, but because he himself remains the poet Russians most love to contemplate. His writings and the quickly emergent legends about his life enabled others to write, paint, sculpt, film, and dramatise ideas that had great powers of national definition. His individual, specific traits have assumed larger-than-life significance, but he is also the symbol of the poet; he stands in the minds of Russians for all that poetry is meant to be.

In the language of psychoanalysis, as rephrased by Adam Phillips: the figure of the poet is 'a highly valued internal object, and one who is often linked . . . with fantasies of freedom and independence: the poet represents the apotheosis (at least for some people) of self-becoming, of individuality, of difference wrought to a distinctive pitch through style.'[8] A number of different individuals may occupy this symbolic pride of place in a given culture, but Pushkin, as noted by Lidiia Ginzburg in the epigraph given above, is obligatory. That obligation translates into an intense emotional investment that accompanies any glance in his direction. Love has many complexities: it can involve anger, possessiveness, poor judgement, and projection. A first love is often the source of embarrassment and error. Through the decades, love for Pushkin has been tempered by irritation, disputatiousness, and a desire for distance. From every side, Pushkin and his writings have been passionately possessed, and they have become vehicles for ardent self-expression and determined argumentation. These emotional, individual responses to Pushkin have contributed to larger cultural debates about what it means to be Russian, what role the poet is fated to play in the drama of national self-definition, and how all who live after Pushkin's death can comprehend themselves as Russians through and against his experience.

This process continues in Russia today, where essays dispute the political implications of reading him as uniquely Russian, quarrel about the religious meanings of his poems, and put forth differing versions of why he still matters for Russian culture in these days of chaotic change. No story has offered the promise of greater national coherence than has Pushkin's, and the allure of some remnant of shared national self-definition propels many ongoing disputes and dialogues.

The prestigious status of Pushkin's story in Russian culture invites one to think of it as a myth. That term is worth clarifying, as it names several things. First, myths as we know them from ancient cultures are explanatory narratives, tales that tell us how the world has come to be, how nature's forces change, or how human actions are ordained by the gods. Myths point to origins, offering us explanations of how something came into existence. The Pushkin story is a myth in this sense – a narrative in which modern Russia sees signs of its own beginnings. For example, he is taken as the first modern Russian writer because he worked in a European and not purely Russian context, and because he was a professional writer trying to earn his livelihood through his work. These aspects of his experience become symbolic stages in the culture's emergence into modernity.

Mythic origins are also sacred origins, a fact not diminished by narratives about secular and national beginnings. Anthropologists have noted that modern cultures create '"mythical" beings' who are 'excluded from everyday life and relegated to the vague and frightening zone where everything that was an object of religious belief was assumed to belong'.[9] Legends of gods and heroes who inhabit this other zone can play powerful roles in the cultural attitudes of modern people: attitudes, preferences, and appropriate forms of behaviour may be modelled on them. Since 1837 Pushkin has inhabited this special zone for Russians, but it is difficult to assess how much this placement depended on his own piety, Orthodoxy or sense of spiritual quest. Particularly in the 1990s (reprising more harshly a concern from a century earlier), arguments over the broad question of Pushkin and Christianity raged, a symptom of the culture's larger anxiety about how to reclaim its own traditions of Orthodoxy in the post-Soviet era.[10]

Myths in the modern world also suggest a third meaning: explanatory systems that are false. A myth can be an erroneous belief, perhaps widely shared but also strengthened by official ideologies. This aspect of the Pushkin story complicates the simpler elevation of him to quasi-divine status, since false stories about him and his work have flourished. At times a Pushkin cult has perniciously distorted his reputation. The boundaries separating false from true are not always well defined, however, and false stories have long challenged dedicated readers to re-establish the truth. The fear of a pervasive false image has kept alive a passion for the 'real' Pushkin, always just beyond reach. Which aspects of the Pushkin story are worth fighting over changes: for some the central questions are political, for others religious, and for still others as mundane as the question of whether Pushkin loved his wife, slept with his sister-in-law, and fathered a child by one of his serfs.

Some aspects of the Pushkin myth can, then, be named, for they have recurred across the decades since his death, subject to repetition, resistance, and revision. The first element is that Pushkin was a beacon amid the seeming morass of Russian history, a spot of light and clarity that promises to illuminate the future as well as the past. Russian expressions of self-consciousness have often turned on an image of shared national tragedy and apocalyptic rhetoric. When Russia's influential writers, poets, and philosophers take up the task of defining their nation, they speak in tones of prophecy and lament, concentrating on Russia's history of destruction and loss. Against this tragic national self-image, some (including Rassadin, quoted earlier) say that Pushkin has offered Russians hope. His role has been restorative, palliative, and spiritually enriching.

Yet for every Russian who beams happily at the thought that Pushkin once lived and wrote, another finds in him the very national tragedy he is imagined as curing. Tragic tales of Pushkin abound. Many of them focus on Pushkin's death, an event through which Russians proclaim themselves unified in grief. Some of his writings have seemed retrospectively to speak to these themes. Fedor Dostoevskii made excellent use of Pushkin's Romantic narrative *The Gypsies* (*Tsygany*, 1824) and his lyric poem 'The Prophet' (*Prorok*; 1826) in his influential speech in 1880 at the dedication of Pushkin's statue in Moscow; others have found tragic notes in Pushkin's historical writings, including his problematic and brilliant play *Boris Godunov* (1825) and his late tale *The Captain's Daughter* (*Kapitanskaia dochka*; 1836). The variety within Pushkin's *oeuvre* has meant that serious or agitated writing could always be balanced by what the scholar Victor Erlich called Pushkin's 'sacred play', just as those who sought political justifications for their admiration for Pushkin could point to one set of poems and stories whereas others interested in aesthetic complexity could insist on the importance of another.[11]

In addition to these quite different views of Pushkin's place within Russia's tragic self-definition, there is a third position, distinguished by its rejection of the tragedy altogether. It was well expressed in the work of the Tartu scholar Iurii Lotman (1922–93), who lauded Pushkin's brilliant adaptation to repressive social mechanisms. For him, Pushkin's life and work are tightly bound to one another, each dense in self-expression and interpretable meaning. Lotman and others after him have also seen how the myths of Pushkin have paradoxically repeated some of the very repression Pushkin fought. An early almanac for an avant-garde poetry movement, *Latin Quarter* (*Latinskii kvartal*; 1990), had as its cover photograph a picture of a Pushkin monument encased in scaffolding (fig. 11.1); this irreverent image created a literalising parody of the then pervasive political term 'restructuring' (*perestroika*), yet contributors to *Latin Quarter* presented themselves as reinventing Russian culture. As poets, they would rescue Pushkin from the confining structures of scaffolding and thus liberate Russian culture for future glory.

This variety of responses to a Pushkin myth begins to answer the question of why *Pushkin* became Russia's national poet. The timing was also vitally important: Pushkin appeared at that moment early in the nineteenth century when post-Napoleonic Romantic nationalism made nations search for a native genius. The only other writer and poet who might then have fitted the bill was Pushkin's slightly younger and even shorter-lived contemporary Mikhail Lermontov (1814–41). However, Pushkin's having written with authority and clarity in every genre, and his having died in a duel marked by romantic intrigue, rather than the all-male dispute of Lermontov's duel, helped him become the more appealing figure. Pushkin's death was itself a poetic subject that catapulted the young Lermontov to fame when he wrote a widely circulated poem on the subject, 'The Death of the Poet' (*Smert' poeta*; 1837).

The circumstances of Pushkin's death were especially conducive to the mythmaking process. Contemporaries saw his death as a time of coming together, and their belief in a national reaction to tragedy became a foundational moment in myths of Pushkin. Nicholas I's government recognized the magnitude and danger of the response at once: Pushkin's body was wheeled out of Petersburg in the dark of night to be buried at the distant Sviatogorsk Monastery near Pushkin's family estate at Mikhailovskoe. The absence of the body enabled an especially spiritual aspect of the Pushkin myth, although his meagre property was treated with a reverence that belies any absolute denial of the material. The relics of his life include his library, sanctified by Pushkin's gesture of farewell to his books as he was dying, as well as the expected paraphernalia of death that can still be seen in Russian museums: death masks, the waistcoat with its bullet hole, the duelling pistols, the divan on which he lay.

The removal of Pushkin's body was brought about by political considerations (the Tsar's informers claimed that the crowds would get out of hand, and the very idea of such attention being paid a mere writer, and one whom they also found politically untrustworthy, was not to be borne), and then the death itself came to seem politically meaningful. Pushkin had

ЛАТИНСКИЙ
КВАРТАЛ

11.1 Cover photograph for the poetry almanac *Latin Quarter* (*Latinskii kvartal*), 1990.
Courtesy of the editor, Victor Kulle

died from a duel motivated by a gentleman's sense of family honour, but the intervention of the Tsar into funeral arrangements reminded friends that he might have prevented the duel altogether. Lermontov's widely circulated poem blamed Russian high society. Particularly when compared to other elegies on Pushkin's death, Lermontov's offers a vividly disembodied poem, and it initiated the politics of Pushkin as state martyr in a way that required this negation of the body. One hundred years later, when Stalin urged Russians to celebrate the anniversary of Pushkin's death, the 1937 Pushkin Jubilee engaged the rhetoric of martyrdom fiercely and coincided with the height of Stalin's purges.

Monuments to Pushkin have often been erected during anniversary celebrations, including those of 1937 and 1949. They act as what Pierre Nora has called 'lieux de mémoire', his name for sites, events, and artifacts that keep alive an otherwise fragile memory. Nora aptly calls them the markers of 'commemorative vigilance'.[12] Pushkin monuments have proliferated, repeating a small number of iconographic poses to fix images of the poet declaiming his verse, relaxing on a park bench, or standing contemplatively, head bowed. The monuments' stillness and similarity suggest a static, rather than dynamic Pushkin, which is ironic: erecting a monument to a private person in 1880 was actually quite a daring thing to do in a nation that previously so honoured only autocrats and generals. But the monuments are consonant with a disembodied version of the Pushkin myth where there is no place for stories and legends of the poet that suggest bodily energy, erotic inventiveness, transgressive desire, and physical difference. This myth long shaped the inherited canon of Pushkin's writings, expurgating letters and lyrics and keeping obscene texts, like *Gavriliad* (*Gavriliada*; 1821), almost entirely out of the hands of readers.[13] But like all myths these, too, have generated resistance. Opponents include the poets Vladimir Maiakovskii (1893–1930) and Marina Tsvetaeva (1892–1941), and the creators of popular legend and endless anecdotes. Perhaps the best example of the anecdotal rejection of Pushkin as a monument comes in the expression that asks 'Who's going to do that? Pushkin?' In this rhetorical expression, the verb is endlessly replaceable by activities of daily life – sweeping, mending, laundering. Another almanac cover from the *perestroika* period brought this expression to life with its picture of Pushkin innocently holding a broom, ready to sweep (fig. 11.2). The wish to bring Pushkin down from his monument reacted against mindless elevations of him in official discourse, at the same time as it reinvigorated and renewed affection for him, keeping his image alive before a changing public.

11.2 Cover illustration for the almanac *Citizens of the Night* (*Grazhdane nochi*), 1990

A vivid sense of the range of Pushkin's public image emerges when we examine some of the best-known clichés about him. He was a 'radiant name' (*svetloe imia*) from the beginning, a 'happy name' and the 'sun of Russian poetry'. These names share metaphorical references to light and to gaiety, and they reflect great optimism. The light-filled aura of Pushkinian presence has him illuminating Russia as the sun lights the earth, but it also lends impermanence and fragility to his image: Pushkin's death was described as the setting of the sun as early as 1837,[14] and the metaphor later informed an essay by the modernist poet Osip Mandelshtam (1891–1938) that evoked 'the poet's sun-filled body', and placed the sun 'in its coffin at night'.[15] Mandelshtam's 'night sun' reminds us of the tragedy hidden in the bright light of official cheer (and refers to the dark time when Mandelshtam lived).

In the early Soviet period, another cliché about Pushkin began to seem more appropriate, 'Pushkin is our everything' (*Pushkin – eto nashe vse*).[16] This emphasis on unity suggests a gigantic vessel able to contain any experience shared by Russians. The word *our* is also important, emphasising that Pushkin absorbed fully Russia's being, its spirituality. 'Pushkin is our everything' implies a levelling in which all of the experiences that could be drawn into the vessel *Pushkin* have equal value and equal meaning. Its claim lifts Pushkin out of history into an absolute realm where heroes do not change and where nations are defined by their heroes. The association of Pushkin with light is ahistorical because of its grounding in the world of nature, but the association of Pushkin with 'everything' goes further, obliterating distinctions like nature vs. culture, past vs. present. It contemplates him in an emotional rather than rational way, demonstrating by its own extravagance that attitudes toward Pushkin properly exist in the superlative.

These verbal formulae exemplify a shared perception of Pushkin as light-filled and clear, as capacious and profoundly Russian. Through them, Pushkin becomes as inevitable as sunshine, as all-encompassing as the world around us. The clichés concentrate a number of the implicit myths of Pushkin: the national poet whose brilliant achievements demonstrate the greatness of the nation that produced him; the protean writer in whom successive generations of Russians saw themselves (and their political or aesthetic agendas); the martyred artist whose early death helped a nation understand its own tragic fate and showed the ruthless power of an indifferent state; and the integrity-filled man of genius, an inspiring example to later generations of artists, thinkers, and citizens. Now, over 150 years after Pushkin's death, it is difficult to read any of his texts without this mediating interpretative activity, without these myths.

2. ANNIVERSARIES

As a case study in the workings of the Pushkin myth we can consider the cultural production generated around Pushkin anniversaries, and in particular the celebrations of the bicentennial of his birth. Pushkin has been celebrated in a number of anniversary years – 1880, 1899, 1921, 1924, 1937, 1949, 1987, and the bicentennial in 1999. Nearly all marked 'round' numbers of years from the times of Pushkin's birth or death and they occasioned public rituals of remarkable continuity. They stand in self-conscious relation to one another and their effect is cumulative; amid much repetition, the rituals have changed in response to political and cultural pressures. Anniversary dates are thus abstractly valuable, a narrative device that organises the Pushkin story in Russian culture. They cluster larger numbers of responses to Pushkin in a single day or month, urging writers, thinkers, and public figures to note their attitudes and reflections on particular texts. These statements and images in turn drive a more generally intensified attention to Pushkin among the larger population. The anniversary appears not to be an artificial occasion – its timing is determined by a fateful repetition, the day or year when something important happened 50 or 100 or 150 years ago. Yet there is rich artifice in any anniversary celebration, particularly in the elaborately coordinated events of the twentieth century. This paradox of a natural, powerful love for the poet made manifest in a centrally organised celebration is itself a constituent feature of the Pushkin myth in Russia.

The most complex and influential celebration in the twentieth century was in 1937, with its centralized control of jubilation against a background of terror. It is also the best test case against an either/or theory which would see official celebrations as false, unworthy of those who 'truly' love Pushkin: even in 1937, remarkable individuals participated and important new views of Pushkin emerged. No imposition of a mandated approach to Pushkin could ever be wholly successful, and each anniversary shows interesting fractures of belief and commitment. Commemorations typically include a great range of events, and within this broad diversity one finds unexpected signs of Pushkin's enduring capacity to help Russia invent itself over time. In 1937, as in 1999, a transitional society used public rituals for the purposes of cultural exploration and stabilisation.

In 1999, the commemoration was meant to demonstrate that the new Russia could function as a governing state, to put it simply. Its celebration was a financial as much as an ideological triumph, against great odds. Moscow spent some four million dollars. Another five million was allocated for restoring the three Pushkin museums in the Pskov region. Money, lots of it, became the measure of respect for Pushkin in the bicentennial of his birth. One recipient of a Pushkin medal hoped (in vain) that he would receive a cash award.[17] Despite worries that the crumbling Russian economy would never support a sufficiently lavish celebration, it was quickly obvious that Pushkin, having survived the Stalin Terror in the 1937 Jubilee, would do fine in the era of financial default.[18] His image was put to good commercial use, resulting in memorable advertising campaigns: 'Pushkin knew how to put words together into a poem. We know how to assemble an excellent automobile', promised one company; another did a direct mailing that began 'Dear Muscovites! We congratulate you on the two-hundredth anniversary of the birth of Aleksandr Sergeevich Pushkin! If you want to rent a cottage in the country, please call us.'[19] An exhibit that compared Pushkin and Goethe memorabilia (1999 was also the 250th anniversary of the great German national poet's birth), provoked a splendid riff by the post-modernist poet Lev Rubinshtein on 'Pushkin as an object of kitsch'. He laughed at the symbolism of Pushkin appearing on a vodka label whereas Goethe was used to sell brandy; when he saw Goethe's image on a package of women's stockings, he found it regrettable that Pushkin's name was not put to the same use – after all, Pushkin had famously celebrated women's legs in *Eugene Onegin*.[20]

Russian commentaries predictably found the commercialization of their national poet and the show-business atmosphere tremendously off-putting. There was much condemnation of supposedly wrong-headed books or films or exhibits. The critic Valentin Nepomniashchii took on the English film *Eugene Onegin* (directed by Martha Fiennes) but mostly to air his somewhat stale ideas on Western vs. Russian art, a grand gesture very much in the Jubilee tradition.[21] Some critics praised the Jubilee as spiritually purifying; they found public complaints about vulgar events to be a sign that the masses retained their instinctive tact and good taste.[22] Most publications implied that past commemorations had been better in all senses and had been more significant in shaping attitudes toward Pushkin. The Kultura television station aired a new documentary, *The Bronze Pushkin: Seven Jubilees* (*Mednyi Pushkin: sem' iubileev*), about previous Pushkin jubilees.[23] This nostalgia for past commemorations sweetened the bitter cynicism of some coverage. The prominent Moscow critic and editor Natalia Ivanova fled to St Petersburg, still many Russians' fantasy site for authentic culture, where she was gratified to find an atmosphere of happy celebration: 'surprising as it seems, it all worked'.[24]

What made it work, though, if that is what happened, is that there was a tremendous mix of events, publications, promises, and predictions. The end of censorship meant that almost anything was possible, including a remarkable slew of errors – in the most noted, the nineteenth-century dictum, 'Pushkin is our everything', was attributed to Boris Eltsin (still President of Russia in 1999). More than any earlier celebration, television played a large role in setting the tone, conveying information, and exemplifying modes of celebration. A cameraman for channel ORT stopped people on the streets to recite one line from *Eugene Onegin*, and a stanza was given every night in these different voices and faces. The vast number of responses, much in the tradition of factory workers and farmers reciting Pushkin across the Soviet land, imitated an old idea of democratic 'levelling' and broad access to high culture, but it also suggested in microcosm the variety of voices that could be heard in 1999.

In this atmosphere, the possibility for carnival was vast, and one critic noted that the real motivation for large-scale events was the urge to celebrate something, anything.[25] Various balls were announced for the public squares in Moscow, collectively named 'Love! Russia! Sun! Pushkin!' Sergei Penkin blasted out his rock-and-roll version of an intimate Pushkin lyric ('I loved you'; *Ia Vas liubil*) on Moscow's Manezh Square.[26] Newspapers joined in the foolishness with mockeries of their own. The high-brow newspaper *Ex libris* treated Pushkin as if he were a contemporary writer, with all due disrespect. Several Pushkin texts were reviewed as if just published by the imaginary 'Our Everything' (*Nashe vse*) Press in Moscow, with laments that poor Pushkin had received neither the Booker nor the Anti-Booker prize that year. The issue asked various contemporary writers why they were not the same as Pushkin, and the always outrageous prose writer Eduard Limonov blasted back, 'I don't want to be Pushkin. To be him means to be a poet of calendars, a poet who founds cities, rivers . . . I would not want to be this monument monster.'[27] Another high-profile publication printed a spicy story heard from Semen Geichenko, the staid director of Mikhailovskoe (Pushkin's family estate, now a museum), about a strophe of *Eugene Onegin* that was accidentally used by the poet as toilet paper.[28]

Such irony and irreverence marked a striking departure from Soviet anniversaries. The leading *Literary Gazette* (*Literaturnaia gazeta*) trumpets its direct link to the Pushkinian tradition by printing his famous self-portrait in profile on the front page of every issue, along with a banner announcement that the paper was founded in 1830 with the participation of Pushkin, then 'renewed' in 1929. It had an entire section about the Jubilee in its 6 June 1999 issue, as one might expect, but on the front page of its next issue it had a small boxed epigraph, just under the Pushkin profile, quoting a letter from Pushkin to his wife: 'I am sitting out all these festivities at home.'[29] The most vibrant mix of homage and verbal irreverence may have been the collection *Pushkin's Overcoat* (*Shinel' Pushkina*; 2000), with its brilliant introduction by the cultural critic and literary scholar Andrei Zorin that described Pushkin as the modern incarnation of safe sex for Russia: 'rarified pleasure practically guaranteed without the slightest undesirable consequence.'[30] Zorin concluded that Pushkin's relevance to Russian self-definition had conclusively been proven by the 1999 commemorations: he was an equally appropriate national hero for tsarist, Soviet, and commercially self-obsessed post-Soviet Russia.

New poems to Pushkin, often prominent in earlier commemorations, were less important, as if the genre were almost too *retro* for renewal. Several poetry publications involved a form of recycling. Bella Akhmadulina, well known as a poet who gained prominence in the 1960s, gathered all her writings on Pushkinian themes in *Enclosed in Winter* (*Zimniaia zamknutost'*; 1999), subtitled *An Offering for the Two-Hundredth Anniversary of A. S. Pushkin*, but her volume attracted little attention. More interesting was the older avant-garde poet Genrikh Sapgir's completion of Pushkinian fragments, written in 1985, quietly published in 1992, and made widely available in the journal *The Peoples' Friendship* (*Druzhba narodov*) in May, 1999. Sapgir chose little-known Pushkin poems for completion, although he includes the famous line 'And I could have . . .' that Pushkin wrote above a sketch of gallows in his notebooks, long taken as a contemplation that he might have shared the fate of five hanged Decembrist conspirators in 1826.[31] Sapgir did three poems based on this broken line, keeping the well-known context of the gallows but amplifying it with references to dance, and layering Pushkin's intonation of fear and regret with notes of pride. The three poems subtly increase in possible violence, creating a successful if entirely inadvertent resonance with the violence of daily life in Russia in 1999.

Another republication project was the conceptualist poet Dmitrii Aleksandrovich Prigov's 1992 rewriting of *Eugene Onegin*.[32] It appeared in 1998, a supposed facsimile of the only surviving portion of the project. A preface claimed it was the fruit of Prigov's wish to copy out this 'sacred' text of Russian culture. Prigov also said he was inspired by a late Soviet legend of a mother whose son would only read samizdat literature, so she copied out Tolstoi's *War and Peace* for him on a typewriter. He made *Onegin* his own, changing all epithets to either 'insane' or 'unearthly' (*bezumnyi, nezemnyi*), choices which made the text more Lermontovian, he said.[33] The changes are more interesting than that, however, substituting *bezumnyi* (insane) so often as to render the familiar text truly otherworldly and crazed. In the 1998 edition, illustrations by Aleksandr Favorskii add a quaintly loony touch (the bottom right corner of each page features a line drawing of Pushkin, with top hat and cane, just enough different from one page to the next that, if you flip through the pages quickly, you get the effect of a cartoon image, doffing his hat). Because the tissue-thin 'facsimile' pages are imitations of *samizdat*-era typescript, there is something nostalgic about the entire production, despite its use of clever formatting.

The 1999 anniversary also offered films about Pushkin, some quite innovative. The documentaries were perhaps more interesting than the feature films, but they were sadly ignored. Andrei Khrzhanovskii's two small Pushkin films were screened to a negligible audience at the Sochi film festival and a few other festivals. The short films, each under half an hour, are enigmatic and charming, particularly the second, the nearly wordless *'Let's Fly Away!' (The Pushkin Can Now Take Off)* (*'Davai, uletim! . . .'* (*Pushkinu vzlet razreshen*)). Its title comes from a helicopter sculpture with Pushkin's face as its front window, and from a real helicopter named *The Pushkin*.

'Let's Fly Away!' focuses on an art exhibit that opened in October 1998, featuring thirteen soft and kinetic sculptures created by children. It begins with the Russian flag fluttering in the wind and intercuts many images from the 1999 commemoration: buildings draped with banners showing Pushkin's face or body; shop windows with Pushkin's name or image on boxes of chocolates; shopping bags with *Pushkin 200 Years* imprinted on them; billboards with words like 'passion', 'love', 'beauty' alongside Pushkin's face; and Pushkin rugs, with the selling price visibly marked. As such, the film is an excellent compilation of visual imagery from the Jubilee, and a fine demonstration of how Pushkin was marketed to the new Russia. *'Let's Fly Away!'* preempts the cynical inference that one might draw from the commodification of Pushkin – that his 'image' has lost all value – when it lingers over the sculptures in the children's exhibit, entitled *Pushkin, Again* (a title with its own irony). By showing the process of making the sculptures, Khrzhanovskii indulges his own favourite cinematic moment, showing how art is created. We see the application of lips to face, of red paint to the lips, of extra pieces of tape to hold things together, which means that we see the pleasure and efforts of the young creators as vividly as we see the final product. The editing and camera work de-naturalises the sculptures, using extreme close-ups and rhythmically repeating shots to make the faces grotesque. They are already grotesque in several instances, with disproportionate lips or eyes and garish colours thickly applied. An early sequence has one of the sculptures carried by unseen people through the streets, with a stop-start action that has interesting effects. The film-maker suggests that Pushkin as ghost walks the streets of the city that commemorates his birth. Khrzhanovskii has several Pushkins in this watchful role – the artworks of children, the images on billboard and shop window that look out onto the Moscow scene, and a small Pushkin monument unveiled at the end of his film that looks as if it is made of wax and is also the work of a child. All defamiliarise Pushkin, a remarkable feat in a film that shows how exceedingly familiar his image was in the 1999 celebrations.

Moving the Pushkin sculpture through the Moscow streets almost makes it seem to come alive. The movement is not naturalized: the puppet remains an object, manipulated by film-maker and viewers. The same is true of the art objects in the exhibit *Pushkin, Again*: some can be activated by visitors, for example the chair shaped like Pushkin's body (his arms are the chair's arms). Others have motors, like the helicopter, or internal mechanisms. One mattress-like face invites children to lie on its cheeks, making the face move. An eerily beautiful wire sculpture, seen from several angles, casts its shadow on a wall. But the real suggestion of movement in these images is not just human movement, it is flight. The reality of Pushkin's never having left Russia and his various experiences of limitation are as important as the dynamism, as when images of Pushkin are shown behind the bars of a shop window – the film's first words are Pushkin's 'I am imprisoned behind bars' from 'The Prisoner' (*Uznik*; 1822). How to liberate Pushkin? asks the film. The answer is shamelessly romantic – put him in the hands of children, let the imagery be grotesque and irreverent and loving, let him soar if only in our imaginations.

Somewhat less successful is Pavel Gromov's *Three Songs of Pushkin* (*Tri pesni o Pushkine*; 1999), but it is a valuable film for its historical retrospective and use of documentary footage. Like the Dziga Vertov film from which it takes its title (*Three Songs of Lenin*; *Tri pesni o Lenine*; 1934), *Three Songs of Pushkin* is a compilation, mixing documentary footage from newsreel and other sources to recreate historical moments from a past that seems distant. It is didactic in the extreme, using relentless voice-over to hammer home its message of the lasting evil of Stalin's regime. Its first 'song' interprets the 1937 Jubilee as a terrible celebration in a desperate time. As the film moves forward in time, it tries to do the same with the regimes of Nikita Khrushchev and Leonid Brezhnev from the late 1950s to the early 1980s, but less exclusively, and much of the footage about the 1960s and 1970s shows the young poets who emerged at that time. The film's last 'song' looks at what has been built on the ruins of the past in contemporary Russia. Signs of commercialisation are shown, the most expressive a Pushkin *matrioshka* doll lined up next to one of President Bill Clinton with his saxophone. People on the street are asked about Pushkin, each responding with more clichés than the next. At the film's end, old footage from earlier in the movie is intercut into contemporary street scenes, suggesting that past Pushkins live into the present, which implies, in this film's view, that the Pushkin created in 1937 cannot be displaced.

If you take that image as a residue of violence and autocratic excess, then the one 1999 feature film based on Pushkin's works proves Gromov's point: the epic production of *The Russian Uprising* (*Russkii bunt*), directed by Aleksandr Proshkin. This self-described 'big-budget' film reflects its creation during the disorganised advent of capitalism of the 1990s and it was not released in Russia until the autumn of 2000. The result is hard to watch, an aesthetically confused film more bloody than Pushkin's *The History of Pugachev* (*Istoriia Pugacheva*; 1834) and considerably more romantic than *The Captain's Daughter* (*Kapitanskaia dochka*; 1836), to name the film's two source texts. Like Soviet film adaptations that turned Pushkin's restrained writings into over-the-top spectacles, *The Russian Uprising* has some good acting, and elaborate costumes and sets, but it differs in its treatment of sex and violence.

The violence in the film corresponds to the new taste: a severed head is delivered to Russian officers when Belgorsk fortress is stormed, bodies of just-hanged men twitch in the agony of death, and the camera lingers on battlefield injuries and assaulted peasants. The Captain's wife, Vasilisa Egorovna, is improbably made to witness more than her fair share of these injuries, including the severed head, which she unwittingly removes from its cloth cover for all to see. As in Pushkin's tale, she finds her husband hanged, but Proshkin adds a camera shot of her pendulous breasts as she rips her shirt in mourning, just before she is felled by a pistol shot. Women and their sexuality are meant to bring life to the film, as when Masha Mironova and the young officer Petr Grinev nearly have sex in a threshing barn, with close-up shots of spilling grain unsubtly duplicating Masha's eager sexuality. Never mind that such an encounter, especially at Masha's initiative, was unthinkable for the characters Pushkin created in *The Captain's Daughter*, where an epigraph stresses the point of honour. It make some sense for the film to pile on details about Catherine's decadent life at court, but Pushkin did not imagine his young heroes as similarly dissolute. When the villain Shvabrin forces himself on Masha, her sense of honour and her personal revulsion equally help her resist his advances. He responds by ripping open her shirt for another gratuitous flash of women's breasts.

For whom are these bodies on display? *The Russian Uprising* hoped for an overseas audience as well as one at home. The same income could be generated in the 1990s by a single showing on European television as by an entire year of revenues in the Russian market. Russian films made in the 1990s often keyed into the desires and expectations of a foreign audience, and *The Russian Uprising* is no exception. For every idealizing shot of countryside loveliness meant to stir the hearts of Russians nostalgic for a landscape destroyed by Soviet ecological disasters and urban growth, the film also provides an allegory of the 'Russian soul' as the West has come to fantasize it. The director, perhaps anticipating criticism for his deviations from historical accuracy, tried to make the film seem less about the past than about the moral effects of the past on the present. He claimed that his goal was ethical, meant to expose the cruelty of such national heroes as Pugachev and of the government's reaction to them. Proshkin compared Pugachev's uprising to the present-day war in Chechnia: 'We live in a society where we are daily shown blood and dead bodies on TV. We have grown accustomed to the sight of death.'[34] Whatever one thinks of the film, then, its director's ambitions follow the Jubilee tradition of using Pushkinian material for contemporary commentary, and of taking on issues no less significant than the nature of good and evil.

Art exhibits during the Jubilee also addressed ethical issues. At the prestigious Moscow gallery of Marat Gelman, Ira Valdron showed seven tapestries under the title *Fak-iu, Dantes* (i.e. 'Fuck you, D'Anthès' – Georges D'Anthès being the man who killed Pushkin). The images are as dramatic as that title, mixing words with animals and faces, and Valdron success-fully mixes scandalous images with Pushkin's words of grief and outrage, but the gallery's website directs our attention not just to her mix of high and low but to a historical moment when all values are being reassessed, when Pushkin remains perhaps the only shared national language.[35] The constructivist Iurii Avvakumov chose a more direct indicator of his interest in the question of value in his exhibit *Pushkin and Money* (*Pushkin i den'gi*) which opened at XL Gallery in Moscow on 29 January 1999 (the day of Pushkin's death according to the pre-revolutionary calendar). Avvakumov used graphic works and computer-generated voice-over, relying entirely on Pushkin's own plaintive requests for money.[36] The voice-over made it seem as if Pushkin himself were in the gallery, but the exhibit's mode was not realist. The graphic works were stylized, changing the handwriting and let-tering to suggest a personal letter, a desperate note, a public announcement. Pushkin is presented as the nation's currency, he is solid gold to those who value him but pure exchange value to his cynical detractors. Avvakumov suggests that he was vulnerable to the difficulties of getting money, but also strangely usable as if he were himself made of coin.

Two new monuments in Moscow were unveiled, both to Pushkin and his wife, a first in Pushkin commemorations and a sure sign of both the continuing fascination with his marriage and the ebbing tide of criticism toward the woman who married Pushkin. In Petersburg, a proposal to erect a chapel on the site of Pushkin's duel surfaced, but it was linked to an odd wish to demolish the obelisk now there. A letter signed by the head of the Union of Russian Writers, Valerii Ganichev, repeated an old Petersburg

11.3 Pushkin Monument, Moscow: photograph by Lev Melikhov, from *New Literary Review* (*Novoe literaturnoe obozrenie*), 1999

rumour that the obelisk placed on Chernaia Rechka by the Soviets in 1937 had been illicitly taken from someone else's grave.[37]

The idea that Pushkin monuments might be tainted by some secret or might themselves contain a secret is old, as old as Pushkin's own writings, where a monument (to Peter the Great) turns out to have terrifying magical powers in *The Bronze Horseman* (*Mednyi vsadnik*; 1833). The revolutionary poet Vladimir Maiakovskii in his 1924 anniversary poem (*Iubileinoe*) had a Pushkin monument come beneficently to life. Representations of monuments have remained as significant as the objects themselves, as was shown dramatically by a series of photographs published in a 1999 issue of a prestigious Moscow literary theory journal: four photographs by Lev Melikhov of the Moscow Pushkin monument used the style of Soviet Constructivist photography to distort the familiar monument by using extreme close-up (of Pushkin's hat and the drape of his coat), odd camera angles, or, in the example reproduced here, placing the monument into the background, with a man's head seen from the rear and in extreme close-up in the foreground (fig. 11.3). The man wears earphones and watches a hand-held television that is nearly obscured from view. A woman to his right watches as well. Here is Pushkin truly in the background, standing guard over a man absorbed in the technological innovations of the late twentieth century, but in the layout of the photograph, the monument seems to arise from the man's head as if it were his idea, as if whatever he watches on his tiny screen also has to do with Pushkin.

Pushkin's words and ideas were used in films, stories, poems, advertisements, dramatic spectacles, and popular festivals at anniversaries across the twentieth century. Individual Russians continued to find his words and his image compelling. From the top down, there was every attempt at self-importance, but in 1999 there were voices to answer in many tones, including lightness: as the theatre director Kamo Ginkas put it, Pushkin never goes out of Russian consciousness precisely because of his unbearable lightness.[38]

Afterword

In a posthumously published essay which has come to be known as 'The Author's Confession' (*Avtorskaia ispoved'*), Nikolai Gogol writes of his quest to discover Russia as he was working on his novel *Dead Souls*. It was a quest conducted mainly while he was living abroad. Gogol explains the problem, brought into focus by his two trips back to Russia in 1839 and 1841:

Twice I returned to Russia [. . .] but the strange thing was that in the midst of Russia I could barely see Russia [. . .] I noticed that almost everybody had formed their own Russias in their own heads. Hence the interminable arguments. That wasn't what I needed at all. [. . .] Throughout my stay in Russia, in *my* head Russia disintegrated and dissolved. I couldn't gather it up as a whole. [. . .] but as soon as I departed from it, it put itself back together again in my thoughts.[1]

Gogol was relieved when Russia 'put itself back together again' in his thoughts. He needed an integral vision of Russia, one that made sense, one that was . . . one. He needed a unitary vision of Russia to suit his pur poses. Unitary Russias do tend to be projected for a purpose. They come with political or social or moral agendas. Unitary visions of Russia imply prescription rather than description, what people should think rather than what they do think, what people should become rather than what they feel or believe themselves to be.

In the present book, our purpose and procedure is the opposite. Though we do look from abroad, the aim is emphatically *not* to arrive at an integral coherent picture of what Russia 'is', or 'was'. In a sense, Russia 'is' precisely that multiplicity of imagined and often competing Russias which Gogol found so irritating. If one tries to adjudicate, to resolve those 'interminable arguments', to determine which is the 'real' Russia, then one not only invalidates huge areas of cultural discourse which are just as 'real' as any other, but one also misrepresents the central issue of how 'identity' is constituted. Our aim, therefore, has been to look at the theme of national identity in Russian cultural discourse from a range of angles, in a range of dimensions, to explore and illustrate some of the varied, contrasting, perhaps contradictory ways in which Russia and Russianness have been imagined and represented. Individually, such Russias may be plausible or implausible, but none is adequate The more persuasive and authentic 'entity' – though the assertion sounds paradoxical – is that which is formed by all such Russias collectively.

We have not, of course, actually covered 'all' the Russias. Plenty of others are possible. How is it, for example, that we have got though a whole book on Russia and Russianness with no mention of cabbage soup, caviar, pancakes, or samovars? Or of gesture and body language or manners and mannerisms (all that expansiveness)? Or of the weather (ah, the cold . . .)? Completeness in detail is far beyond sensible aspiration, but these and many similar and dissimilar Russias can be accommodated within the basic grid. Moreover, the surveys which have been included are sufficient to indicate the likely general pattern of analysis for topics which have not been included: in particular, that the plain obviousness of the stereotype is undermined on more careful inspection, giving way to a more nuanced and altogether more interesting picture.

However, the aim of this book has not just been to advocate one approach to the question of national identity. Just as important as the broad surveys are the case studies, the often highly specific readings of cultural 'texts'. These 'texts', after all, constitute the tangible, visible, audible reality. Without them to articulate it, no Russia exists. Here any claim to completeness would be patently absurd, but a sense of breadth and diversity has been crucial. Once the grid itself becomes familiar it might start to resemble a formula, but there is – we hope – very little repetition in the type of material illustrated from chapter to chapter, as the chronological and generic horizons continually expand. Our 'texts' range across a full millennium, from c.1000 to c.2000. They include novels and poems, films and paintings, buildings and sculptures, guide-books and childcare manuals, travelogues and diaries, postage stamps and banknotes, words and grammatical forms, encyclopedias, saints' lives, posters, journalism, play and recreation, television, critical and philosophical essays, song, opera, peep-shows, chocolate wrappers.

This book is not an introduction to Russian national identity 'as such' (whatever that may mean). It is an introduction to cultural discourses of Russian national identity. It is therefore an introduction to ways of 'reading' a particular theme in Russian culture, and hence an introduction to the range of things that there are to be 'read'; and hence, ultimately, it cannot help but reflect and introduce something of the rich diversity of Russian culture itself.

Notes

1 'ALL THE RUSSIAS . . .'?

1. C. E. Vaughan (ed.), *The Political Writings of Rousseau* (2 vols., Cambridge, 1915), II, p. 319.
2. Henry Norman, *All the Russias: Travels and Studies in Contemporary European Russia, Finland, Siberia, the Caucasus, and Central Asia* (London, 1902), p. 1.
3. Benedict Anderson, *Imagined Communities: Reflections on the Origin and Spread of Nationalism* (London, 1983).
4. Homi Bhabha (ed.), *Nation and Narration* (London, 1990), p. 2.
5. In fact the English phrase distorts its Russian source, which was singular, not plural: either the adjective *vserossiiskii* ('All-Russian') or the more archaic expression *vseia Rusi* ('of all Rus'). Thus the English version is even more imperialistic than its original.

2 RUSSIA IN TIME

1. A. N. and V. N. Storozhev, *Rossiia vo vremeni. Kniga 1. Drevniaia istoriia sibirskikh i slavianskikh narodov* (Moscow, 1997), p. 85.
2. Further on this see Chapter 6.
3. *Povest' vremennykh let*, ed. D. S. Likhachev and V. P. Adrianova-Peretts (2 vols., Moscow, Leningrad, 1950), I, p. 83; cf. *The Russian Primary Chronicle*, transl. S. H. Cross and O. P. Sherbowitz-Wetzor (3rd printing; Cambridge, Mass., 1973), p. 119.
4. Metropolitan Ilarion's *Sermon on Law and Grace*: *Biblioteka literatury Drevnei Rusi*, I (St Petersburg, 1997), p. 38; transl. Simon Franklin, *Sermons and Rhetoric of Kievan Rus'* (Cambridge, Mass., 1991), pp. 13, 14.
5. In the Bible: Matthew 20:1–16; cf. Matthew 19:30; Mark 10:31; Luke 13:30. In the eleventh-century 'Lection' on Saints Boris and Gleb, and the *Life of Feodosii of the Caves*, both by the Kievan monk Nestor, see *Die altrussischen hagiographischen Erzählungen und liturgischen Dichtungen über die heiligen Boris und Gleb*, introd. L. Müller (ed. D. Abramovich, Petrograd, 1916; repr. Munich, 1967), p. 3; *Biblioteka literatury Drevnei Rusi*, I, p. 352; transl. Paul Hollingsworth, *The Hagiography of Kievan Rus'* (Cambridge, Mass., 1992), pp. 5, 34; cf. p. 222.

6. *Biblioteka literatury Drevnei Rusi*, XI (St Petersburg, 2000), pp. 278–89; see also pp. 290–305 for texts on Moscow as the Third Rome.

7. See also Chapter 4.

8. On the history of Russian and Soviet anthems see Chapter 7.

9. See Chapter 11.

10. Genesis 18:1–10.

11. See also Chapter 10.

12. See also Chapter 6.

13. See Volodymyr Shvets', *Kataloh ukrains'kykh hroshei vid 1917 roku* (Lviv, 2000), pp. 20–49.

14. For examples, see M. P. Sotnikova, *Drevneishie russkie monety X–XI vekov* (Moscow, 1995), pp. 46–96.

15. The forms of names can themselves be emblematic. 'Vladimir' is the modern Russian form, which happens also to reflect the early Church Slavonic form, which was used by the prince himself in his own coin inscriptions. 'Volodymyr' is the modern Ukrainian form, closer to the local Easy Slav vernacular form which tended to be favoured in the early chronicles.

3 RUSSIA AS SPACE

1. Walter Benjamin, 'Moscow,' in *Reflections: Essays, Aphorisms, Autobiographical Writings*, ed. Peter Demetz (New York, 1978), p. 118. RSFSR: Russian Soviet Federative Socialist Republic. The USSR was formed in December 1922.

2. 'Model' mira', *Vokrug sveta*, 11 (1931), 23.

3. Aleksandr Herzen, 'Du développement des idées révolutionnaires en Russie', in A. I. Gertsen, *Sobranie sochinenii v 30-i tomakh*, VII (Moscow, 1956), p. 16.

4. A. A. Blok, *Zapisnye knizhki*, 2 vols. (Leningrad, 1930), I, p. 83.

5. See Chapter 2.

6. *Povest' vremennykh let*, ed. D. S. Likhachev and V. P. Adrianova-Peretts (2 vols., Moscow, Leningrad, 1950), I, p. 9.

7. See pp. 3–4.

8. *Entsiklopedicheskii slovar'* (St Petersburg, 1895), XV (a), pp. 633–40.

9. Marquis de Custine, *La Russie en 1839* (4 vols., Paris, 1845), IV, pp. 108–10.

10. V. O. Kliuchevskii, *Sochineniia*, 8 vols. (Moscow, 1956), I, p. 70.

11. See Chapter 2.

12. F. I. Tiutchev, *Polnoe sobranie stikhotvorenii* (Leningrad, 1987), p. 229.

13. D. S. Likhachev, *Zametki o russkom* (Moscow, 1984), p. 10.

14. I. A. Bunin, *Sobranie sochinenii v shesti tomakh* (Moscow, 1988), V, p. 37.

15. Nikolai Gogol', *Sobranie sochinenii v vos'mi tomakh* (Moscow, 1984), V, p. 248.

16. Ibid.

17. A. A. Blok, *Stikhotvoreniia*. 3 vols. (St Petersburg, 1995), III, p. 286.

18. M. Iu. Lermontov, *Polnoe sobranie sochinenii v 10 tomakh*, II (Moscow, 2000), p. 171.

19. M. Gor'kii, L. Averbakh, and S. Finn (eds.), *Belomorsko-Baltiiskii kanal imeni Stalina: istoriia stroitel'stva* (Moscow, 1934), insert.

4 'US': RUSSIANS ON RUSSIANNESS

1. For a detailed analysis of Pushkin's experience, see Monika Frenkel Greenleaf, 'Pushkin's "Journey to Arzrum": the Poet at the Border', *Slavic Review* 50 (1991), 940–53.
2. See Richard Wortman, *Scenarios of Power: Myth and Ceremonies in Russian Monarchy* (2 vols., Princeton, 1995, 2000).
3. Hans Rogger, *National Consciousness in Eighteenth-Century Russia* (Cambridge, Mass., 1960), p. 158.
4. See Chapter 7.
5. Cited in Hans Lemberg, *Die nationale Gedankenwelt der Dekabristen* (Cologne, Graz, 1963), p. 60.
6. The change was not absolutely unprepared: see Chapter 6, on the film *Aleksandr Nevskii*, made in 1938.
7. Simon Saradzhyan, 'Russia To Educate More Patriots', *The St Petersburg Times*, no. 652 (13 March 2001).
8. 'Ulichnoe poboishche v Peterburge', *Nedelia*, no. 24 (11 June 1878), 798–800.
9. Eugen Weber, *Peasants into Frenchmen: The Modernization of Rural France, 1870–1914* (London, 1979).
10. Cf. also Chapter 10.
11. Jeffrey Brooks, *When Russia Learned to Read. Literacy and Popular Literature, 1861–1917* (Princeton, 1985), p. 241.

5 'THEM': RUSSIANS ON FOREIGNERS

1. The words of Louis-Sébastien Mercier, quoted by Paul Langford, *Englishness Identified: Manners and Character 1650–1850* (Oxford, 2000), p. 138.
2. *Zemlia tatarskaia*: Tatars (or by older English convention Tartars) were one of the Mongol tribes. In the present book we generally use 'Mongol' when referring to those who were overlords of Rus c. 1237–1480, and 'Tatars' for later periods.
3. All the examples are taken from *Slovar' russkogo iazyka XI–XVII veka* (Moscow, 1975), I, p. 73; II, pp. 17–18; VI (1979), pp. 243–5; XI (1986), pp. 178–9. For 'Latin' meaning 'Catholic' see below, Chapter 6.
4. See the wide-ranging essay by Lindsey Hughes, 'Attitudes towards Foreigners in Early Modern Russia', in Cathryn Brennan and Murray Frame (eds.), *Russia and the Wider World in Historical Perspective: Essays for Paul Dukes* (London, 2000), pp. 1–23. It is from this study that several of the following quotations are taken.
5. Quoted in George Vernadsky (ed.), *A Source Book for Russian History from Early Times to 1917*, II (New Haven, 1972), p. 362.
6. See above, Chapter 2.
7. The words of the Croat Iurii Krizhanich, quoted in Anthony Cross, *Russia under Western Eyes, 1517–1825* (London, 1971), p. 23.
8. N. K. Gudzii (ed.), *Zhitie protopopa Avvakuma im samim napisannoe i drugie ego sochineniia* (Moscow, 1960), p. 136.

9. *Polnoe sobranie zakonov rossiiskoi imperii*, I (St Petersburg, 1830), no. 607 (6 August 1675).

10. *Polnoe sobranie zakonov rossiiskoi imperii*, IV, no. 1910 (16 April 1702).

11. United Society for the Propagation of the Gospel, London, Correspondence A.I/138.

12. Andrew Swinton, *Travels into Norway, Denmark, and Russia, in the Years 1788, 1789, 1790, and 1791* (London, 1792), pp. 229–30.

13. As reported in the *New York Times* (19 September 2000), p. A3.

14. 'V Rossiiu s liubov'iu?', *Moskovskie novosti* (7 September 1989).

15. Although, confusingly, in the foreign passport *grazhdanstvo* ('citizenship') is rendered in English as 'nationality'.

16. Giles Fletcher, 'On the Russe Commonwealth', in Lloyd E. Berry and Robert O. Crummey (eds.), *Rude and Barbarous Kingdom: Russia in the Accounts of Sixteenth-Century English Voyagers* (Madison, 1968), p. 172.

17. Quoted by Lyall in an appendix to his *Travels in Russia, the Krimea, the Caucasus, and Georgia*, II (London, 1825), pp. 519, 520.

18. See V. P. Adrianova-Peretts, *Ocherki po istorii russkoi satiricheskoi literatury XVII veka* (Moscow, Leningrad, 1937), pp. 239–51.

19. D. I. Fonvizin, *Sobranie sochinenii*, I (Moscow, Leningrad, 1959), p. 72.

20. P. N. Berkov (ed.), *Satiricheskie zhurnaly N. I. Novikova* (Moscow, Leningrad, 1951), p. 63.

21. C. Hibbert, *The Grand Tour* (London, 1974), p. 25.

22. Berkov (ed.), *Satiricheskie zhurnaly N. I. Novikova*, pp. 328–29.

23. N. Ianovskii, *Novyi slovotolkovatel'*, I (St Petersburg, 1803), p. 150. 'Angloman' was used as a pseudonym by M. I. Pleshcheev, writing some thirty years earlier in *Opyt trudov Vol'nogo russkogo sobraniia*, II (1775), p. 261.

24. N. M. Karamzin, *Sochineniia*, II (St Petersburg, 1848), p. 773.

25. Quoted in H. M. Hyde, *The Empress Catherine and the Princess Dashkov* (London, 1935), p. 107.

26. *Arkhiv kniazia Vorontsova*, XXX (St Petersburg, 1893), p. 391.

27. Karamzin, *Sochineniia*, II, p. 659. In this redaction (1794) Karamzin did not mention the admiration for England's 'political perfection' that was clearly spelt out in one of his pre-travel works, 'Pustynnik', *Detskoe chtenie dlia serdtsa i razuma*, XV (Moscow, 1788), 41–2.

28. Karamzin, *Sochineniia*, II, pp. 778–9.

29. Nikolai Korsakov, 'Journal des voyages en Angleterre et en Ecosse', Lenin Library, Moscow, Fond 137, Korsakovy, papka 2, ed. khr. 12, f. 42.

30. Karamzin, *Sochineniia*, II, p. 723.

31. *Annual Register, or General Repository . . . for the Year 1803* (London, 1804), p. 302.

32. *Russkaia starina*, XXIII (1883), 437.

33. Karamzin, *Sochineniia*, II, p. 773.

34. Karamzin, *Sochineniia*, II, pp. 780–2, 674.

35. *Sochineniia i perevody Petra Makarova*, II (2nd edn., Moscow, 1817), pp. 43–4.

36. Karamzin, *Sochineniia*, II, p. 780.

37. 'Rossiianin v Anglii', *Priiatnoe i poleznoe preprovozhdenie vremeni*, XI (Moscow, 1796), 262.
38. 'O voine' (*Osennie vechera*, nos. 2–3 (St Petersburg, 1803), 24); reprinted in V. F. Malinovskii, *Izbrannye obshchestvenno-politicheskie sochineniia* (Moscow, 1958), p. 103.
39. *Vestnik Evropy*, IX (May 1803), 74.
40. 'Rossiianin v Anglii', XI, 257.
41. Ibid., 257–64.
42. Karamzin, *Sochineniia*, II, p. 468.
43. *Severnyi vestnik*, V (St Petersburg, 1805), 152–3.
44. *Arkhiv kniazia F. A. Kurakina*, V (Saratov, 1894), p. 385.
45. Karamzin, *Sochineniia*, II, p. 684.
46. Ibid., p. 475.
47. *Severnyi vestnik*, V, 248.
48. Karamzin, *Sochineniia*, II, p. 684.

6 IDENTITY AND RELIGION

1. Archbishop Iuvenalii of Kursk and Rylsk, in *Nash sovremennik* 1996, no. 1, p. 106.
2. *Biblioteka literatury Drevnei Rusi* [*BLDR*], I (St Petersburg, 1997), p. 112.
3. *BLDR*, I, pp. 40, 38; Simon Franklin, *Sermons and Rhetoric of Kievan Rus'* (Cambridge, Mass., 1991), pp. 15, 14.
4. *BLDR*, I, p. 162.
5. The earliest is Novgorod birch bark document no. 941; for this and other documents, see the word-lists in A. A. Zalizniak, *Drevnenovgorodskii dialekt* (Moscow, 1995), pp. 626, 678.
6. *BLDR*, I, p. 38; Franklin, *Sermons and Rhetoric*, p. 14.
7. *BLDR*, I, p. 72.
8. Ibid., p. 158.
9. For references to the texts see Sophia Senyk, *A History of the Church in Ukraine. Volume I: to the End of the Thirteenth Century* (Rome, 1993), pp. 316–18.
10. *BLDR*, IV, pp. 366, 368.
11. On Church Slavonic and some of its implications see below, Chapter 8.
12. For more examples of the reforms see below, Chapter 8.
13. See Chapter 10.
14. See Chapters 4 and 7.
15. See Chapter 4.
16. See Chapter 7.
17. See Chapters 2 and 10.
18. N. S. Leskov, *Sobranie sochinenii v 11 tomakh*, IV (Moscow, 1957), p. 400.
19. Ibid., pp. 433–34.
20. Ibid., p. 434.
21. Sergei Eisenstein, *Battleship Potemkin, October and Alexander Nevsky*, ed. Jay Leyda, transl. Diana Matias (London: Lorrimer Publishing, 1974), pp. 110, 132.

22. Other examples appear under various headings in the present book.
23. *Sviataia Rus'. Entsiklopedicheskii slovar' russkoi tsivilizatsii*, ed. O. A. Platonov (Moscow, 2000).
24. *Sviataia Rus'*, pp. 790–1.
25. Ibid., p. 764.
26. Ibid., pp. 687, 688.

7 MUSIC OF THE SOUL?

1. Percy A. Scholes, *God Save the Queen! The History and Romance of the World's First National Anthem* (London and New York, 1954).
2. See Chapter 4.
3. V. V. Krutov, *'Bozhe, tsaria khrani!': istoriia pervogo rossiiskogo gimna* (Moscow, 1992), p. 95.
4. Krutov, *'Bozhe, tsaria khrani!'*, p. 98.
5. V. F. Odoevskii, 'Starinnaia pesnia' (1863), 'Pis'mo Kn. V. F. Odoevskogo k izdateliu ob iskonnoi velikorusskoi muzyke' (1863), 'Russkaia i tak nazyvaemaia obshchaia muzyka' (1867); see V. F. Odoevskii, *Muzykal'no-literaturnoe nasledie* (Moscow, 1956), pp. 252–4, 276–86, 318–30.
6. See Chapter 4.
7. See A. D. Kastal'skii, *Osobennosti narodno-russkoi muzykal'noi sistemy* (Moscow, 1961); idem, *Osnovy narodnogo mnogogolosiia* (Moscow, Leningrad, 1948).
8. A. N. Radishchev, *Sochineniia* (Moscow, 1988), p. 30.
9. Radishchev, *Sochineniia*, p. 148.
10. A. S. Pushkin, *Polnoe sobranie sochinenii v 10 tomakh*, VI (Leningrad, 1977), p. 350.
11. Ibid., IV, p. 237.
12. N. V. Gogol', *Polnoe sobranie sochinenii*, VIII (Leningrad, 1952), p. 294.
13. Ibid., VI (1951), pp. 220–1.
14. Ibid., VIII, p. 289.
15. I. S. Turgenev, *Polnoe sobranie sochinenii v 30 tomakh*, III (Moscow, 1979), p. 222.
16. See the commentary in Turgenev, *Polnoe sobranie sochinenii*, III, pp. 492–3.
17. Ibid.
18. I. S. Zil'bershtein and V. A. Samkov (eds.), *Sergei Diagilev i russkoe iskusstvo: stat'i, otkrytye pis'ma, interv'iu, perepiska, sovremenniki o Diagileve* (Moscow, 1982), p. 420.

8 IDENTITY IN LANGUAGE?

1. See Anna Wierzbicka, 'Russian Language', in her book *Semantics, Culture and Cognition* (Oxford, 1992), pp. 33–88; E. S. Iakovleva, *Fragmenty russkoi iazykovoi kartiny mira (modeli prostranstva, vremeni i vospriiatiia)* (Moscow, 1994); T. V. Bulygina and A. D. Shmelev, *Iazykovaia kontseptualizatsiia mira*

(na materiale russkoi grammatiki) (Moscow, 1997); N. D. Arutiunova, *Iazyk i mir cheloveka* (Moscow, 1998).

2. Lavrentii Zizanii, *Hrammatika slovenska, Wilna 1596*, ed. Gerd Freidhof (Frankfurt am Main, 1980).

3. *Povest' vremennykh let*, ed. D. S. Likhachev and V. P. Adrianova-Peretts (2 vols., Moscow, Leningrad, 1950), I, p. 153.

4. See Chapter 2.

5. *Zhitie Avvakuma i drugie ego sochineniia* (Moscow, 1991), p. 33.

6. *Povest' vremennykh let*, I, p. 162; transl. in Basil Dmytryshyn (ed.), *Medieval Russia: A Source Book, 850–1700* (New York, 1991), pp. 71–2.

7. *Zhitie protopopa Avvakuma*, p. 31; transl. in Serge Zenkovsky (ed.), *Medieval Russia's Epics, Chronicles, and Tales* (New York, 1974), p. 401.

8. Epifanii Premudryi, *Zhitie sv. Stefana, episkopa Permskogo*, ed. V. G. Druzhinin (St Petersburg, 1897; repr. The Hague, 1959), p. 87.

9. Ibid., pp. 71–2.

10. Ibid., p. 106; transl. Zenkovsky (ed.), *Medieval Russia's Epics, Chronicles, and Tales*, p. 262.

9 *BYT*: IDENTITY AND EVERYDAY LIFE

1. Igor' Shaitanov, ' "Bytovaia" istoriia', *Voprosy literatury*, no. 3–4 (2002), p. 3.

2. Svetlana Boym, *Common Places: Mythologies of Everyday Life in Russia* (Cambridge, MA, 1994), p. 31.

3. A recent case in point is Dale Pesmen's quasi-anthropological study, *Russia and Soul: An Exploration* (Ithaca, 2000).

4. G. R. Derzhavin, *Stikhotvoreniia* (Leningrad, 1981), pp. 137–9.

5. Nathaniel Knight, 'Science, Empire and Nationality: Ethnography in the Russian Geographical Society, 1845–1855', in *Imperial Russia: New Histories for the Empire*, ed. Jane Burbank and David L. Ransel (Bloomington, IN, 1999), p. 127.

6. Robert Service, *Lenin: A Political Life*, II (London, 1991), p. 153.

7. See 'Zverskoe ubiistvo Morozovykh', *Pionerskaia Pravda*, no. 102 (1932), 4. On Pavlik, see also Catriona Kelly, *Comrade Pavlik: the Rise and Fall of a Soviet Boy-Hero* (London: Granta; forthcoming).

8. A. P. Chekhov, *Polnoe sobranie sochinenii i pisem* (30 vols., Moscow, 1969–1978), *Pis'ma*, I, pp. 223–4.

9. In Gerry Smith's sardonic formulation in his book *D. S. Mirsky: A Russian–English Life* (Oxford, 2000), p. 19: 'The classic lifestyle of the Russian male intellectual aims to eliminate demeaning involvement in *byt* through the exploitation of dependent wives and servants, and leave him free to pursue intellectual and other forms of self-gratification, justified and rationalized through all sorts of variously pretentious moral and ethical excuses.'

10. Marina Tsvetaeva, *Stikhotvoreniia i poemy* (Leningrad, 1990), pp. 555–68; Arsenii Tarkovskii, *Izbrannoe* (Moscow, 1982), p. 115.

11. G. Speranskii, *Ukhod za rebenkom rannego vozrasta* (4th edn., Moscow, 1929), pp. 117, 107, 129.
12. Beatrice King, *Changing Man: the Education System of the U.S.S.R.* (London, 1936), p. 99.
13. Rousseau, *Emile*, Book II, quoted here from the Everyman Library translation by B. Foxley (London, 1995), p. 188.
14. Dzh. Kolozza (Giovanni Colozza), *Detskie igry: ikh psikhologicheskoe i pedagogicheskoe znachenie*, transl. anon. (Moscow, 1909).
15. See *Metodicheskie pis'ma po doshkol'nomu vospitaniiu 13: Igra i trud doshkol'nika* (Moscow, 1927), passim.
16. Ibid., p. 11.
17. Ibid., pp. 15–16, 22, 25, 20.
18. A. N. Tolstoi, *Polnoe sobranie sochinenii*, XII (Moscow, 1948), p. 52.
19. 'Nash dnevnik: rabota vo dvore', *Vorobei* 9 (1925), p. 26.
20. See 'Zabyli organizovannykh', *Pionerskaia Pravda*, no. 19 (1927), p. 1, and L. Shnaider, 'Dom No. 53 po Smolenskomu bul'varu', ibid., p. 7.
21. Z. Lilina, *Roditeli, uchites' vospityvat' svoikh detei* (Moscow, 1929), pp. 5–9.
22. 'Up till now, we have been hanging round the streets of the town and living an ordinary childish life, one with no purpose. But on 12 September a new page of life opened up for us. We were transformed into a Communist collective.' Letter from Rostov City Troop of the Pioneers to I. V. Stalin, 23 October 1924, Tsentr khraneniia dokumentov molodezhnykh organizatsii (TsKhDMO) f. 1 op. 23 d. 458 l. 17.
23. 'Kto umeet igrat' druzhno, ne ssorias', tot umeet i zhit' druzhno': I. Surozhskii, 'Pioner v zhizni', *Pioner*, no. 2 (1924), 8.
24. Tsentral'nyi arkhiv obshchestvennykh dvizhenii Moskvy [TsAODM] f. 1884 op. 1 d. 52 l. 20 (plan of Venevskii uezd, Moskovskaia guberniia). For similar activities in a city courtyard, see 'Dvor stal pionerskim', *Pionerskaia Pravda*, no. 81 (1933), 4–5.
25. *Pioner*, no. 4 (1924), 15: on the term 'American Fascists', see *Pioner*, no. 7 (1924), 17.
26. Rossiiskaia Akademiia Obrazovaniia (formerly Akademiia pedagogicheskikh nauk), Nauchnyi arkhiv [RAO NA] f. 1 op. 1 d. 145 l. 59. (Meeting of 19 March 1924.) According to I. Shangina, *Russkie deti i ikh igry* (St Petersburg, 2000), p. 27, in Russian villages blankets were scarce items, to be found only in wealthy households.
27. See e.g. Belev, 'Zabytyi uchastok', *Sovetskaia iustitsiia*, no. 13 (1932), 26.
28. TsAODM f. 634 op. 1 d. 35 l. 82.
29. Ella Winter, *Red Virtue: Human Relationships in the New Russia* (London, 1933), p. 215.
30. See e.g. Shnaider, 'Dom no. 53'.
31. V. Shefner, 'Imia dlia ptitsy, ili Chaepitie na zheltoi verande', in the same author's *Lachuga dolzhnika* (St Petersburg, 1995), pp. 543–4.
32. See the memoirs of 'Ol'ga Nikolaevna' in Clementine G. K. Creuziger, *Childhood in Russia: Representation and Reality* (Lanham, MD, 1996), p. 40.

33. Shefner, *Imia dlia ptitsy*, p. 542.
34. RAO NA f. 1 op. 1 d. 49 l. 313.
35. See E. I. Zamiatin, 'Sovetskie deti' (1932), in *Sochineniia*, IV (Munich, 1988), p. 565.
36. K. Chukovskii, *Ot dvukh do piati* (Leningrad, 1934), pp. 79–80.

10 MONUMENTS AND IDENTITY

1. V. A. Petrov, *A. Savrasov. Iz sobraniia gos. Tret'iakovskoi galerei* (Moscow, 1986); more below on all these monuments.
2. See Chapter 2.
3. 'Petition of the City of Moscow on Being Relegated to Oblivion', in Marc Raeff (ed.), *Russian Intellectual History: An Anthology* (New York, 1966), p. 53.
4. A. I. Bogdanov, *Opisanie Sanktpeterburga* (St Petersburg, 1997), pp. 99, 371.
5. Quoted in E. B. Mozgovaia, *Skul'pturnyi klass Akademii khudozhestv v XVIII veke* (St Petersburg, 1999), p. 24.
6. V. Ruban, *Nadpisi k kamniu, naznachennomu dlia podnozhiia statui Imp. Petra Velikago* (St Petersburg, 1770).
7. V. Bur'ianov, *Progulka s det'mi po S.-Peterburgu*, 3 parts (St Petersburg, 1838), II, p. 41.
8. P. Svin'in, *Dostopamiatnosti Sanktpeterburga i ego okrestnostei*, 5 parts (St Petersburg, 1816–28), I, pp. 1–2.
9. Svin'in, *Dostopamiatnosti*, III, pp. 44–51.
10. See Chapter 4.
11. *Puteshestvie po sviatym mestam russkim* (St Petersburg, 1846), part 1, p. 188.
12. V. Dorofeev, *Bol'shoi Uspenskii sobor v Moskve. Chteniia dlia moskovskikh fabrichno-zavodskikh rabochikh* (Moscow, 1904), pp. 16, 21, 48.
13. *Putevoditel' po S.-Peterburgu. (Ekskursii nachal'nykh shkol)* (St Petersburg, 1914), p. 6.
14. A. Varshavskii, 'Bogatyri', *Znanie-sila*, no. 5 (1963), 92.
15. Quoted in O. Galerkina, *Khudozhnik Viktor Vasnetsov* (Leningrad, 1957), p. 143.
16. N. I. Punin, 'Andrei Rublev', *Apollon*, no. 2 (1915), 1–23. Here quoted from *Andrei Rublev* (Petrograd, 1916), pp. 13–14, 23.
17. N. Kuz'min, 'Andrei Rublev', *Novyi mir*, no. 10 (1960), 206.
18. N. A. Mudrogel', *Piat'desiat vosem' let v Tret'iakovskoi galeree* (Leningrad, 1962), pp. 118, 122.
19. F. S. Roginskaia, T. A. Bystrova, *Antireligioznaia ekskursiia po Tret'iakovskoi galleree* (Moscow, 1933).
20. A. Romm, *Pamiatnik Petru I v Leningrade* (Moscow, Leningrad, 1944), p. 24.
21. N. Shchekotov, *Zaporozhtsy. Kartina velikogo russkogo zhivopistsa I. E. Repina* (Moscow, Leningrad, 1943), p. 9.
22. E. Polishchuk, *V. M. Vasnetsov. Bogatyri* (Moscow, 1950), p. 7.
23. Galerkina, *Khudozhnik*, p. 155.
24. *Muzei sobor Vasiliia Blazhennogo* (Leningrad, 1928), p. 19.

25. A. Briullov, *Entsiklopedicheskii leksikon Pliushara* (St Petersburg, 1835), III, p. 275.
26. V. V. Suslov, *Tserkov' Vasiliia Blazhennogo v Moskve* (St Petersburg, 1912), pp. 17, 21.
27. *Novyi Lef*, no. 10 (1927), 3. Quoted in Abbott Gleason, Peter Kenez and Richard Stites (eds.), *Bolshevik Culture: Experiment and Order in the Russian Revolution* (Bloomington, Indiana, 1985), p. 12.
28. Ivan Fomin's memoirs, quoted in A. Tarkhanov, S. Kavtaradze, *Stalinist Architecture* (London, 1992), p. 40.
29. N. Serebriakova, 'Dom moi domom molitvoi narechetsia', *Derzhava* 4, no. 7 (1996), 59.
30. Dan Richardson, *Moscow. The Rough Guide* (London, 1998), p. 73.
31. *Mukhina. Literaturno-kriticheskoe nasledie* (3 vols., Moscow, 1960), I, pp. 105–6, III.
32. N. Vorkhunova, *Simvol novogo mira* (Moscow, 1965), p. 64.
33. *Katalog posterov proizvedenii iz sobraniia Gosudarstvennoi Tret'iakovskoi Galerei* (Moscow, 1997), p. 26.
34. *Komsomol'skaia Pravda*, 14 April 1937, p. 1.

11 'PUSHKIN' AND IDENTITY

1. Lidiia Ginzburg, 'Iz zapisei 1950–1970-kh godov', *Literatura v poiskakh real'nosti* (Leningrad, 1987), p. 331.
2. Some of the many items imprinted with Pushkin's profile, writings, and/or signature, produced for the 1999 Jubilee.
3. Stanislav Rassadin, 'Bez Pushkina, ili nachalo i konets garmonii', *Znamia*, no. 6 (1991), 220, emphasis in original.
4. The poet Evgenii Baratynskii (1800–44).
5. 'Coldness and Rationality: An Interview with Elena Shvarts', in Valentina Polukhina (ed.), *Brodsky Through the Eyes of His Contemporaries* (London, 1992), p. 226.
6. Irina Surat, '"Da pristupliu ko smerti smelo . . .": O gibeli Pushkina', *Novyi mir*, no. 2 (1999), 166.
7. F. I. Tiutchev, *Polnoe sobranie stikhotvorenii* (Leningrad, 1987), p. 140.
8. Adam Phillips, *Promises, Promises: Essays on Psychoanalysis and Literature* (New York, 2001), p. 19.
9. Reidar Th. Christiansen, 'Myth, Metaphor, and Simile', in *Myth: A Symposium*, ed. Thomas A. Sebeok (Bloomington, Indiana, 1955, rcpr. 1965), p. 65.
10. See Chapter 6.
11. See Victor Erlich, *The Double Image: Concepts of the Poet in Slavic Literatures* (Baltimore, 1964), pp. 16–37.
12. Pierre Nora, 'Between Memory and History: Les Lieux de Mémoire', *Representations* 26 (Spring, 1989), 12.
13. An edition of *Gavriliada* was published in 1921, and then reissued only in 1991.

14. The phrase entitled the obituary for Pushkin in the journal *Literaturnye pribavleniia k Russkomu Invalidu*, no. 5 (30 January 1837), 48.

15. Osip Mandelshtam, 'Pushkin and Scriabin', in Mandelshtam, *The Complete Critical Prose and Letters*, ed. Jane Gary Harris (Ann Arbor, 1979), p. 90. For the Russian original, see Osip Mandel'shtam, *Sobranie sochinenii*, 3 vols., ed. G. P. Struve and B. A. Filippov (New York, 1971), II, pp. 313–19.

16. The phrase originates with Apollon Grigor'ev, 'Vzgliad na russkuiu literaturu so smerti Pushkina' (1859), reprinted in *Svetloe imia Pushkina*, ed. V. V. Kunin (Moscow, 1988), p. 78.

17. V. Nepomniashchii, 'Iubileinye obryvki', *Iskusstvo kino*, no. 1 (2000), 61.

18. V. Radzishevskii, 'Orden dlia Pushkina', *Literaturnaia gazeta*, no. 1–2 (5728) (13 January 1999), 1.

19. Both cited by Evgenii Bunimovich in the column 'Lichnaia zhizn'', *Literaturnaia gazeta*, no. 22 (5745) (1 June 1999), 13.

20. Lev Rubinshtein, 'Pushkin kak ob"ekt kitcha', *Itogi*, no. 17 (27 April 1999). Here, and subsequently, the absence of a page number indicates an item read on the web through the Universal Database of Russian Newspapers.

21. V. Nepomniashchii, 'Poor boy Onegin', *Iskusstvo kino*, no. 2 (2000), 65–67.

22. Nepomniashchii, 'Iubileinye obryvki', p. 61.

23. 'Pushkin v medi(a)', *Ex libris NG*, no. 21 (93) (June 1999), 1.

24. Natal'ia Ivanova, 'V Peterburge, s Pushkinym', *Znamia*, no. 9 (1999) p. 239.

25. Andrei Novikov, 'Ia ustal ot slova "kul'tury"! O Mednom vsadnike kak glavnom geroe Pushkinskogo iubileia', *Znamia*, no. 7 (1999), 208–12. This is an angry diatribe by a member of the Writers' Union and the Moscow Journalists' Union.

26. Dmitrii Abaulin, 'On sterpel nashe vse', *Literaturnaia gazeta*, no. 23 (5746) (9 June 1999), 9.

27. *Ex libris NG*, no. 21 (93) (June 1999), 1–2, quotation from Limonov on p. 4.

28. Andrei Zorin, 'Moi Pushkin', *Neprikosnovennyi zapas*, no. 2 (4) (1999), 40.

29. *Literaturnaia gazeta*, no. 23 (5746) (9 June 1999), 1.

30. Andrei Zorin, 'Bezopasnyi seks', in *Shinel' Pushkina: sbornik k 200-letnemu iubileiu A. S. Pushkina* (Moscow, St Petersburg, 2000), p. 6.

31. Genrikh Sapgir, 'Chernoviki Pushkina', *Druzhba narodov*, no. 5 (1999), 110–15.

32. *Faksimil'noe vosproizvedenie samodel'noi knigi Dmitriia Aleksandrovicha Prigova 'Evgenii Onegin Pushkina'* (St Petersburg, 1998).

33. D. A. Prigov, 'Pop-geroi', an interview conducted by Sergei Shapoval, *NG – Figury i litsa*, no. 11 (32) (5 June 1999).

34. Aleksandr Proshkin and Anzhelika Artiukh, '"Eto nasha beda, chto my sdelali iz razboinikov natsional'nykh geroev"', *Iskusstvo kino*, no. 5 (2000), 26.

35. See www.guelman.ru/actions/dantes and, for more on Ira Valdron, see www.guelman.ru/artists/waldron.html.

36. See www.geocities.com/SoHo/8070/pushpics.htm.

37. Mikhail Kuraev, 'Ganichev i drugie na fone Pushkina', *Literaturnaia gazeta*, no. 7 (5733) (17 February 1999), 9.

38. Mariia Sedykh and Kamo Ginkas, 'Igrai, da ne zaigryvaisia!' *Literaturnaia gazeta*, no. 22 (5745) (2 June 1999), 12. Ginkas draws the collocation from the 1988 American film *The Unbearable Lightness of Being*, without mentioning Milan Kundera's novel on which the film was based.

AFTERWORD

1. N. V. Gogol', *Polnoe sobranie sochinenii*, VIII (Leningrad, 1952), pp. 451–2.

Selected further reading in English

Aizlewood, R., 'Revisiting Russian Identity in Russian Thought: From Chaadaev to the Early Twentieth Century', *Slavonic and East European Review* 78 (2000), 20–43.

Auty, R., and D. Obolensky (eds.), *Companion to Russian Studies*. 3 volumes. Cambridge and New York, 1976–80.

Barker, A. (ed.), *Consuming Russia: Popular Culture, Sex, and Society since Gorbachev*. Durham, NC, 1999.

Bassin, M., 'Russia between Europe and Asia: The Ideological Construction of Geographical Space.' *Slavic Review* 50: 1 (1991), 1–17.

Berlin, I., *Russian Thinkers*. London, 1978.

Berry, E. E., and A. Miller-Pogacar (eds.), *Re-entering the Sign: Articulating New Russian Culture*. Ann Arbor, 1995.

Berton, K., *Moscow: an Architectural History*. London, 1990.

Billington, J. H., *The Icon and the Axe: An Interpretive History of Russian Culture*. New York, 1966.

Boym, S., *Common Places: Mythologies of Everyday Life in Russia*. Cambridge, MA, 1994.

Brandenberger, D., *National Bolshevism*. Cambridge, MA, 2002.

Brooks, J., 'Russian Nationalism and Russian Literature: The Canonization of the Classics', in I. Banac et al. (eds.), *Nation and Ideology: Essays in Honor of Wayne S. Vucinich*. Boulder, 1981, pp. 315–34.

When Russia Learned to Read: Literacy and Popular Literature, 1861–1917. Princeton, 1985.

Brown, A., M. Kaser, and G. S. Smith (eds.), *The Cambridge Encyclopedia of Russia and the Former Soviet Union*. 2nd edn. Cambridge, 1994.

Brumfield, W., *A History of Russian Architecture*. Cambridge, 1993.

Burbank, J., and D. L. Ransel (eds.), *Imperial Russia: New Histories for the Empire*. Bloomington, 1999.

Carter, S., *Russian Nationalism: Yesterday, Today, Tomorrow*. London, 1990.

Cherniavsky, M., *Tsar and People: Studies in Russian Myths*. New York, 1969.

Chulos, C. J., and T. Piirainen (eds.), *The Fall of an Empire, the Birth of a Nation: National Identities in Russia*. Aldershot, 2000.

Condee, N., and V. Padunov (eds.), *Soviet Hieroglyphics: Visual Culture in Late Twentieth-Century Russia.* Bloomington, 1995.

Cormack, R., and D. Gaze (eds.), *The Art of Holy Russia: Icons from Moscow, 1400–1660.* London, 1998.

Cornwell, N. (ed.), *A Reference Guide to Russian Literature.* London, 1998.

The Routledge Companion to Russian Literature. London, New York, 2001.

Cracraft, J., and D. Rowlands (eds.), *Architectures of Russian Identity: 1500 to the Present.* Cornell, 2003.

Cross, A. G., *Russia under Western Eyes, 1517–1825.* London, 1971.

Debreczeny, P., *Social Functions of Literature: Alexander Pushkin and Russian Culture.* Stanford, 1997.

Ellis, J., *The Russian Orthodox Church: A Contemporary History.* London, 1986.

Ely, C., *This Meager Nature: Landscape and National Identity in Imperial Russia.* DeKalb, IL, 2002.

Figes, O., *Natasha's Dance. A Cultural History of Russia.* London, 2002.

Fitzpatrick, S., *The Cultural Front: Power and Culture in Revolutionary Russia.* Ithaca, NY, 1992.

Freeze, G. (ed.), *Russia. A History.* Oxford, 1997.

Frierson, K., *Peasant Icons: Representations of Rural People in Late 19th Century Russia.* Oxford, 1993.

Graffy, J., and G. Hosking (eds.), *Culture and the Media in the USSR Today.* Basingstoke, 1989.

Grayson, J., and G. Hosking (eds.), *Ideology and Russian Literature.* London, 1990.

Hamilton, G. H., *The Art and Architecture of Russia.* London, 1983.

Hellberg-Hirn, E., *Soil and Soul: The Symbolic World of Russianness.* Aldershot, 1998.

Hosking, G., *A History of the Soviet Union.* London, 1985.

Russia and the Russians. A History. Cambridge, MA, 2001.

Russia: People and Empire, 1552–1917. Cambridge, 1997.

Hughes, L., 'Restoring Religion to Russian Art', in G. Hosking and R. Service (eds.), *Reinterpreting Russia.* London, 1999, pp. 40–53.

Jahn, H., *Patriotic Culture in Russia during World War I.* Ithaca, London, 1995.

Jahn, H., and J. von Geldern (eds.), *Birches, Bolsheviks, and Balalaikas: Popular Culture in Russian History* (= *Journal of Popular Culture* 31:4 [1998]).

Johnson, P., *Krushchev and the Arts: The Politics of Soviet Culture, 1962–1964.* Cambridge, MA, 1965.

Jones, M., and R. Feuer Miller (eds.), *The Cambridge Companion to the Classic Russian Novel.* Cambridge, 1998.

Kaiser, D. H., and G. Marker (eds.), *Reinterpreting Russian History, Readings 860–1860s.* Oxford, 1994.

Kelly, C., and D. Shepherd (eds.), *Constructing Russian Culture in the Age of Revolution: 1881–1940.* Oxford, 1998.

Russian Cultural Studies: an introduction. Oxford, 1998.

Knight, N., 'Narodnost' and Modernity in Imperial Russia', in Y. Kotsonis and D. L. Hoffman (eds.), *Russian Modernity: Politics, Knowledge, Practices.* Macmillan, 2000, pp. 41–67.

Lieven, D., *Empire: The Russian Empire and its Rivals*. London, 2000.

Milner-Gulland, R., *The Russians*. Oxford, 1997.

Milner-Gulland, R., with N. Dejevsky, *Cultural Atlas of Russia and the Former Soviet Union*. Oxford, 1998.

Modern Encyclopedia of Russian and Soviet History. Gulf Breeze, FL, 1976–.

Modern Encyclopedia of Russian and Soviet Literature. Gulf Breeze, FL, 1977–.

Moser, C., *The Cambridge History of Russian Literature*. Cambridge, 1992.

Nakhimovsky, A., and A. Stone Nakhimovsky (eds.), *The Semiotics of Russian Cultural History*. Ithaca, London, 1985.

Obolensky, D., *The Byzantine Commonwealth*. London, 1971.

Pesmen, D., *Russia and Soul: An Exploration*. Ithaca, 2000.

Pipes, R., *Russia under the Old Regime*. London, 1994.

Raeff, M., *Russian Intellectual History: An Anthology*. New York, 1978.

Riasanovsky, N., *A History of Russia*. 6th edn. New York, 1999.

   Nicholas I and Official Nationality in Russia, 1825–1855. Berkeley, 1959.

Rogger, H., *National Consciousness in Eighteenth-Century Russia*. Cambridge, MA, 1960.

Russianness: Studies on Nation's Identity: Essays in Honor of Rufus Mathewson, 1918–1978. Ann Arbor, 1990.

Rzhevsky, N. (ed.), *The Cambridge Companion to Modern Russian Culture*. Cambridge, 1998.

Sandle, M, 'Searching for a National Identity: Intellectual Debates in Post-Soviet Russia', in C. Wiliams and D. S. Thanasis (eds.), *Ethnicity and Nationalism in Russia, the CIS and the Baltic States*. Aldershot, 1999, pp. 64–90.

Sandler, S., *Commemorating Pushkin: Russia's Myth of a National Poet*. Stanford, 2003.

Seton Watson, H., *The Russian Empire 1801–1917*. Oxford, 1967.

Shukman, A. (ed.), *Semiotics of Russian Culture*. Ann Arbor, 1984

Smith, H., *The Russians*. London, 1977.

Smith, J., *Beyond the Limits: The Concept of Space in Russian History and Culture*. Helsinki, 1999.

Stavrou, T. G. (ed.), *Art and Culture in Nineteenth-Century Russia*. Bloomington, 1983.

Stites, R., *Russian Popular Culture: Entertainment and Society since 1900*. Cambridge, 1992.

Stites, R. (ed.), *Culture and Entertainment in Wartime Russia*. Bloomington, 1995.

Suny, R. G., *The Revenge of the Past: Nationalism, Revolution, and the Collapse of the Soviet Union*. Stanford, 1993.

Szporluk R. (ed.), *National Identity and Ethnicity in Russia and the New States of Eurasia*. Armonk, NY, London, 1994.

Taruskin, R., *Defining Russia Musically: Historical and Hermeneutical Essays*. Princeton, 1997.

Terras, V., *Handbook of Russian Literature*. New Haven, 1985.

   A History of Russian Literature. New Haven, 1991.

Thaden, E., *Conservative Nationalism in Nineteenth-Century Russia*. Seattle, 1964.

Thompson, E. M. (ed.), *The Search for Self-Definition in Russian Literature*. Amsterdam, 1991.

Tolz, V., *Russia: Inventing the Nation*. Oxford, 2001.

Vinokur, G., *The Russian Language – A Brief History*. Cambridge, 1971.

von Geldern, J., and L. McReynolds (eds.), *Entertaining Tsarist Russia: Tales, Songs, Plays, Movies, Jokes, Ads and Images from Russian Urban Life 1779–1917*. Indiana, 1998.

Walicki, A., *A History of Russian Thought from the Enlightenment to Marxism*. Oxford, 1980.

  The Slavophile Controversy: History of a Conservative Utopia in Nineteenth-Century Russian Thought. Oxford, 1975.

Westwood, J., *Endurance and Endeavour: Russian History 1812–1992*. 4th edn. Oxford, 1993.

Williams, R. C., *Russia Imagined: Art, Culture and National Identity, 1840–1995*. New York, 1997.

Wood, A. (ed.), *The History of Siberia: From Russian Conquest to Revolution*. London, 1991.

Wortman, R., *Scenarios of Power: Myth and Ceremony in Russian Monarchy*, 2 vols. Princeton, 1995/2000.

Zenkovsky, S. A. (ed.), *Medieval Russia's Epics, Chronicles, and Tales*. New York, 1974.

Index